INVITE DR. TROY CLARK
to speak for your adult group:

Perfect Bible Sunday
Bible Conference / Seminar
College-Seminary Guest Lecturer
Camp Meeting / Tent Meeting
Adult Sunday School Class
Church Retreat / Rally
Book Signing Event
Bible Revival

Info@TroyClark.net

THE

Perfect

BIBLE

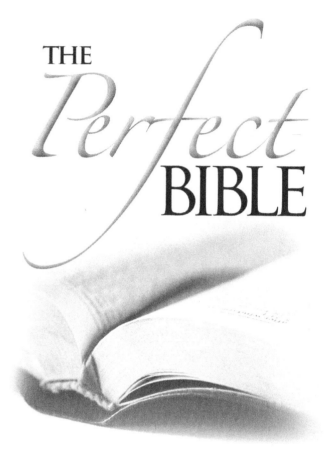

TROY G. CLARK, PH.D.

PSALM 19:7

The law of the LORD is perfect,

converting the soul.

DEDICATION

To my Lord Jesus Christ

Who saved my soul one perfect April 14, 1973 night
Who yields His perfect love through my family
Whose resurrected life delivers perfect hope
for those who need a 2nd chance
to honor His Word

**I take up the King James Translation.
I consider it to be a perfect Bible.**

T. DeWitt Talmadge
(1832-1902)
1st Presbyterian Church, Washington, DC
Pastor, Renowned Bible Expositor

per ♦ fect

Middle English parfit, from Latin perfectus,
1 a: being entirely without fault or defect:
FLAWLESS
d: faithfully reproducing the original;
3 a: PURE b: lacking in no essential detail

Merriam-Webster's Dictionary
11th Collegiate Version 3.0, 2003 ©

RECOMENDATIONS

In 1987, Troy Clark, a young college sophomore, found himself at a crossroads in life. When told that the King James Bible was not the Word of God, he faced a crisis. This crisis started a burning fire in his soul to discover where the Word of God is located. The results of that challenge has enabled him to reproduce a well written and powerfully researched defense of the Word of God as found in The King James Version of the Bible.

We owe a debt of gratitude to Troy Clark for giving us this excellent addition to our library. He once again confirms what we have known through the years. God has preserved His Inspired Word in the King James Bible.

We are honored that our Dear Lord has raised up another generation to hand to their generation the pure Word of God. Troy Clark has done a masterful job in drawing the appropriate line in the sand that The King James Bible is indeed The Word of our God!

Dr. Ron Baity, Pastor
Winston Salem, NC
Return America, **Founder**

I commend the preparation, presentation of historical facts, and honest reporting. I found this book to be one that will be deeply appreciated by God's servants who study and preach the precious truths of God's Word. God bless you for a job well done, and may our Lord get all the honor and glory.

J. Earl Green, Pastor
Greenville, SC

The Perfect Bible book will help many understand the foundation of the 1611 King James Bible, and that it came by God. Also, each chapter will guide and ground many believers to future belief in the perfection of Holy Scripture.

Dr. Troy Clark makes many great statements about our providentially preserved Bible. One statement is, "Word equals Word". Another is, "The King James Bible is not a version (paraphrase). It is the Holy Bible". These two validated points are worth the entire book.

Dr. Clark clarifies that we have a perfect Bible so an imperfect world can see our perfect Savior. I recommend this great time consuming work.

Dr. Jimmie M. Clark, Evangelist
Lexington, NC
Farmer Christian Academy, **Founder**

I would like to recommend the book entitled "The Perfect Bible" by Dr. Troy Clark and thank God for a man who stands by the King James Version of the Bible. There are so many different versions in print today that leave out words and parts of the Scriptures. Dr. Clark has spent many years in research and does an excellent job in explaining why we believe in the King James Version.

It is an honor to recommend this book to you, and I believe it will be a help and blessing to those who truly want to know the truth. In II Timothy 3:16 we read, "All scripture is given by inspiration of God, and is profitable for doctrine, for reproof, for correction, for instruction in righteousness:" I do believe that "The Perfect Bible" will help each of us have a greater understanding of the wonderful Word of God.

Dr. Bobby Roberson, Pastor
Walkertown, NC

FOREWORD

This book is not limited to the "King James Bible crowd". Any individual who reads *The Perfect Bible* will glean a clearer understanding and reap deeper appreciation for the precision of each inspired word within our Holy Bible. After 20 plus years of exhaustive research, Dr. Clark validates the fact that we have confidently in existence today an every-Word-of-God Bible.

The Perfect Bible reads in easy-to-get layman terms. Dr. Clark takes this complex issue and simplifies it to the benefit of both new Christian as well as saged theologian. It is an excellent resource for teachers, students, pastors, and any inquirer of the Word. Because this can be a divisive issue among all brands of Christianity, Dr. Clark tactfully focuses on the facts without trying to upset varied convictions on this topic.

Common questions and accepted misnomers about the 1611 King James Bible are tastefully answered by Dr. Clark. Enjoy viewing clearly the highlighted perfection of God's Scripture that purely survived the age of the Earth, the more you read *The Perfect Bible.*

Mine rich historical documentation and background information supporting all sides of the Bible issue that Dr. Clark addresses. This book is a treasure chest bursting with gems of Bible history and truth. *The Perfect Bible* reads in chronological order of events, timelines, and cultural way marks that shape the present course of Scripture translations.

Hearts will be stirred. Minds will be changed. Ignorance will be enlightened. Falsehood will be challenged after reading *The Perfect Bible.* It is the perfect gift for one who is confused, or one who sees little difference in the plethora of bible versions perched atop bookstore shelves today. This book encourages the faith and growth of believers who desire to live out and rest assured in God's Holy Words.

Most importantly, we see how God is the author of the 1611 Holy Bible. Every word. Thanks to massive documental research and simplistic layout of facts, *The Perfect Bible* creates a wealth of hope for mortal humans to believe in a perfect God. His Divine Words reach out to us in love that has never or will ever expire.

Cecil Johnson, Ph.D.

Christian Bible College, President
Author of
Revelation
Ruth
Hypocritical Separation vs. Biblical Separation
An Analysis of the Charismatic Heresies

PREFACE

Would you say anything on Earth has ever been *perfect*? The Garden of Eden set into motion the first trace of perfection upon baby Earth. Jesus Christ would later embody human and religious law for 33 years as the perfect God-man. Divine Writ was perfectly inspired through the quill of anointed writers. What happened to Heaven's perfection on planet Earth?

Inhabitors of the Garden were conned out of it, by trusting a statement with merely one word difference from what God had already said. Consequences later wreaked death upon the faultless Saviour's flesh.

Evil intends to annul every witness on Earth of a *perfect* God who is converting the souls of mankind.

The last vestige of perfection is being cloned for profit sharing in the religious market, charming society with optional "Scriptures".

In America, there are over 50 English bible versions. Over 50. Just how many Bibles did God write anyway? Which one is God's Word? All of them? None of them? Maybe two or three of them? Confusion reigns.

Congregational unison reading is no longer possible in church. We've got more bible flavors today in churches than Baskin-Robbins 31®.

Cotton candy bibles are fluffed with "improved readings" creating doctrinal cavities within new believers. Subpar scriptures require **endless** updates in committee.

Should we wonder why the world scoffs Christianity, who profess infallible truth about God, Heaven, and hell, which comes from an *fallible* book? When are we gonna' get it? The Christian community's pro choice treatment of our Holy Bible is doing us more harm than good.

We forget precise truth requires precise words. This book answers one simple question. Does there exist today an every-Word-of-God Bible? One that equals the original, inspired Scripture. One not requiring constant updating. One without any error. A perfect Bible. How can we live today by the Word of God if we do not have God's perfect Words? Matthew 4:4 verifies, *"Man shall not live by bread alone, but by **every word** that proceedeth out of the mouth of God."*

Marking Scriptural perfection is necessary in a new century of religious vagueness, so as to help the reader avoid the question, "Which one is he referring to?"

The 1611 King James Bible is the **perfect** Bible. Every single word is, in fact, a faithful Creator's heritage on Earth for mankind.

It is a common misbelief that "little changes" have gradually compounded over centuries due to human error within translation of the 1611 King James Holy Bible.

The Perfect Bible chronicles epic **word-equals-word** translation of Holy Writ crowning the English King James Bible to be an exact mirror image of the original source, God-breathed manuscripts.

The intent to be clear is not meant to outrage King James Bible critics. Our focus is not to lend fuel to an already divisive debate. Nor are we to vilify one another's opinions, or smirk at honest critique. It is this bit of intellectual snobbery within the textual criticism community that I think we can all live without. Truth will set us free.

The purpose of this book is not to pick up the fight, but to pick up the facts, that the Divine Inspiration and Divine Preservation of God's Holy Oracles are unique to the King James Bible in modern times.

Being led by this Spirit of assurance, we open before you a reservoir of Holy Bible history about its Heavenly provenance and pristine flow into present day.

It is important for Scriptural faith to rest in beliefs that square with documental truth. To that end, dear reader, may you acquire a more perfected opinion toward our *perfect* Bible.

Troy Clark, Ph.D.

TABLE OF CONTENTS

Chapter One

The Perfect
Old Testament

*The Bible does not contain the Word of God;
it is the Word of God.*

Dr. Lee Roberson
(1909-2007)
Tennessee Temple University, Founder
10,000 member Highland Park Baptist Church, 40-year Pastor

The Holy Bible is God's written revelation of Himself to man. His truth to mankind has been faithfully revealed for every age, every millennia, in specific ways that appeal directly to each various culture. Not every civilization communicated in harmony with God exactly the same way. Different methods were employed for different people.

For example, in the Garden of Eden audible, personable conversation was how Adam and Eve knew God. A visible relationship revealed God's guidelines to them about life and death on planet Earth. This visible, audible, and interpersonal relationship fit into the creation at this time.

As cultures formed, shifted, and changed over centuries, so did the language of God's revelation of Himself. He appeared in dreams. God gave visions. He once spoke through a donkey. Through prayer, the *inaudible* voice of God directed people. Inclement weather, droughts, and plagues warned certain people. His truth was heralded through the voice of prophets, the advice of sages, and out of the mouth of babes.

Each method of God's revelation of Himself to man appealed directly to the culture of its day. We may view some of these channels used by God as ludicrous in our day. Of course, we see our culture as a bit more progressive than ancient days and times preceding us.

In our present age, a <u>written</u> document appeals best to our legal sense of authenticity. Any agreement between two is not binding in our society, unless it is signed, authorized (notarized), and documented. It then becomes truth to us.

Today's written revelation of God to man comes to us perfectly so. The authenticity of Holy Writ from its Divine source is forever validated by and in historical facts. This record substantiates the God-inspired, every-word-preserved Scripture unique to one Holy Bible of modern times. His Words come to us perfectly as it was originally given by God Himself. Registered truth appeals to the legal sensibilities of our current culture. We will see the Holy Bible's perfection authorized in documental candor. So, where did Divine Scripture come from? How did it get here? How can it be as perfectly preserved today as it was first given?

HISTORIC OVERVIEW

The word Bible is an extract of a 14th century Phoenician city called, Byblos, from which papyrus (scrolls made of dried plant leaves) were exported.

The Holy Bible contains 39 books in the Old Testament and 27 books in the New Testament. The Holy Bible is a time-honored Book. Sixty-six letters of love, written through forty authors, living on several different continents, are each marked in time across 16 centuries. The exact words of its text have been woven together by a golden, unhampered thread. This thread of grace is called *Divine Preservation*. It is a New Testament church doctrine of Scripture.

Matthew 24: 35
Heaven and earth shall pass away, but **my words shall not pass away**.

God not only originally inspired the words of Scripture, but He built them to last. This permanent preservation is why we have a perfect Bible today.

Consider the words of Bible history authorities Dr. Bill Grady, then Gail Riplinger.

Without infallible preservation, we are forced to
conclude that God's breath evaporated with the
deterioration of His originals.[2]

God did not promise inaccurate translations and
lost original books. What God did promise is to
preserve His Words.[3]

Other verses related to the promise of Divine
Preservation are pledged by Scripture itself: Psalm 12:6,7;
78:1-7; 105:8; 119:89,111,152,160. Proverbs 22:20-21.
Ecclesiastes 3:14. Matthew 4:4; 5:17-18. I Peter 1:23-25

If you believe in the 6-day Genesis account of
creation, our Earth is approximately 6000 years young.
This accurate age of planet Earth is clearly laid out by
virtue of the Scripture's own genealogical timeline dating
up to the birth of Christ (1 A.D.) set forth in Genesis 5,
11, Matthew 1, and Luke 3.

At approximately 4000 B.C., God created the
heavens and the Earth. For the first two and a half
millennia God's revelation of Himself to man was mostly
interpersonal. That is, face to face. People who came into
union with God were noticeably changed, revered, and
believed. Unlike our culture would treat them today, *they*
were not seen as the quacks of society. They were intently
listened to. A world-wide flood ravaged the entire globe
at approximately 2400 B.C., when society failed to adhere
to God's prediction through Noah.

How many appearances of Christ can we point to
in the Old Testament? How many visions redirected
people in walks of life to warn, instruct, or reveal God's
Plan? Military leaders, kings, parents of prophets,
prophets themselves, a servant girl, a widow with a son,
and a prisoner, were a few. Who can forget Job's
whirlwind dialogue with God? How many other
appearances were unrecorded? Atop Mount Sinai, Moses

received a glimpse at the "hinder parts" of God, as well as the first Holy Writ.

2600 years after 4000 B.C., at approximately 1400 B.C., the first written revelation of God to mankind began to be recorded. Spanning roughly 1600 years, until approximately 100 A.D., all 66 books of the Bible would be initially written by 40 separate authors. These 66 books would conclusively be collated (put together) into English during the 16th century A.D. to become our Holy Bible.

The books of the Old Testament were written between 1400-200 B.C. The New Testament books were written between 30-100 A.D. The earliest copies and fragments of these books still in existence today date well into the actual days of Christ during the first century A.D.

Consider this recent discovery:

> There has been a remarkable recent discovery which made front page news in the *London Times*. The **oldest remains** of any New Testament manuscript were discovered. Using a high-magnification device and the epifluorescent confocal laser scanning technique, the small fragment was dated A.D. 66. Close examination shows that it contains the King James Bible's reading from Matthew 26:22, "hekastos auton", - "every one of them". [4]

The article goes on to say that the King James Bible is the *one and only* Bible today that has this correct reading. Perfection repeats itself. The more New Testament fragments of ancient Scripture are found, the more paraphrased versions have to correct themselves. Due to a plethora of historical facts, the popular *Nestle-Aland 26th edition* Greek New Testament had to correct itself back to the King James Bible text approximately 500 times. All modern English bible versions translated from the *Nestle-Aland 26th edition* Greek New Testament have yet to catch up (NIV, NASV, KNJV, TNIV, RSV, ESV, CEV, NCV, NRSV, NAB, NLB, et al).

The Holy Bible is testimonied in approximately 5,200 ancient Scriptural manuscripts (hand-written *copies*) extant (existing) today. Here is a small chart comparing other existing famous works of art to the steadfast King James Bible.

Written Work	When Written	Earliest Copy	No. of copies
NT (KJB)	30-100 AD	60 AD	5,200
Homer	900 BC	400 BC	643
Aristotle	384-322 BC	1100 AD	49
Caesar	100-144 BC	900 AD	10
Plato	427-347 BC	900 AD	20
Aristophanes	450-385 BC	900 AD	10
Thucydides	460-400 BC	900 AD	8
Tacitus	100 AD	1100 AD	20
Herodotus	480-425AD	900 AD	8

TWO SCRIPTURE STREAMS

The Christian community at large has shifted its focus toward the Holy Bible. The historic doctrine of Divine <u>Preservation</u> of Scripture is now replaced with modern "restoration" of Scripture. This explains the constantly updated, unreliable new version paraphrases.

Contemporary critics are moving Divine Inspiration of Scripture away from the King James Bible you hold in your hands to the nebulous, non-existent "lost original books". Whether we realize it or not, this makes

God's "true" Word inaccessible and of no value to anyone. If the "lost original books" contain the only inspired Bible, perhaps a "Tomb of the Unknown Bible" could tangibly signify the nonexistence of God's "real" Words due to the centuried battle over the Scriptures. Do we need a symbolic marker to recognize where His Words are located in present day? Are God's perfect Words dead?

So, the question still begs, *Are any of the 50 English versions on the bible market today the Word of God?*

The answer is simple. You have a choice. There are two streams of Scripture that flow separately down through history. Let the record clearly show **two** streams of Scripture. Any expert who says otherwise, or that ALL scriptures today are tributary from the same source, is not being intellectually honest or historically pure. All bibles on the market today originated from *one of two* textual streams, both coursing through history, yet carving a separate path.

The dichotomy of Scripture is key to understanding the difference. So, the choice is **not** to be made out of 50 different versions, but simply between the two Scriptural text streams. The clear choice is not between 50, but between 2.

The **Majority Text** and the **Critical Text** are the two, severed Scripture manuscript streams marked and recorded in history. The King James Bible is the perfect product of the Majority Text. All other bible versions (including "New" King James bibles) are the repositories of the ever-evolving Critical text.

This is ultimately your 2-fold choice. The Majority Text, or the Critical text. Which one are God's Words? Can both Scripture lineages mirror the exact Words of God? Ask yourself. Why do their labels have different names? Why indeed. Things that have different labels are not the same thing. Both scriptural manuscript streams do not flow from the same upstream source.

Proverbs 25:26
A righteous man falling down before the wicked *is as* a troubled fountain, and a **corrupt spring**.

As a side note, you will notice that I use the word *Bible* when referring to the 1611 King James Holy Bible. I will never call inspired Scripture a "version". A version is a paraphrase. It was only when the first, failed English Revised *version* (paraphrase) of 1885 was later combined together with the Holy Bible to form the American Standard bible *version* in 1901, was the word "version" first glued onto the label of contemporary bibles.

This is why I choose to spell modern day bible versions with a small "b" and refer to them as they are - mere versions (paraphrases) of the actual Holy Bible.

For centuries the King James Bible had no competitors. It was referred to only as **Holy Bible**. For virtually 300 years, since 1611, it was stamped "Holy Bible" on the cover. Not "King James version". Therefore, to be true to history, the 1611 King James Bible is therefore, not a *version* of the Bible, it *is* simply - the Holy **B**ible. The paradox of renaming it did not occur until after 1901, when opportunists first attempted to clone Holy Scripture and sell it as a "better version".

The Words of God are not found in a version. The Words of God rest in the Holy Bible. The Holy Bible, to be clear, is what it has always been, the 1611 King James Bible, as many call it today.

Of course, you understand the King James Holy Bible was not originally written in English, right? The modern day English language was not developed until the

1500's. Our *Modern English* language (1500 A.D.-present) grew out ye 'ole broken *Middle English* (1100-1500 A.D.), which grew out of the unrecognizable *Old (Anglo Saxon) English* (700-1100 A.D.).

Nearly all portions of the Old Testament were originally written in Hebrew. Some minute passages are found written in Aramaic (Ezra 4:8-6:18, 7:12-26; Dan. 2:4-7:28, Jeremiah 10:11, and two words in Genesis 31:47). Not to be confused with Arabic, the Aramaic language, sometimes called Syriac, has its roots within the Semitic (Jewish) culture of Upper Mesopotamia and Syria.

The Old Testament was written by Jewish authors in their native Hebrew tongue. The Old Testament writers were inspired by God to write beginning with Moses around 1400 B.C., and inked its way over a thousand years later to 200 B.C. when the last Old Testament book (Ezra) was written.

The New Testament epistles were written roughly 30-100 A.D. It is obvious to conclude that they were not writing in English. These books were originally penned in Greek. The *Koine Period*, 300 B.C. - 300 A.D., predominately used the Koine' Greek dialect in writing, being spoken in every day language. Although global languages have taken turns in world predominance, Majority Text Holy Writ are purely Divine Words kept equally intact in language translation. Perfection repeats itself.

The King James Bible Old Testament is the original Hebrew Old Testament in English. The King James Bible New Testament is the original Greek New Testament in English.

OLD TESTAMENT SCRIPTURE

What advantage hath the Jew?...
...unto them were committed the oracles of God.
Romans 3:1-2

How did the Bible actually get here? How was it first written down? How were the authors moved by God to write each book, each inspired Word? The determination of Scripture refers to the Words written down on Earth that were spoken or supernaturally revealed by God Himself.

Matthew 22: 29-31
Jesus answered and said unto them, Ye do err, not knowing the **scriptures**, ...have ye not **read that which was spoken** unto you **by God**.

Obviously, the words of God originate where God is. Heaven. God's Word began in Heaven first. Holy Scripture is forever established in the provenance of God's Heaven. In Heaven today, there is an actual, perfect Book of God's Holy written Words. The Bible itself shares this fact.

Psalm 119:89
For ever, O LORD, thy word is settled in heaven.

John 1:1-2
In the beginning was the Word, and the Word was with God, and the Word was God. The same was in the beginning with God.

Other written Books and works of our Creator-God include:

The 10 Commandments,

Exodus 24:12, 31:18

And the LORD said unto Moses, Come up to me into the mount, and be there: and I will give thee tables of stone, and a law, and commandments which **I have written**; that thou mayest teach them. And he gave unto Moses, when he had made an end of communing with him upon mount Sinai, two tables of testimony, tables of stone, **written** with the finger of God.

The Book of Members,

Psalm 139:16

Thine eyes did see my substance, yet being unperfect; and in thy book all *my members* were **written**,

The Book of Life, Exodus 32:32, Luke 10:20, Revelation 20:12,

Yet now, if thou wilt forgive their sin--; and if not, blot me, I pray thee, out of thy book which **thou hast written**.

Notwithstanding in this rejoice not, that the spirits are subject unto you; but rather rejoice, because your **names are written** in heaven. And I saw the dead, small and great, stand before God; and the books were opened: and another book was opened, which is the *book of* life: and the dead were judged out of those things which were **written in the books**, according to their works.

The Book of Seven Seals,

Revelation 5:1
And I saw in the right hand of him that sat on the throne **a book written** within and on the backside, sealed with seven seals.

So, how did God's **written** Word in Heaven get written down equally on Earth? The transferring of God's Words into human language is called *Divine Inspiration.* That is, God inspired human authors to write down what has already been written in Heaven. God miraculously spoke His Words into the writer's heart.

II Timothy 3:16
All scripture *is* given by **inspiration** of God, and *is* profitable for doctrine, for reproof, for correction, for instruction in righteousness:

You see, the perfect Bible would be one that duplicates God's written Word in Heaven. Literally, inspired means, "God breathed". Consider Webster's dictionary definition:

in · spired
Middle English, from Anglo-French & Latin; Anglo-French inspirer, from Latin inspirare, from in- + spirare to breathe14[th] century
1 a : to influence, move, or guide by divine or
supernatural inspiration
2 a archaic : to breathe or blow into or upon
b archaic : to infuse (as life) by breathing
3 a : to communicate to an agent supernaturally
Merriam-Webster's Dictionary
11th Collegiate Version 3.0, 2003 ©

Again to be clear, God "breathed" His written Words in Heaven into spiritual, yet human servants on Earth who recorded what was already written in Heaven. That is Divine Inspiration. God put *His* Words into the writer's hearts.

It was a supernatural act of God to man, not an act of man's intellect. Men did not create God's Words. Men dictated the Divine Words that were superimposed on them by God Himself. Holy men simply wrote down equally what was already written in Heaven. The word "inspiration" rests twice in Scripture - II Timothy 3:16 and Job 32:8.

Job 32:8

But *there is* a spirit in man: and the inspiration of the Almighty giveth them understanding.

Stamped upon Jewish tradition is Divine authority to dictate, as well as, preserve the written "oracles of God" (Romans 3:1-2). Oracle means "revelations delivered by God to prophets".

Biblical author Josh McDowell points out,

The Jews became a people of one Book, and it was this Book that kept them together.[5]

The accepted list of Old Testament Hebrew books are broken down into three groups: The **Law** (*Torah*, also called Pentateuch) – Genesis through Deuteronomy; the **Prophets** (*Nebhiim*) – Joshua, Judges, Samuel, Kings, Isaiah, Jeremiah, Ezekiel, Hosea through Malachi; and the **Writings or Psalms** (*Kethubim*) – Job, Song of Solomon, Ruth, Lamentations, Esther, Ecclesiastes, Daniel, Ezra-Nehemiah, and Chronicles.

The Hebrew language, and its sister - Aramaic, have characteristically been Semitic (Jewish) languages. The Hebrew Old Testament Scriptures are the exact same 39 Old Testament books found in the King James Bible. However, it is composed as 24 books in the earliest writings, because the two-part books (I & II) were combined as one. Other books were paired together also.

The entire Hebrew Bible is referred to as the *Tenach* by Jewish people. The first letter of the three divisions T (Torah), N (Nebhiim), and K (Kethubim), combine to form Tenach. Today, the Tenach is also referred to commonly as the Old Testament **Masoretic Text.**

The Lord Jesus, Himself, authorized the traditional Masoretic Text in

Luke 24:44
And He said unto them, These *are* the words which I spake unto you, while I was yet with you, that all things must be fulfilled, which were written, in the **law** of Moses, and *in* the **prophets**, and *in* the **psalms**, concerning me.

Tenach is the correct, original Jewish label of God's inspired Words. The Masoretic Text is the correct, modern label of the same, which reflects the name of the Masoretes, who were largely responsible for its preservation. The ancient stream of Tenach Hebrew manuscripts have formed a single line of historical documents known today as the Masoretic Text. The Tenach, or the Hebrew Masoretic Text, mirrors precisely the King James Bible Old Testament in English. Just how has this Old Testament Scripture been perfectly preserved?

TRANSLATION

Why did Holy Scripture need to be copied, or translated?

First of all, the original written revelations of God to mankind were not recorded in our English language. Modern English emerged as a national language in roughly the 16th century. What you see in the King James Bible Old Testament is the original Hebrew Old Testament in English. What you see in the King James Bible New Testament is the original Greek New Testament in English.

Secondly, the Old Testament books of the King James Bible were originally written on vellum parchment (dried animal skins) from 1400 B.C to 200 B.C. The New Testament books of the King James Bible were originally written on papyrus (dried plant leaves) from 30-100 A.D. Paper was not invented until the 14th century A.D. The printing press was invented in 1439. Can we imagine what condition these scrolls and leaves should be in today after 1000, 2000, up to 3400 years from the time of Moses? Ever seen the *Declaration of Independence* up close? This parchment has to be kept inside of an air-tight, helium-filled chamber to keep it from falling apart. It is only 225 years old.

I list more in depth reasons in Chapter 4 why the original Scripture manuscripts were not allowed by God to survive. So, they were copied - very accurately.

The reality is, the first written books of Divine Scripture have gone the way of all the Earth and returned to dust. Fear not, though. The very Words of God are as Divinely Preserved as they are Divinely Inspired. God's promise for eternal preservation of Holy Writ extends to every word, not the paper upon which they were written. His Words are unending. This is key to understanding perfection within the King James Bible. *Translation does not mean lost inspiration.*

53 verses in the King James Bible mention the word "Scripture". These are **not** referring to the *original* books of Scripture, but to *equally prepared copies.* Mirror-perfect copies of God's Words are called inspired Scripture again and again in the Holy Bible. Jesus Christ never read from the original books of Holy Writ during His earthly ministry, but from equal copies. He never pointed to one mistake in the Masoretic Text Scripture He used then. If there were mistakes in the copies of Scripture Jesus used, the Son of God would have definitely pointed to them as error. However, Jesus read exact *copies*, and Jesus Himself verified these to be the Words of God. God called equally preserved copies, His Scripture.

Luke 24:27
And beginning at Moses and all the prophets, he expounded unto them in **all the scriptures** the things concerning himself.

John 5:39
Search the **scriptures**; for in them ye think ye have eternal life: and they are **they** which **testify of me**.

I Corinthians 15:3-4
For I delivered unto you first of all that which I also received, how that Christ died for our sins **according to the scriptures**; 4 And that he was buried, and that he rose again the third day **according to the scriptures**.

Proverbs 25:1
These *are* also proverbs of Solomon, which the men of Hezekiah king of Judah **copied** out.

So, does the Bible pronounce <u>only</u> the *original* books of Scripture are inspired - Yes or No? Does the Bible itself insure that we may trust an equal *copy* of God's inspired Words - Yes or No? The Bible makes it clear. Perfectly preserved copies of God's Word are called Scripture. In order for copies to be called Scripture however, they must be mirror-perfect.

Majority Text Holy Scripture comes to us by **Formal Equivalency** translation. The entire King James Bible has been translated from the original books *the whole way* by formal (verbal) equivalency. That is, each word being translated into the new language must be the same, literal <u>word</u> being translated from. Word equals Word. The Holy King James Bible is a purely preserved, fixed document. This is also key to understanding perfect preservation of inspired Scripture.

It is a common yet misguided belief that "little changes" have compounded over centuries due to human error in translation within the King James Bible. The drumbeat of critics have sunk into the heads of believers this fallacy. Although *printing press* and *spelling* adjustments have been made over time, as the English language was settling down and printing has become a more exacting craft, the TEXT of Divine Writ has remained equally the SAME in the Majority Text Holy Bible.

Suppose a scientist were being interviewed by NASA to write code for satellites orbiting Earth. NASA asks the scientist being interviewed his methods for calculating the exact, precise coordinates for orbital flight. The scientist responds, "If my calculations are off one inch, it won't really matter. It's to be expected. Calculations are accessed by the drawing room, to the processing center, to the production room, to the evaluation center, and finally to the Command Center. Human error is to be expected in such nanoscale measurements, right? If it's off just one inch, no big deal." Would this scientist be hired by NASA? He would be horse-laughed back out to the front curb.

We will see how God's caretakers of His Word, the Sopherim and Masoretes, spared no excruciating detail to *perfectly* "write the code" (copy) the inspired Words Almighty God entrusted to their calculations. Their translation methods were not off "one inch", one tittle, or one jot.

So, the inspired Scripture given by God and recorded by spiritual, yet human men, were copied very accurately. And copied. And copied. And copied. And copied, as various languages such as, Hebrew, Greek, Italian, Syriac, and English, etc., gained international prominence, the Words of God remained the same in the perfectly preserved Majority Text Holy Scripture. The pure meaning of translation is to merely **copy or duplicate** the original. This has been done.

Another misguided belief is "double inspiration". Among theological debaters, critics of *every word inspired* Scripture today falsely assert this notion. That is to say, each time God's Word was translated, it must be *re-inspired*. So, in order for the King James Bible to retain Divine Inspiration, one must believe by default that God re-inspired, then re-re-inspired, and then re-re-re-inspired, ad nauseam, each formal translation from the original books forward, over centuries of time leading up to the 1611 King James Bible. God is forced to "re-breathe" His Words over again, and again, and again, as the original inspired books were perfectly copied, and copied, and copied, beginning at 1400 B.C. and ending at 1611 A.D. Hence, "double inspiration". Therefore, since this phenomenon did not occur, the King James Bible cannot be inspired Word for Word by God, says the critic. Whew boy.

Question. Does God Himself manually "re-breathe" the breath of life into each human being born after Adam? Of course not. God breathed into the first man (Adam) the breath of life, and man became a *living* soul. God's life **continued** in the birth of Adam's son, Seth. God's life **continued** in the birth of Seth's son, Enos. God's life then **continued** in Enos' son, Cainan. Going forward into the lineage of humanity, God's life continues today in the *living soul* of you and I.

Likewise, there is no need for God to manually "re-breathe" His Words over and over again to accomplish the Divine Preservation and flourishing life of inspired Scripture. The King James Bible comes to us by way of **continued original inspiration**. That is, the 1611 King James Bible embodies *preserved Words of original inspiration.* Holy Writ perpetuated through impeccably pure copies. The King James Bible has no need for "double inspiration". His unending Words already inspired are perfectly copied. Always remember, formal translation does not mean lost inspiration.

"Double inspiration" is a slick misideology simply meant to camouflage a Bible scholar's aversion to say that ANY Bible today is inspired by God word for word. It is a way for Bible critics to appear spiritually enlightened "more than the rest of us" on the subject. Yet, it is also a failure to take a correct, and unpopular, conservative position in religious circles of lower and higher criticism, that Holy Scripture inspiration perpetuates itself into present day. "Double inspiration" is an intelligent sounding cop-out for those unable or unwilling to settle into one inspired Bible today.

Contemporary critics razz fundamental believers whose Scripture position is a <u>visible</u> "King James only" Bible, while plugging *invisible* "original books ONLY" are inspired word-for-word. Which would you prefer - visible or invisible - Words of God?

The Holy Bible translated from its original Hebrew (Old Testament) and Greek (New Testament) into English by formal equivalency method, stings the sensibilities of today's new version mindset. Why? It severely limits the carefreeness of modern critics who want to make endless word changes in Scripture.

Formal translation is juxtaposed to the cut-and-paste, "sky is the limit" *dynamic* style of translation work milling out consumer-driven bible versions today. The "American Dream" ideal has shifted the purpose of marketing bibles from a pursuit of Creator-friendly to customer-friendly results.

The method of Critical text translation is **Dynamic Equivalency**. Dynamic implies *change* or movement. Webster's dynamic is defined, "pertaining to *change* or process."[6]   New bible version committees believe dynamic equivalency grants the authority needed to make endless changes to neo-scripture. Here, scripture text evolution opens up "the better rendering" latitude for the "new and improved" copyright law versions. This has been a big mistake.

When translating scripture by dynamic equivalency method, parts of speech may be switched by the person translating, as it is carried over from one language to another. There are no governing rules either. Verbs may change in tense. An adjective might become a noun. Plurals become singular. One word becomes three words. Anything goes! There is no loyalty to the original text being translated from. Words and parts of speech mutate.

This type of problematic "word cloning" engenders grotesque DOCTRINAL imperfections in Scripture to say the least. More examples are openly laid out in Chapter 6. God calls them "added" words and places a stiff warning in doing so. From the beginning to the end of the Holy Bible, God's wishes are crystal clear concerning HIS Words.

Deuteronomy 4:2
Ye shall **not add unto the word** which I command you, neither shall ye diminish *ought* from it, that ye may keep the commandments of the LORD your God which I command you.

Revelation 22:18
For I testify unto every man that heareth **the words** of the prophecy of this book, If any man shall **add unto these** things, God shall add unto him the plagues that are written in this book:

Don't say we haven't been forewarned. Don't say the consequences for giving Holy Scripture plastic surgery aren't going to have permanence. How does the King James Bible stay in compliance to God's Word policy? The Majority Text King James Bible is the only Bible is existence today that has NEVER been sutured together by dynamic equivalency translation. Rather, Word-equals-Word Formal Equivalency kept each Divine Word in its place as inspired Scripture rolled over into the international language of each century.

Let's be clear, so as to not miss the obvious. Dynamic equivalency reduces critical scripture translation to a series of unnecessary options that merits "this reading" over "that reading", "this manuscript" over "that manuscript", "this word" over "that word", left up to the discretion of the editor. It brings the critic to an area where personal opinion, even personal bias, can easily determine translation decisions. It leaves the scholar free to choose words in or out of Scripture in terms of his own prejudice.

How does this occur? Where do the free-style gyrations of new scripture begin?

Critics go on fault-finding missions. In the minds of bible critics bent toward "scripture correction" is the misnomer that the basic "idea, thought, or message" of scripture is more important than actual **WORDS** of Scripture. The broad stroke of dynamic critique operates in stark contrast to the fixed Scripture itself.

Exodus 4:30
And Aaron spake all the **words** which the LORD had spoken unto Moses...

Psalm 12:6-7
The **words** of the LORD *are* **pure words**: *as* silver tried in a furnace of earth, purified seven times. Thou shalt keep them, O LORD, **thou shalt preserve them** from this generation **for ever**.

Proverbs 30:5-6
Every word of God *is* **pure**: he *is* a shield unto them that put their trust in him. **Add thou not** unto his **words,** lest he reprove thee, and thou be found a liar.

Jeremiah 15:16
Thy words were found, and I did eat them; and **thy word** was unto me the joy and rejoicing of mine heart: for I am called by thy name, O LORD God of hosts.

Matthew 4:4
It is written, Man shall not live by bread alone,but by **every word** that proceedeth out of the mouth of God.

John 6:63
...the **words** that I speak unto you, *they* are spirit, and *they* are life.

How important are the *Words* of Scripture in the Holy Bible? Which are most important in the Bible - the Words, or the basic message of Scripture? Does the Bible guarantee the preservation of basic ideas, thoughts, or message of Scripture - Yes or No? Are the actual <u>Words</u> of God guaranteed survival in the Bible - Yes or No?

Formal equivalent translators of the inspired Majority Text Scripture carefully and most definitively copied every single word without any mutation from the original source. God wants *every word* equally preserved.

The error of present day bible versions are the means by which they were translated. These dynamic equivalent paraphrases are *further removed from the original books* of Scripture. New, earthy word choices embody unreliable, shifty scriptures requiring high maintenance. In new versions, the original Words of God are fragmented.

This means only one thing. Modern bible translation rules are "living".

For example, let's dust off a board game to play a rousing game of Monopoly®. What if we, before the game begins, decide to play with the rules being "living"? Meaning, the rules can change in the middle of the game whenever someone wants them to change. Suppose I decide later on that I collect $400 for passing "Go". You collect only $200 for passing "Go". It's a fluid (changing) concept based on what is best for me at the moment.

Modern bible translators **rely heavily on this technique** *while picking and choosing the words* for modern bibles. The Holy Bible is treated as a "living document", meaning subject to wild text changes based on the "experts" whim, public opinion, or personal bias.

Too often, open market bible translations key on textual reversals that are motivated by what *people or the public wants changed* in Scripture (ye, thou, thee words, etc.). How would a marriage work if the wedding vows were "living", unfixed, unsettled, or reversed at any time on cultural whims? Where would be the accountability? By contrast, conservative judges view the United States Constitution as a "fixed document". Liberal judges view the United States Constitution as a "living document". That is, to be shape-shifted to however the present culture wants it to be interpreted.

How can any modern-day bible translator be certain that the very words being randomly selected to "update" a bible verse equally match what is already written in Heaven? Of course, this is a human impossibility. God's perfectly inspired and preserved Words were never meant to be altered from the get-go. It has been gotten right the first time. New version translators trump this fact by being drawn into a seductive translation technique specifically designed for limitless "updates" in their bible texts.

Furthermore, how can bible versions on the market today put a copyright on a written work that they claim was originally written by God? A copyright denotes ownership. The fact that a bible is copyrighted by a human corporation means by default that God is not the author. The King James Bible is the only Bible on planet Earth that is NOT COPYRIGHTED. If you see a copyright on the front flap of a King James Bible, it is a copyright only on the marginal reference notes, additional materials, maps, etc. (all the other "extras" included), but it is not a copyright on the Scripture text itself.

I ask you to consider. Who inspired your Bible? Answer - Whoever has ownership. No one can put a copyright on the King James Bible, simply because man can not take credit for its original source or equal copies. If mankind can not claim ownership of the King James Bible, who can? Ahem, there are only three choices. Either animals, God, or aliens are responsible. Which one would you want to believe gave us a perfect Bible?

To establish a copyright, each new bible version must contain *different* words, which have not been copywritten by previous new version committees. Therefore, each new version becomes *further removed from the original books* that God breathed. Why? A version is a paraphrase. Always remember, bibles that are different are not the same.

Dallas   Theological   Seminary's   Dr.   Wilber Pickering said,

> New versions differ from the originals in some
> six thousand places. They are several times
> removed from the originals than the King James.
> 7

Translation purity does not mean to improve the text. It purely means to <u>copy</u> it in another language. Word for word formal translation equals the Word. That is, each word being translated into the new language must be the same, literal Word being translated from, to retain its original source. Word for word equals Word. New version bibles never were translated based on this principle.

D.A. Carson scholarizes in his book, *The King James Version Debate,*

> ...the purpose and goal of textual criticism is to
> get as close to the originals as possible. To fail
> to recognize this is to misapprehend what textual
> criticism is all about. [8]

TRANSCRIBE means *"to express in different terms and especially different words"* (Merriam-Webster's Dictionary 11th Collegiate Version 3.0, 2003). Perhaps committees assembled to spawn new bible versions need to accurately label themselves **transcribers**, not translators.

TRANSLATE, derived from its roots, are two Latin terms. *Trans* means "across"; *Latus* is the past participle root of *Hatus* and means "to lift or carry". The literal meaning of translation is "to lift or carry across." That is, accurate Bible translation occurs as the picking up of words from the Hebrew (Old Testament) and Greek (New Testament), carrying those words over into English, or any language being translated into, and setting them down very gently without losing any parts, gaining any parts, or changing any parts. It simply means to copy from language to language. This is Word-equals-Word purity.

For example, in 1611 conservative Bible translation scholars copied into English the King James Bible *correctly* putting this principle into practice. Even the "out of date" and "archaic" words *of that time* would not be changed remaining in Scripture. The committee understood that even though these words would need to be looked up in a dictionary at that time, they could not call their translation pure if the text were altered in any way. Perfection begets perfection. Word for word equals Word. They took the high road to follow **Aristotle's dictum:**

> The benefit of the doubt is to be given to the document itself, and not arrogated by the critic to himself.[9]

God breathed His Words directly to mankind through spiritual, yet human writers. This means God *inspired* His Words. God then kept His exact Words perfectly intact through all ages without loss or error. This means God *preserved* His Words. The Divine Inspiration and Divine Preservation of Holy Scripture are two pillars that foundationalize Christ-centered, Bible doctrine.

I can't even begin to count the number of revisions the book you are now reading went through before it was finalized. The King James Bible was finalized from the moment God first breathed His Words through human writers. From then on, HIS exact Words were fixed. No revisions. No additions. No subtractions. No "easier and better" readings. Just His Words. Scrupulously guarded. Translated formally by Word-equals-Word. The King

James Bible locked them into place for English speaking people. With blessing the 1611 King James Bible preserved the inspired Scripture word by word in English. Its formal translation from Hebrew and Greek to English was honored by perfection. "It appears the KJV translators 'reshaped English' to fit the Biblical mold. Hence, God honored the KJV and used it as the fountainhead of the English language."[10]

> We ought invariably and in the church and on public occasion to use the Authorized Version [King James Bible]; all others are inferior....it is the most beautiful monument erected with the English alphabet.

> **Ladies Home Journal Magazine, 1921**

OLD TESTAMENT PRESERVATION
From Abraham to King David (2000-1000 B.C.), Egypt is recognized in history as a great and predominant power, and primary enemy to Israel. Shortly after the reign of King Solomon, a shift of national supremacy is overtaken by Assyria (1000-625 B.C.) throughout the region of Palestine. Babylon (Mesopotamia) is a secondary national power bordering southern Assyria. Egypt loses first rank to Assyrian domination.

In the perpetual Old Testament rebalancing of power, Babylon eventually conquers Assyria (625-400 B.C., end of the Old Testament books) and destroys Jerusalem (587 B.C.) to become supreme national superpower. Egypt and Israel disappearance in history as a world power with the conquests of Babylonian Emperor Nebuchadnezzar II (605-562 B.C.). Babylon is eventually taken over by Persia under Cyrus (539 B.C.).

Abraham made his Genesis 11:31 trek from southern Babylonia (Ur of the Chaldees) to northern Babylonia in Genesis 12:5 (Haran - modern day Turkey), then through Egypt to Palestine (Canaan). Abraham lived during the time of early Babylonian King Hammurabi (2000 B.C.). Records of his reign are found in several dozen letters, contracts, and documents in a code of laws that bear his name, discovered in 1901, known as *Hammurabi's Code*.

The *Cuneiform* system of writing existed in Mesopotamia long before the time of Hammurabi in *Amarna* letters (382 ancient clay tablets representing diplomatic letters between Egypt, Babylon, Assyria, Canaan, and Cyprus). These documents show Hebrew was written sometimes in this script. The places mentioned in these letters are largely Hebrew, such as Palestine and Syria. Furthermore, the sons of Abraham, Isaac, and Jacob are given Hebrew names as the King James Bible correctly records for us. We conclude the Hebrew language was viable from Abraham's day (2000 B.C.) all the way up to the first written Hebrew books of Moses (Genesis through Deuteronomy).

God inspired Moses around 1400 B.C. to record the first 5 books of Holy Scripture, as they were already written in Heaven. Some conservative Bible historians agree that Adam originally wrote Genesis 2:4-5:1. These sacred, inspired books were officially recognized, and sanctioned into Jewish law around 400 B.C., called the *Torah*. A specific group of Jewish linguist specialists (scribes) whose sole life responsibility was to accurately record, *copy*, and preserve inspired Scripture from the time of Moses. They were called *Sopherim*.

About 627 B.C., under Josiah, the "book of the law" was found in the temple (II Chronicles 34:15). It was probably Deuteronomy, which means "law". During the

5th century B.C. the "priestly code" (Leviticus) was also brought to light. The Law (Torah - Genesis through Deuteronomy) was canonized about 400 B.C. "This date is based largely on the approximate time the Samaritans split with the Jews and recognized the Torah as Scripture"[11]

To canonize simply means "*to sanction or approve by ecclesiastical authority*" (Merriam-Webster's Dictionary 11th Collegiate Version 3.0, 2003). The priests, by authority of the King, officially recognized the inspired Law of Moses, and enacted it into Jewish cultural law.

Also, about 250 B.C., Ezra, read the law to the people and, again, canonized the Pentateuch (same as Torah). Here again, the sacred Scriptures of God by way of Moses (Genesis-Deuteronomy) are being admitted as Divine authority and preserved (Nehemiah 8-10).

Notice the legal standard of law itself was upgraded to reflect the inspired Scripture given by God to Moses, the Torah. The Torah was not being changed at all. It was the culture that changed to fit the Words of God. This kept the stream of Scripture manuscripts pure and honest, as it continued to flow from the original inspiration God gave it.

The 2nd section of the Jewish Old Testament designated as "Prophets" was finalized about 200 B.C. This is evidenced by *Jesus Ben Sira*, a book on wisdom written around 180 B.C. The book offers praise to every famous Bible prophet from Joshua through Malachi. This historically validates the actual existence of these books immediately following their inspired origin.

By 132 B.C., various writings of the 3rd section "Writings or Psalms" were known. In 180 B.C., Judas Maccabees, son of a priest, began a Jewish liberation movement in opposition to the Syrian dynasty. Jewish independence was won in 162 B.C. from the King of

Syria, Demetrius II. Today's Catholic bible contains I & II Maccabees. They originated from the Jewish Maccabees sect at approximately 132 B.C. Although these books have correctly never been included as part of the inspired Hebrew Old Testament (Tenach), they do provide solid *historical* verification of certain facts. These books mentioned praises to saged Jewish men of God, including all the Bible prophets. It specifies the "Writings or Psalms" section of inspired Scripture was established by 140 B.C.

Furman Professor, T.C. Smith, amplifies a voice from this era in his book, *How We Got Our Bible,*

> The third section of the Hebrew scriptures, the 'Writings', was known by 132 B.C. when the grandson of Jesus ben Sira translated his grandfather's book into Greek from the Hebrew. In his prologue...he said, Whereas many great teachings have been given to us through the law, and the prophets and the others and then later 'the **law** itself, the **prophecies**, and the **rest of the books**.' He did not call the third section writings, but he simply labeled the remaining books as 'others' and 'the rest'.[12]

Another earliest recording of the 3-fold division of the Old Testament is lodged in the prologue of the book, *Ecclesiasticus* (130 B.C). It calls to reference "the Law, and the Prophets, and the other books of the fathers (Writings or Psalms)."

Josephus, the great Jewish historian, wrote in 93 A.D., his work, *Against Apion 1,8.* He expressly verifies a timeline of books from Moses to Artexerxes, King of Persia (423 B.C.), and numbered 22 Divine books containing records of all past Jewish times. He linked Ruth together with Judges, and Lamentations to Jeremiah, to arrive at 22, instead of the more recognizable 24 books. In Josephus' own words,

> For we have not countless books among us…but only twenty-two books, which contain the records of all past times; which are justly believed to be **divine**; and of them **five belong to Moses**, which contain his laws and the traditions of the origin of mankind till his death.[13]

In 90 A.D., following a synod (sacred meeting) of Jewish rabbis near Jaffa, the complete Hebrew Bible was fully recognized.

A precise list of all 39 Old Testament books appear in the *Baraita*, as quoted in the Babylonian Talmud from the period 70-200 A.D.

The Masoretic Text, or Hebrew Bible, or Tenach, or King James Bible Old Testament, however you choose to refer to God's Word, all tie together as one in the same Holy Scripture. The names associated with all of these are not indicative of different Bibles, but of different labels on the same, duplicated, Scriptural Old Testament stream flowing down through iconic ages.

The *oldest* Old Testament manuscripts <u>existing in present day</u> are from the caves of Qumran, where the Dead Sea Scrolls were found. "Scholar Solomon A. Burnham ventures to date them as far back as the fifth century B.C. Many other scholars date the fragments in the 4th to 3rd centuries B.C."[14]

Of the 830 documents discovered, roughly one-fourth of them (202) were Biblical texts. They contained fragments of the Pentateuch, the Minor Prophets, Psalms, and the complete book of Isaiah. These reflect exclusively none other than the text of the King James Bible Old Testament, or the Masoretic Text. In fact, 3 letters in the Dead Sea Scroll's Isaiah Chapter 53 comprising the word 'light' were added without changing the meaning of the verse. After 2400 years of preservation, the only "questionable" difference of the Dead Sea Scroll Isaiah to the King James Bible Isaiah amounts to 3 letters.

By contrast, an embarrassed Mr. Burroughs, Revised bible version committee chairman, said he was wrong when he made at least 13 changes in the Old Testament, after the discovery of the Dead Sea Scrolls in 1947. When will scholars learn that perfection can not be improved upon by the newest, latest, "greatest" versions? More historic details of the Dead Sea Scrolls are in Chapter 4.

Old Testament scholar Gleason Archer concluded that the Dead Sea Scrolls 'proved to be **word for word identical** with the standard Hebrew Majority Text in more than 95% of the text. The 5% of variation consisted chiefly of obvious slips of the pen and spelling variations. F.F. Bruce dittoed that the text of the Hebrew Bible which the Masoretes edited has been handed down in time with conspicuous fidelity (exactness) over a period of nearly 1,000 years.

The King James Bible Old Testament is the final reservoir of Jewish manuscripts from a cascading stream of historical documents known as the **Masoretic Text**. The Masoretic Text mirrors the King James Bible Old Testament. These books come to us Divinely Inspired **as well as** Divinely Preserved by Word-equals-Word perfect transcription (the act of copying) of the text. This *Formal*

Translation method is the key, certifying perfect preservation is not only possible, but validated.

SOPHERIM, MASORETES, MASORETIC TEXT

The *Mishnah* was written in 200 A.D. to establish traditional Jewish oral law. It supplies us with an unbroken historical record of linguists (language experts) responsible for the preservation of inspired Scripture from the time of Moses through the first century.

The Mishnah is part of the Jewish *Talmud* today. The Talmud is the complete authoritative body of Jewish tradition, which includes the Masoretic Text.

The Mishnah says, Moses received the Law from Mount Sinai, who committed it to the men of the Great Synagogue. Who are these "men of the Great Synagogue"? This group of scribes called *Sopherim* (meaning "counters") are highly credited with the transcription and care of the Old Testament for centuries leading up to 500 A.D. These revered scribes earned their reputation based on an excruciating detailed manner in which they checked the accuracy of their textual copying. Their rules for copying Scripture are legendary in the Jewish Talmud:

1. The parchments must be made from the skin of clean animals. The skins must be fastened together by strings taken from clean animals.
2. Each column must not extend more than 60 lines, or less than 48. Each line must consist of 30 letters. Nothing written could touch. Between every letter the space of a hair or thread must intervene. Between every section, the breadth of 9 letters. Between every book, three lines.

3. No word or letter could be written from memory. The scribe requires an authentic copy before him. He must read and pronounce each word aloud before writing it.
4. The pen is reverently wiped clean before writing the name of God (Elohim). The scribe must wash his whole body before writing the name of Jehovah (LORD in the KJB).
5. The ink used must be no other color than black and prepared in accordance to a special recipe' used only for writing Scripture.
6. Every letter and every word was counted. If a sheet of parchment had one mistake on it, the sheet was condemned. If there were three mistakes found on any page, the whole manuscript was condemned. Each scroll had to be checked within 30 days of its writing, or it was considered unholy. If a letter were omitted, an extra letter inserted, or if one letter touched another, the manuscript was condemned and destroyed at once.
7. The copyist must sit in full Jewish dress. Should a king address him while writing the name of God, the scribe must take no notice of him.

There are over 20 rules altogether for these scribes to follow while copying the sacred text. A scribe copyist had to pronounce each word aloud before copying, not just see it in his mind. This was to avoid any errors, duplications, or omissions. What if a scribe wrote from Genesis all the way to Malachi and found 4 mistakes on one page? According to Rule 6, he would have to start over from Genesis and go all the way through Malachi again. Jews were ordered to guard the purity of all 791,328 of God's written Words.

Romans 3: 1,2
What advantage then hath the Jew? or what profit *is there*
of circumcision? Much every way: chiefly, because that
unto them were committed the oracles of God.

Some of these copyist rules may appear to be
extreme and a little "over the top". The logistics of these
procedures is mind-numbing. The flip side is that this
Word-equals-Word method is precisely why the King
James Bible Old Testament in our English language today
mirrors perfectly the Hebrew Old Testament originally
given by inspiration of God. This helps to illustrate the
veracity of perfect Scripture preservation in Jewish hands.

The Hebrew Masoretic Text has been perfectly
copied and professionally preserved by centuried Jewish
tradition to later become the King James Bible Old
Testament in English.

Correct Bible translation occurs as the picking up
of words from the Hebrew (Old Testament) and Greek
(New Testament), carrying those words over into English,
or any language being translated into, and setting them
down very gently without losing any parts, gaining any
parts, or changing any parts. Word for word equals Word.
Translation purity simply means to copy.

The Sopherim became specialists in preserving not
only the Scripture, but recording the laws, history, and the
cultural traditions of the Jewish people. These translation
specialists flourished in Palestine and Babylon and began
to be known between 500 to 1000 A.D. as the **Masoretes**,
from the Hebrew word *mesar* meaning "to hand down".
These experts meticulously continued to copy to the
"enth" degree with equal tradition to scrupulously guard
against error.

These Jewish traditionalists inserted vowels into
the consonantal-only text, using the very same methods

mentioned previously. "The consonantal text of the Old Testament used only consonants, no vowels. The Masoretic text supplied the vowel points."[15]

The Hebrew language is traditionally a language of only consonants. That's why it ceased to be a predominantly spoken language. Not only did the Masoretes treat the language with the most unimaginable reverence when supplying the vowel points underneath the consonants (1, 2, or 3 dots), but they devised a more complex system of safeguards against scribal slips. The inconceivable detailed manner of accuracy employed by the Masoretes is not fully comprehended by us today, because the average believer doesn't take it as seriously as they did.

Masoretes numbered the verses, words, and l e t t e r s of every book. The middle word and letter was located on every line. Every line. This acute attention to every grammatical iota would ensure not one jot or tittle (letter, or tiny part of a letter) of the Scripture should pass away or be lost as it was God-given.

These Jewish scholars, chosen via the Jewish nation upon Divine authority, were highly skilled to the greatest care of sacred Scripture. Each copy was kept intact as originally given by God from the beginning. The Masoretic Hebrew Old Testament Bible in English is exclusively the 1611 King James Bible Old Testament.

God is in every syllable. [16]
Erasmus
(1466-1536)

A wonderful Sunday School teacher, and former president of the world's largest furniture manufacturer, is a dear friend of mine. Once to his church class, he described a picturesque example how to maintain purity in factory production. When producing a line of furniture, they set the first piece matching the original blueprint aside. Everything coming through the assembly line is compared to it. Why? If you compare and modernize every piece of furniture thereafter with the one immediately preceding it, little changes occurring down the line would eventually cause a <u>different</u> product at the end of the production order.

The first piece of Holy Scripture from God's revelation production line is the Masoretic Text, later translated into English, the King James Bible Old Testament. It is not a revised product of the version before it, of the version before that one, of the version before that one, of the version before that one, etc. etc. etc., ad infinity. It is a flawlessly copied product matching the blueprint *ORIGINAL*, God-inspired Scripture, because we know *how* it was copied. Word for word equals Word. The two words "Masorete perfection" mirror one another to have equal meaning.

The Masoretic Text in modern times was first labeled the *First Rabbinic Bible* in 1516, as edited by Daniel Bomberg. (Edit means: to prepare for publication or public presentation, to organize or assemble, to reissue). In 1524, Bomberg published a second edition, edited by Jacob Ben Chayyim (pronounced Ra-eme) iben Adonijah, a Jewish refugee who became a Christian. This **Ben Chayyim Masoretic Text**, called the *Great Second Rabbinic Bible* became the standard Old Testament Text for the next 400 years leading up to the 20th century. This is the Hebrew Old Testament Text mirroring the English 1611 King James Bible Old Testament. It is perfectly inspired, and equally preserved by Word-equals-Word formal equivalency method from the original, God-breathed Old Testament books.

Professor Robert Wilson (1856-1930), Ph.D. of Princeton, was a stalwart defender of the verbal (word for word) inspiration of Holy Scripture. In particular, he held the highest regard for the Masoretic Text Old Testament, which he intensely studied for 45 years. Professor Wilson could read the New Testament in **nine different languages** *by age 25*. From memory, he could recite a Hebrew translation of the New Testament without missing one syllable. He could repeat the same feat with large portions of the Old Testament.

Dr. Wilson inconceivably studied *every consonant* (1,250,000) in the actual Masorete Hebrew Old Testament, including the Masoretes' notes. After life-long examination, listen to the bearing this scholar of massive learning places upon the Holy Masoretic Text:

> For forty five years continuously since I left college I have devoted myself to the one great study of the Old Testament in all of its languages, ...being immediately inspired by God, by His singular care and providence been kept **pure** in all ages.[17]

SUMMARY

What have we learned so far? Moses wrote as inspired by God. Heaven's written revelation begins on Earth. From approximately 1400 B.C., dozens of inspired Jewish authors transmit the Words of God through 200 B.C., completing the Old Testament books. The written Word in Heaven came down to man by Divine Inspiration. Next, the Divine Preservation and utmost care of the *"oracles of God"* were charged to the safeguarded tradition of certain Jews - Sopherim, then Masoretes (Romans 3:2). The Masoretic Text became the cornerstone of Jewish culture as a nation.

- King Josiah canonizes Torah (Law of Moses: Genesis-Deuteronomy) 627 B.C.
- Samaritans canonizes Torah 400 B.C.
- Ezra canonizes Torah 250 B.C.
- Maccabees verifies Tenach (Law, Prophets, and Writings) 180 B.C.
- *Ecclesiasticus* verifies Tenach 130 B.C.
- Jaffa Jewish synod verifies complete Hebrew Bible (Tenach) 90 A.D.
- Josephus, Jewish historian, verifies timeline of all Old Testament books 93 A.D.
- *Mishnah* supplies Jewish oral law and historical line of people responsible for preservation of Scripture from Moses through the first century - 200 A.D.
- Talmud records translation specialists are the Masoretes 500-1000 A.D.
- 1st Rabbinic Bible 1516 A.D.
- 2nd Rabbinic Bible 1524 A.D.
- Masoretic Text translated into the English King James Holy Bible 1611 A.D.

- Dead Sea Scrolls (3rd-5th century B.C.) verifies Masoretic Old Testament in the King James Bible 1947 A.D.

Specialized copyists, the Sopherim later called Masoretes, perfectly copied the sacred Old Testament Scripture. The complete Masoretic Text purely comes to us today in English. It is exclusively the 1611 King James Bible Old Testament. All diverse, modern English bible versions of the Old Testament today *do not* originate from the Hebrew Masoretic Text. In spite of popular demand for new bible versions, the experts agree on the superiority of the Masoretic Text.

Professor Robert D. Wilson of Princeton, who held several doctorates and mastered 45 languages and dialects of the Near East, including all of the Semitic languages exudes:

> I have come to the conviction that no man knows enough to attack the veracity of the Old Testament. Every time when anyone has been able to get together enough documentary 'proofs' to undertake an investigation, the biblical facts **in the original texts** have victoriously met the tests. [18]

Dittos from Biblical text expert D.A. Waite,

> The results of those 30 years' study which I have given to the text has been this: I can affirm that there is not a page of the Old Testament in which we need have any doubt. We can be absolutely certain that substantially we have the text of the Old Testament that **Christ and the Apostles had** and which was in existence **from the beginning.** [19]

Everything God communicated to human writers was perfect. His many promises to preserve these Words were perfectly carried out. Every commandment was perfect. Everything God planned in His Word is perfectly carried out. Scriptural prophecies are perfectly timed. Jesus Christ did all that He did, and said all that He said, in perfection. God's faithfulness is perfect. All of this is found in a *perfect* Bible. If you want to know what perfection looks like, if you want to know where it exists today, if you want to know what a perfect person would do, read the Holy King James Bible. If obeying the Bible could make a person perfect, mustn't the Holy Bible itself be perfect? God put perfection there for all to profitably benefit and enjoy.

Those responsible for keeping the Word perfect are marked as great by Divine standards.

Psalm 68:11
The Lord gave the word: great *was* the company of those that published *it*.

Most Old Testament Scripture manuscripts can be observed at the following ancient manuscripts centers:
1. Ancient Biblical Manuscript Center (Claremont, Ca., owned by the Mormons)
2. Andrews University (7th Day Adventist)
3. Biblical Institute of Germany (owned by German government with the Roman Catholic Church)
4. Ekol Biblique of Jerusalem (Roman Catholic Church)
5. West German Institute for New Testament Textual Research (Munster, Germany)
6. Shrine of the Book (Jerusalem – Dead Sea Scrolls)
7. National Jewish Archives

8. British Museum, London, England (10th century Pentateuch)
9. Karaite Synagogue, Cairo, Egypt (895 A.D. - 6 Old Testament books)
10. Synagogue of Sephardic Jews, Aleppo, Syria (10th century Old Testament)
11. Cambridge University Library (Nash Papyrus 150-100 B.C.)

Chapter Two

The Perfect
New Testament

The King James Version is absolutely inerrant.

Dr. W. B. Riley
(1861-1947)
Northwestern Bible School, Founder
Minnesota Baptist Convention, President
World Christian Fundamentals Association, Founder
The Christian Fundamentalist, Editor

The Bible is no mere book, but a Living Creature,
with a power that conquers all that oppose it.

Napoleon
(1769-1821)

HISTORIC OVERVIEW

The New Testament apostles were inspired by God to write the Gospels (Matthew, Mark, Luke, John), the epistles (letters to the early churches), and the Revelation from roughly 30-100 A.D. It is obvious to conclude that they were not writing in English. These God-breathed books were written in Greek. The *Koine'* period, 300 BC-300 A.D., utilized the Koine' Greek semantic in every day language.

After 100 A.D., most of these inspired books were formally translated into vernacular (native) languages of other countries (Italian, French, Syrian, Dutch, Latin) and spread out across Asia Minor. These were translated so accurately that these Majority Text Bibles say the exact same thing in each language.

Mark 13:10
And the gospel must first be published among all nations.

Approximately 5,200 of these Greek and vernacular Scripture manuscripts exist today. Early Majority Text Bibles were also formally translated into Coptic, Ethiopic, Armenian, Gothic, Slavic, and Arabic. This is an important part of the King James Bible's New Testament heritage. The **Words** of God are equally preserved in these vernacular (native) language Bibles. Perfection repeats itself.

It is the fulfillment of Romans 16:26,

But now is made manifest, and by the **scriptures** of the prophets, according to the commandment **of the everlasting God, made known to all nations** for the obedience of faith:

SCRIPTURE TEXT DOCUMENTS

There are 4 kinds of Biblical, Greek manuscripts that we possess today: 1) papyri 2) uncials 3) minuscules 4) lectionaries.

Papyri are the earliest and fewest in number. Being made of papyrus plant leaves, their fragile condition have left us between 80-170 manuscripts (hand written copies). These scrolls are the kind that John witnessed in his vision in Revelation 5:1,2.

Uncial (pronounced un-see-ll) means "large or inch high letters". These Greek manuscripts are written in ALL   CAPITAL   LETTERS   with nospacebetweenthewords. No punctuation marks and no break in the text are given. They number approximately 212-267.

Minuscule (pronounce min-a-skewl) means "small letter". These manuscripts provided   space between   words, smaller case letters, and longhand "cursive" flow as our writing does today. Estimated between 2,429-2,764 are preserved for us today.

Finally, the **Lectionaries** are portions of Scripture that were read in early New Testament churches on certain days. Lection comes from the Latin root meaning "to read". Lectionaries provide unswerving evidence to show how Scripture looked in centuries past. We have an estimation of 1,678-2,143 lectionaries extant (existing today).

The sum total of Greek and vernacular manuscripts that have survived to this present day add up to over 5,200. "Only about 50 of these 5,000 contain the entire New Testament...Most of the manuscripts, however, do contain the four Gospels."[2] They range in size from small fragments to containing two or three verses to nearly entire Bibles.

Consider a most recent papyri manuscript discovery validating the Holy Bible in our day:

> There has been a remarkable recent discovery which made front page news in the *London Times*. The oldest remains of any New Testament manuscript were discovered. Using a high-magnification device and the epifluorescent confocal laser scanning technique, the small fragment was dated A.D. 66. Close examination shows that it contains the **King James Bible's** reading from Matthew 26:22, *"hekastos auton"*, - "every one of them".[3]

Furthermore, there are also in existence about 1,000 ancient manuscripts of numerous translations from the Greek New Testament into **vernacular** (native) languages of other countries. These strongly reflect as a mirror the precise Word-equals-Word perfect translation of the King James Bible New Testament from equally preserved Majority Text Scriptures.

Do all 5,200 Greek documents perfectly agree with one another? The answer is, no. There are two streams of Scripture that separately flow down through history, remember? All of these 5,200 New Testament documents flow into either the **Majority Text** or the **Critical text** stream of Scripture.

Within the first 100 years after the death of the Apostles, Irenaeus (grand-pupil to John the Apostle) said those who were corrupting Bible manuscripts **said that they were** *correcting* **them.** Corrupted copies were so multiplied that agreement between them was hopeless. The worst, Greek New Testament counterfeits originated within 100 years after it was composed.

While II Timothy **3:16** props the inspired Word: "All Scripture *is* given by inspiration of God...", II Peter **3:16** forewarns the coming of deviant bibles, "...in which are some things hard to be understood, which they that are unlearned and unstable wrest, as *they do* also the **other scriptures**, unto their own destruction."

Between 95-99% of the 5,200 New Testament manuscripts existing today, altogether mirror without question the Greek Majority Text. These overwhelmingly authenticate the King James Bible New Testament. The highest degree of conformity in Greek documents resting as a foundation beneath this Majority Text New Testament is called the *Textus Receptus*, or "Received Text". The Hebrew Old Testament Masoretic Text and the Greek New Testament Textus Receptus combine as one to form the undisputed Majority Text of Scripture manuscript documents. The Majority Text is mirrored exclusively in the 1611 King James Holy Bible.

The Greek Textus Receptus is also called the "Received", "Traditional", "Antiochian" (its roots anchored in Antioch, not Alexandria), and the "Byzantine" text. Byzantium refers to the Eastern Roman Empire, later renamed Constantinople by the 7th century, when Greek was recognized as its official language. Described as "Empire of the Greeks" during this period, the region hails presently as modern day Romania. This eastern outgrowth of the empire founded in Rome was designated "Byzantine" in the 16th century as a popular term among German historian Hieronymus Wolf and French authors Du Cange and Montesquieu. All modern textual critics acknowledge the *Textus Receptus* was the Greek New Testament in general use throughout the Byzantine Period (312-1453 A.D.).

We shall see later how Erasmus arranged Majority Text Greek manuscripts into a single Greek New Testament to embody the *Textus Receptus* in 1515 A.D. This "Received Text" is so aptly named due to its traditional acceptance by doctrinally conservative Apostolic fathers, the early New Testament churches, the disciples of Christ, and the Protestant Reformation churches.

Biblical historian and textbook author, Gail Riplinger, gives us the stats:

> 85% of the papyrus, 97% of the uncials, 99% of the minuscules, and 100% of the lectionaries agree with the Majority Text, or the Textus Receptus (T.R.).[4]

Four-time author of Bible history, Dr. David Otis Fuller in *Which Bible?*, drew a masterful conclusion that the Majority Text Scripture, upon which the 1611 King James Bible is based, is positioned for strongest claim to be regarded as an authentic representation of the **original text**.

Can you feel the strain of new version advocates who base their "updated" scripture texts on less than 5% of all scriptural, historic documents? These are the "latest and greatest" representation of manuscripts? Hardly. Contrary to scholastic popularity is the recent discovery of the world's oldest New Testament fragment, P64 (Magdalen Papyrus, A.D. 60). It corrects several of the new English bible versions, reaffirms the King James Bible text exclusively, and offers no support to the Critical text basis of modern English bible versions.

When comparing Greek texts today, the Textus Receptus is pitted against several other texts (that disagree wildly with each other), so as to make the Textus Receptus to appear in the minority, hence inferior. Don't be fooled, my friend. Critical text manuscripts will always be a minority in real numbers (less than 5%). The Textus Receptus will always represent the undisputed majority of 95-99% of Greek texts that mirror agreement with one other. This obvious reflection of perfection in the King

James Bible blinds most lower textual criticism experts who can't see the truth even when they are looking right at it.

In Chapter 4, I bring to light the blunderous Greek New Testament *Alexandrian* text, which combine together with the defective Hebrew Old Testament *Ben Asher* text, to flesh out imperfect Critical text English bibles. This is the divergent, secondary stream of "scripture manuscripts" that evolved every mutant bible since the first failed Revised version of 1885 A.D. This started the fairly recent phenomenon over the past 100+ years in our country of constantly updating, correcting, modernizing, amending, improving, revising, adjusting, modifying, altering, changing, interchanging, substituting, repairing, qualifying, neutering, reconditioning, restructuring, removing, rephrasing, everything except *preserving* the Words of God.

PRESERVATION OF INSPIRED SCRIPTURE
Shall we begin a stroll through time and catalogue together the Divine Preservation of God's Words in the New Testament? As an overview picture, the first writings of the Old Testament (Moses: Pentateuch, 1400 B.C.) up to the King James Bible (1611 A.D.) are a hefty 3,000 years, using rounded-off numbers. In between the completion of the New Testament writings (John, 100 A.D.) and the King James Bible (1611 A.D.) is roughly 1500 years. Much happened in these 1500 years.

A golden thread of Divine Preservation weaves an unbroken line of inspired New Testament manuscripts that survived more recent centuries, despite the onslaughts of hell on Earth against it. The nimble Majority Text was bequeathed to patient Christians, bullied by civil authority's minority. They sowed Holy Writ in their native tongue through years and tears of abusive suffering.

Saints, sullied in their own blood by religious bigotry, sustained the purity of God's Words that we may reap today the harvest of word-for-word Biblical perfection.

1st - 3rd CENTURY EARLY CHURCH SCRIPTURE

The peace-loving Waldenses inhabited the misty valleys of Vaudois, Italy. Waldensian Scripture, translated from the apostle's epistles into Italian, exclusively match the Majority Text of the King James Bible. P66 is a prime example of this early *papyrus* Scripture manuscript duplicating the Majority Text.

According to the historical research of Dr. Fuller's *Which Bible?*, the Waldensian Church was formed about 120 A.D., from which date on, they passed down from father to son the teachings they received *from the apostles*.

Award-winning religion writer, Jeffrey Sheler, of *U.S. News & World Report* concludes,

> There is little doubt that the earliest texts in what eventually would become known as the New Testament were letters from the apostle Paul written around 50 A.D. It is known from second century sources that **Paul's letters were being copied and widely circulated among the churches of Asia Minor** by no later than the early decades of the second century, along with what were described as "memoirs" of the apostles, which later would be known as the "gospels".[5]

The Waldenses lived by simple virtues. They retained the same religion, kept the same language, and worshiped in primitive churches for more than a thousand years. Yet, their secluded mountain district influenced the most refined and cultured parts of Europe. History and tradition profess constitute remains of their pure, Holy Scripture bequeathed to Waldenses by the first century apostles themselves. The Waldenses became "God's secretaries" who did not change the dictation of His inspired letters to us.

Scripture placed into the hands of common men became illegal by Roman Papal authority. Scripture that varied from the Catholic Vulgate bible was deemed heretical, illegal, and punishable by lawful death. Why? Waldensian Christians could not have doctrines purer than Rome's, unless their **Bible** was purer than Rome's. The sacred and preserved Majority Text passed down by Christ's apostles to the Waldenses was treasured and copied perfectly for centuries throughout steadfast generations, despite enduring inconceivable sufferings leading up the culture-shifting Reformation revivals beginning at approximately 1300 A.D. The Waldenses and their Word-equals-Word Majority Text Bible translation became the object of fury from the Papacy.

Waldensian Churches were among the first in opposition to the church of Rome and its Latin Vulgate bible originating from Critical text manuscripts in 405 A.D. History details long persecutions in Europe of these dear saints from the 4th to the 13th century by the Church of Rome. They seldom were free from intolerant oppression, even persecutions, never conforming to the religion of the state, nor the readings of Vatican scripture. They resiliently sustained the weight of Rome's vicious oppression for hundreds of years.

Lonely mounds topped with flowers in distant lands mark the graves where fell those who forsook comfort and sacrificed their lives to atrocities of civil authority. Why? To the end, that a pure copy of Divine written Words may be placed in our hands this very day. Being tortured, burnt at the stake, executed, and abusive imprisonment were the awful prices the Waldenses willingly paid to keep God's Word as purely copied as the apostles were inspired to write it. What a humbling display of divine love unfolds before all who simply open a King James Bible. To the extent that His Word avoided corruption and annihilation is credited in large part to the Waldenses who passed it down to us today in purest fidelity, and unbroken form.

Sympathetic agents of the Papal Church have destroyed historical records of the noble Waldensian past to malign their character. Jacob Gretser, a Catholic Jesuit (1578), authored 17 volumes of theological writings. In his seventh volume written against heresies of the 12th and 13th centuries, Gretser inserted the name Waldenses at each point where he struck out the names of these heretics. It would be like, if a book were written to record the lawless deeds of some vagabond, like Blackbeard (1718), and the name of George Washington (1732) were substituted.

The Waldensian church in the valley followed on to serve the Lord. She possessed unhampered manuscripts of Divine Revelation which disfigured the excathedra claim of divine "Papal Authority". Generation after generation of Waldensian **skilled copyists** handed down the pure written Word. Their reputation for Scriptural honesty spread far among the nations. In sheer terror, the papacy privately thundered at monarchs to stamp out this grass-rooted threat to their cultural stronghold. Alas, in vain the popish battalions drenched the plains of Europe with martyr blood. Death and damage wreaked its havoc. Yet, the pure Word of God remained unconquered. Thanks to Waldensian devotion more than we could ever imagine.

These saints understood how to pass off a baton. Consider this allegory. The 4x100 Olympic relay race consists of 4 runners. Each runner waits at his stage of the race for the preceding runner to complete his 100 yard leg of the track before he can begin. Not only that, he must be handed a baton by the previous runner to begin.

Suppose the first runner miscalculates. He drops the baton in the hand-off. Could the second runner pull another baton out of his pocket and keep on running? No. He would be disqualified. The second runner would have to go back and pick up the **same baton** to run an honest race.

II Timothy 2:2 describes how this works:
And the things that thou hast heard of me among many witnesses, the same commit thou to faithful men, who shall be able to teach others also.

There are 4 generations in this verse, just like a 4x100 relay race: (1) me, (2) thou, (3) faithful men, (4) others. Paul the apostle is setting the pace to relay the saving Gospel of Jesus Christ in its purest written form down to the generations following.

How can Christ's Gospel have been purely preserved from Paul the apostle to us, I wonder? How about in continuous and equal Scripture that God inspired in written revelation to mankind? Wouldn't a perfectly inspired and perfectly preserved Book of God sustain the pure Gospel inside it? This is why the Gospel of Jesus in its purest form rests exclusively in the 1611 King James Bible.

The first runner hands off the **same** baton to the second runner, who then completes his leg of the race and hands off the **same** baton to the third runner, who then completes his leg of the race and hands off the **same** baton to the fourth runner, who then finishes the race *with the same baton* that the first runner started out with.

Paul gives us this very reason to confess with him, "...I have finished *my* course, I have kept the faith"

(II Timothy 4:7). Likewise, if we desire to hand down to the following generation the <u>same</u> Gospel of Jesus Christ in its purest form, then like the Waldenses, we run the race of life with the **same Bible** "baton" delivered to us. An honest race is run with the same baton from the beginning to the end.

Hebrews 12:1
...and let us run with patience the race that is set before us.

The *canon* is a listing of books that are the standard, the rule, finalizing a written body of work. It is the accepted rule or standard by which to measure all similar books. The canon of the inspired Scripture, for example, are the 66 books we have listed in the 1611 King James Bible. This is the complete measure of inspired writings that we accept as inspired Scripture. The canon of Scripture represents *His* words.

Codex means "book". The canon of New Testament Scripture has been divinely preserved in writings on Papyrus (plant leaves), to vellum (animal skins), to codex (paper bindings in book form). The writings of early Christianity fathers from the 1st and 2nd centuries A.D. (in all 3 forms) testify to the canon of the Majority Text New Testament Scripture, especially the 4 Gospels.

Biblical scholar Hershel Hobbs assesses,

> Irenaeus was a pupil of Polycarp who, in turn, was one of the Apostle John's disciples. In his defense of the Christian faith he quotes from the four Gospels, Acts, the Pauline epistles, several of the general epistles and the Revelation; he regarded all these as inspired Scripture. Tertullian in Northern Africa does virtually the

same...By the end of the 2nd century the **canon** of the Gospels was settled. The same is true also of the Pauline epistles.' He notes that the title 'New Testament' is first used by an unknown writer about 193 A.D.[6]

Before Paul the Apostle's death at 67 A.D., he wrote under the inspiration of the Holy Spirit 13 letters of encouragement and warning, establishing Christianity in the Greco-Roman world. They amount to roughly half of the inspired New Testament books. Because of Paul's skill to speak and write in both Hebrew and Greek (Acts 21:40), his quotes from the original Hebrew Masoretic Text within his New Testament books undoubtedly give credence to the correct English translation of the 1611 King James Bible. These become a way mark of Divine authenticity.

Paul, formerly Saul, was an ecclesiastical Pharisee and murderous zealot of peaceful, early-church Christians. His dramatic conversion on the Damascus Road occurred around 34 A.D. The ministry of Paul's canonical books were collected, heavily copied, and widely circulated by the 2nd century. His vast authorship and undisputed teaching of Jesus Christ were familiar to Bishop Clement, who wrote to Corinthian churchgoers in 96 A.D., reminding them of Paul's faith from forty years earlier.

Ignatius was Bishop of Antioch, Syria. All through the book of Acts (ch.11, especially), missionary activity flows through the church of Antioch. Ignatius (martyred around 116 A.D.), one of the closest disciples to the apostle John, recognized the inspiration and authority of the writings of the apostles in his *To The Romans IV*. He wrote some seven letters in which he quoted from 18 different books of the New Testament.

Every time one of the early church fathers quotes a New Testament text, we can observe what Greek text he was using. These quotes unarguably equal Majority Text Scripture. The King James Bible New Testament therefore is the preserved canon of Scripture text that directly connects to the inspired writings of the apostles from the first century after Christ's resurrection.

John Foxe recorded in the 1500's, a statement about the four Gospels from a certain ancient English book:

> ...the four evangelists wrote the **gospels in divers languages**...since Christ commanded his apostles to preach his gospel unto all the world, and exceptioned no people or language.[7]

Between 100-130 A.D., Bishop Papias of Hierapolis described the disciple Mark as:

> ...Peter's interpreter...wrote down all that [Peter] remembered, whether the sayings or doings of the Lord. Papias also mentioned the apostle Matthew as having composed "the sayings of the Lord"[8.]

Justin Martyr, first century apologist and Christian martyr, referred to the Gospels of Matthew and Luke as *"memoirs of the Apostles"* in a letter to Rome in 150 A.D. The writings of Irenaeus, Bishop of Lyons, from 180 A.D. authenticate both Luke and John's Gospels:

> Luke, also who was a follower of Paul, put down in a book the Gospel that was preached by him [Paul]...John the disciple of the Lord, who leaned back on his breast, published the Gospel while he was a resident at Ephesus in Asia[9]

Bible history author Josh McDowell verifies,

> The number of quotations of the fathers is
> overwhelming, so much so that, if every source
> for the New Testament [Greek manuscripts]
> were destroyed, the text could be reconstructed
> merely on the writing of the fathers.[10]

Supreme importance is placed upon the church at
Antioch for the pureness of Scripture preservation by
King James Bible historians Dr. Thomas Holland, then
Bill Grady,

> The Church of Antioch has a noteworthy
> position in Scripture as the first place believers
> were called Christians (Acts 11:26). It is also
> interesting that where both Antioch and
> Alexandria are mentioned in the same passage,
> Antioch is listed as a place of service and
> Alexandria as a place of disruption (Acts 6:5-
> 10). Could it be that God, Who foreknows all
> things, provides for us our starting point in
> searching for the original text? If so, the
> direction would not be in Alexandria, Egypt.
> Instead, it would be in the cradle of N.T.
> Christianity at Antioch of Syria, where the
> **Traditional text** originated.[11]

The manuscripts which challenge the established
text of the Byzantine world, and hence, the KJB,
are Alexandrian in geographic origin. They are
named after Egypt's capital city of
Alexandria...while Alexandria pioneered the
allegorical or figurative style, Antioch
maintained the strict **literalist** mode of
orthodoxy which would naturally demand a

greater regard for **precise word-for-word copying.**[12]

Both historians capture the same essence of the Majority Text (ie: Traditional Text, Antiochian Text) during the New Testament period. Called by different labels, the same Scripture came from the exact same source - Antioch - the hub of early, apostolic Church leadership, the origin of the apostles' epistles.

The Syrian Christians (early New Testament churches at Antioch and northeast Palestine) used what we now have fragments of called the *Peshitta* Bible (approx. origin 120-145 A.D.). True to its meaning (*rule or straight*), the Peshitta set a standard in early New Testament composition. Written in the Syriac language, an Eastern Aramaic dialect, it is the sister language of Hebrew. It is very similar to the language spoken by Jesus Christ and His contemporaries in first century Palestine.

Herbert May's *Our English Bible in the Making* portrays the Peshitta's background,

> Perhaps it should be connected with the region of Adiabene, east of the Tigris, where in the first century A.D. there was a famous Queen named Helena, who became a convert of Judaism. It may be that the Syriac Old Testament is of Jewish origin...but parts of a Syriac Old Testament may be as early as the **middle of the first century** A.D.[13]

The Peshitta Bible of the Antiochian Church inspires strongest agreement with and validates the Majority Text New Testament of the King James Bible. Since the words of both languages mirror one another in translation, both texts are virtually identical. The inspired

Scripture of the apostles remain intact as documented by this first century witness. Word for word equals Word.

The apostles newly inspired epistles seeped downward into Italy from the thrust of early New Testament church missionary service.

> The first Latin translation of the Bible is known as the 'Old Latin' and was made no later than AD 157 for the young churches established throughout the Italian Alps. The 50 extant manuscripts of this version are classified by either of their eventual twofold areas of expanded circulation – Europe or Asia. Also referred to as the Itala Bible, this venerable [revered] witness was also closely allied with the **Textus Receptus**.[14]

Church father Tertullian (200 A.D.) coined the veracity by which inspired Majority Text Scripture was guarded by early church believers,

> How happy is this Church…she blends the law and prophets with the writings of the evangelists and apostles; and it is thence she refreshes herself…

> **Woe** to them who add or retrench [shorten]
> anything to or from **that which was written**.
> To wish to believe without the Scripture of the
> **New Testament** is to wish to believe against
> them.[15]

John Chrysostom ("Golden Mouth") was perhaps the most eloquent Gospel preacher and Bible expositor of the early church in Antioch, of which he was later Bishop. His homilies of the Sermon on the Mount (398 A.D.) marks a notable, continued usage of the Majority Text. The *Cappadocian Fathers* – Basil of Caesarea (379 A.D.), Gregory of Nazianzus (389 A.D.), and Gregory of Nyssa (395 A.D.), each quoted from the 6th century manuscripts N, O, S, and F.

These three saints are known for their strength in doctrine, opposing the heresy of Aryanism in its heyday, which denies the Trinity. The Majority Text is quoted by all of these fathers in comparison to the Critical text, which cannot be supported by their writings.

Other church fathers who built their initial reputations upon Majority Text Scripture include: Irenaus (192), Hippolytus (236), Vincentius at the 7th Council of Carthage (250), Clement (217), Origen (254), Lucian (312), Epiphanius (365), Diodorus (394), and Theodoret (457). Some of these men later ventured outside of sound doctrine to be excommunicated from the early church and became juxtaposed to the Majority Text, although the structure of their textual knowledge was built upon the anvil of apostolic Scripture.

History would later prove their botched doctrinal errors contributed to frustrate, not enhance, Holy Writ.

British Bible Scholar Dean Burgon pinpointed in the 1880's, the fact remains that a Divine Text has come down to us which is attested by a general consensus of ancient copies, New Testament churches, and early church fathers. Beyond all question the **Textus Receptus** (Majority Text) is the dominant Graeco-Syrian New Testament described by Burgon. The Majority Greek Text began to flourish in full form at 350 A.D. During the Byzantine Era (350-1450 A.D. approx.) all flavors of Greek texts sprang to life. Heretics were busiest then to jump on the early Bible bandwagon to prominence. In 390 A.D., Augustine recorded, "In the earliest days of the faith whenever any Greek codex fell into the hands of anyone who thought that he had a slight familiarity with Greek and Latin, he was bold enough to attempt to make a translation." However, the steady Majority Text expanded into every crack and crevice of the eastern hemisphere, as it poured forth from the fountain of Christ's atoning resurrection in 33 A.D.

Acts 13:49
And the word of the Lord was published throughout all the region.

Consider the litany of specific Majority Text Scripture evidences during the earliest centuries laid out by Dr. D.A. Waite in his book, *The King James Bible's Superiority*:

1) All the Apostolic Churches
2) The Churches in Palestine
3) The Syrian Church at Antioch (33-100 A.D.)
4) The Peshitta Syriac Version (150 A.D.)
5) Papyrus #75
6) The Italic Church in Northern Italy (157 A.D.)
7) The Gallic Church of Southern France (177 A.D.)
8) The Celtic Church of Great Britain

9) The Church of Scotland and Ireland
10) The Waldensian Church (120 A.D. - onward)[16]

DIVERGENT SCRIPTURE STREAM

A divergent scripture stream branched away from early church-accepted, inspired Majority Text Scripture. 1st century scholar Irenaeus, grand-pupil of John the apostle, gives us a realistic depiction. Within the first 100 years after the death of the apostles, Irenaeus spoke out of those perverting the inspired Scripture,

> Wherefore also Marcion and his followers have betaken themselves to mutilating the Scriptures, not acknowledging some books at all, and curtailing the gospel according to Luke and the Epistles of Paul, …**which they themselves have shortened.**[17]

Saint Epiphanius (approx. 310-403 A.D.), served as Bishop of Salamis, Cyprus at the end of the 4th century. Known for being a strong defender of orthodoxy and exposer of heresy, he published a treatise, The Panarion, which became a handbook for dealing with apostate religion shrouded in new scriptures. It describes altogether eighty separate factions of heretical parties, each planning to further its own end **by the misuse of Holy Scripture**. It becomes obviously apparent that corruptions to the New Testament are ongoing from the first 100 years after it was composed.

Do all Greek manuscripts during this infant era of the New Testament perfectly agree with one another? The simple answer is no. Just as the Word Incarnate's resurrection was attacked by Satan's lies only hours after the crucifixion through rumors that his disciples snatched His body and stole it from the empty tomb, the Written

Word was also misaligned in the 1st and 2nd centuries by confirmed heretics. This Critical text of alleged scripture reeks of the same divisive odor.

Because of "doctrinal considerations", intentional word changes on the scripture text were introduced by Marcion's revisions. By spurning the Jewish heritage of Christianity, he removed all references to Jesus' Jewish background. For him, the Gospel began with the third chapter of Luke. The omission of the birth narratives of John the Baptist and Jesus, as well as the genealogies of Jesus, the Pastoral epistles (I & II Timothy, Titus), Matthew, Mark, and John, left him with one Gospel (Luke) and ten epistles to be his bible. Marcion's repudiation of the Hebrew Old Testament (Masoretic Text), and his wild beliefs about Jesus, earned him an excommunication from the church as a heretic around 150 A.D. We can say without sophistry that Marcion is classified as among the first to set forth a corrupted version of the New Testament.

Disciples of John the apostle voice their 2nd century opinion,

> Polycarp, the bishop of Smyrna, called, him the 'first born of satan'. Justin Martyr, the first Christian apologist and martyr for his faith under Emperor Marcus Aurelius about 165 B.C., said of Marcion: 'By the help of devils he has caused many of every nation to speak blasphemies, and to deny that God is the maker of the universe.'[18]

Those following this line-up, whose doctrine is found wanting, are **greatly** responsible for funneling this Critical text pipeline. Other confirmed heretics operating in the mistranslation of scripture are Cyrinthus (50-100 A.D.), Valentinus (160 A.D.), and Sabellius (260 A.D.).

Clement of Alexandria (150-215 A.D.) was reared by pagan parents in Athens, Greece, but chose Catechetical School (to learn by questioning) in 200 A.D. Because he held Greek poets as inspired by God, he agreed with Heraclitus that men are gods possessing divinity. In his *Pedagogus* (202 A.D.), Clement accepts a Father-Mother person of God, the book of Baruch to be divine scripture, and other questionable beliefs such as his preaching against sneezing.

From Clement's writing we understand that one may attain salvation through church membership, baptism, overcoming sensuality, and by faith and works, "...present thyself to God as an offering of firstfruits, that there be not the work alone, but also the grace of God; and **both** are requisite, that the friend of Christ may be rendered worthy of the kingdom, and be counted worthy of the kingdom."[19]

Succeeding Clement as Headmaster at the Catechetical School in Alexandria, Egypt, was Origen (185-254 A.D.). Origen was the first to fully enact the *allegorical* (dynamic equivalency) interpretation and translation of Scripture. He symbolized the Bible in places of literal interpretation, and passages that clearly are symbolic, he presents as literal. As a poignant example, Origen castrated himself, because of his misinterpretation of

Matthew 19:12
For there are some eunuchs, which were so born from *their* mother's womb: and there are some eunuchs, which were made eunuchs of men: and there be eunuchs, which have made themselves eunuchs for the kingdom of heaven's sake. He that is able to receive *it*, let him receive *it*.

Before sharpening his snippers, Origen should have checked out:

Deuteronomy 23:1
He that is wounded in the stones, or hath his privy member cut off, shall not enter into the congregation of the LORD.

He included additional Apocrypha (historical, non-inspired) books *Barnabas, Didache,* and *Shepherd of Hermas*, **as scripture** in his *Hexapla* (a Critical text Old Testament arranged in six columns of Hebrew and Greek translations for comparative study). His wild beliefs contained in 6,000 letters and books would leave a distorted legacy that negatively challenged traditional orthodoxy within the church in 300, 400, and 550 A.D. Ultimately, he was confirmed a heretic, and many of his writings thusly have perished. Just what were his documented beliefs? He questioned the literal interpretation of Scripture, the truthfulness of Genesis, and the fall of man.

New Age Versions author, Gail Riplinger, exposes Origen's own belief system:

> The soul is preexistent (existent in a former state before its union with the body). There was no physical resurrection of Christ. There will not be a second coming of Christ. Man will not have a physical resurrection. All, including Satan, will be reconciled to God. The sun, moon, and stars are living beings. Emasculation (to castrate: deprive of procreation power), of which he partook...In his De Principis, Origen could not determine if the Holy Ghost was born, or if He is the Son of God.[20]

In Origen's own words,

> Who is so foolish as to suppose that
> God, after the manner of a husbandman, planted
> a **paradise in Eden**...I do not suppose that
> anyone doubts that these things figuratively
> indicate certain mysteries, the history having
> taken place in appearance, and **not literally.**
> **He died not for men only** but for all
> other intellectual beings too... it would surely be
> absurd to say that he tasted death for human sins
> and not for any other being besides man which
> had fallen into sins, as for example **for the stars**.
> ...that the Holy Spirit is the most
> excellent and the first order of all **that was**
> **made** by the Father through Christ...although
> **something else existed before** the Holy Spirit, it
> was not by progressive advancement that **he**
> **came to be** the Holy Spirit.
> Heaven...may be safely and most
> confidently placed...for they which have
> undergone **by way of purgation**
> [purgatory]...deserve a habitation in that land.[21]

The laundry list could go on. Bibles-in-transition
in the care of apostate scholars from the catechetical
school of Alexandria, Egypt, pales in stark contrast to the
literalist Word-equals-Word (formal equivalency)
Majority Text Scripture of Antioch. Origen was a prolific
writer and noted textual critic in his day, but to what end?
Dr. Kurt Aland has shown that Origen's Scriptural
citations are Critical text by choice. Later surnamed
Adamantius, "Adam" correctly reflects Origen's legacy to
fall away from the original Words of God. This divorce
from the divinely inspired, original, Greek New
Testament Majority Text originates with Origen. As the
student and protégé of Clement, Origen is commonly
heralded "Father of the Critical (Alexandrian) text."

Origen had so surrendered his better judgment to a fixation on major Bible events being allegories, that he says, "They are of little use to those who understand them as they are written".[22] In order to correctly estimate Origen's translation of Critical text scripture, we remember that he leaned into the teachings of Gnostic heresy like his schoolmaster, Clement. Thus, he lightly esteemed the historical basis of the Majority Text New Testament.

Eusebius (265-340 A.D.) was Bishop of Caesarea, a church historian, and a textual critic responsible for writing *The Ecclesiastical History* in 325 A.D. It contains historical documentation of events in the first three centuries. Modern historian, Will Durant, labels his technique of writing as "honest dishonesty".

Eusebius was commissioned by semi-Christian Emperor Constantine to procure 50 new Bibles in the wake of Diocletian's decade-long persecution (302-312 A.D.). Many believe Codices *Vaticanus* and *Sinaiticus* are two of these 50 copies, representing the Critical text Alexandrian documents. He fished for scripture in the Critical text stream of manuscripts during his translation work. Eusebius disputed James, Jude, II Peter, II & III John, even though these books were recognized by Majority Text early New Testament churches as inspired Scripture. He considered spurious (without genuine authority) Hebrews and Revelation. Eusebius couldn't get enough of Origen's teachings or books, so he co-authored an *Apology for Origen*.

Ancestry of the English Bible author, Dr. Ira Price, connects the Critical text dots between Origen and Eusebius,

> Eusebius of Caesarea, the first church historian,...issued with all its critical remarks the fifth column of Origen's *Hexapla* with

alternate readings from other columns, for use in Palestine.[23]

Jerome (340-420 A.D.) was deeply influenced by the work of Eusebius. Using the Critical Alexandrian Greek text, he translated a bible for the Roman Catholic Church with full financial backing and a full staff of copiers in 405 A.D. It is known today as the Latin Vulgate Catholic bible. Although his work is esteemed by modern day lower criticism scholarship as monumental, his text of choice was the Critical text. We sense the quiet panic of Jerome in the Preface to the Latin Vulgate bible, that his translation was a mistake,

> You [Pope Damascus] urge me to revise...copies of Scripture which are scattered throughout the world...is there not a man, learned or unlearned, who will not...**call me a forger** and a profane person for having had the audacity to add anything to the ancient books, or to make changes.[24]

We see a "chain gang" of doctrinal discord from Marcion (110 A.D.) to Clement (150 A.D.) to Origen (185 A.D.) to Eusebius (265 A.D.) to Jerome (420 A.D.) in the early days of Critical text translation as a divergent stream creating its own path away from inspired Majority Text Scripture. Acceptable or not, these men dangerously stand at odds with the traditional teachings and truths of Christ. Conservative Bible scholars would label them apostate (defection or abandonment of religious truth). Their problematic Greek translations represent a "scriptural halfway house" for bibles-in-transition. It was not the first time God's Words got twisted.

As the Garden of Eden was draped in perfection, satan parlayed woman's innocence by purposefully not recounting the **exact same words** to Eve, then to Adam, that God had already said. *"Yea, hath God said...?"* The *Tree of Knowledge* and the desire to "make one wise" still lures man's sin nature to wander away from the Creator's established Words.

Like Eve, new version translators adhere to a synthetic line of "scriptures" by dismantling God's perfectly inspired and preserved Words to re-assemble them by this world's imposing intellect. Therefore, God's Words become clouded and, perhaps unintentionally, falsified in Critical text-based, new English bibles.

Haven't we learned anything from the origin of human error? From God's *"Thou shalt **surely** die"* to satan's *"Thou shalt **not** die"*, just ONE word change altered the course of human history.

The facts tell us that these men are questionable "scholars" at best. At worst, true church heretics. They dammed up the Majority Text stream to culvert a Critical text artery which flows from seminaries to churches into homes today. Historically, the Critical text culverts together all English bible versions since 1885: The *English Revised version, American Standard version, New International version, New American Standard version, Revised Standard version, Douay-Rheims version, New World Translation (Watch Tower bible), Amplified bible, Moffitt bible, Goodspeed version, New Revised Standard version, Living bible, International Children's bible, English Standard version, New Scofield version, New King James version, 21st Century King James version, New Living bible,* et al. All are tributaries irrupting from the doctrinal disarray of the Critical text.

The facts reveal that Jesus Christ's disciples, apostles, the 2nd and 3rd generation disciples of Christ, as well as the early New Testament church rejected the

Critical text, and received the Holy inspired Majority Text Scripture and relentlessly guarded every Word. Your true New Testament choice today is clear. It lay before you as a crossroad betwixt two. It is the every-Word-preserved, inspired Scripture by way of first century apostles, or heretically-based scripture deviations by way of early church malcontents. It's the Majority Text, or the Critical text. The King James Bible is the perfect bloom of Majority Text Holy Scripture. The Critical text, covered all over with blots of doctrinal weaknesses, is parent to the current, anti-perfect Bible dogma. **ALL** modern English bible *versions* (since 1885) are the repository of the doctrinally-discordant Critical text.

4th - 13th CENTURY SCRIPTURE PERSECUTIONS

One of the first to give direct assent to all 27 books of the New Testament is verified in many *Festal Letters* from Athanasius to a church in Alexandria, Egypt, in 367 A.D.

Described as "Patriarchal Bishop" to Alexandria, Athanasius projected shockwaves of conservative doctrine across the liberal region of Egypt. The common people adored him for it. At the 325 A.D. Council of Nicea, Athanasius stood his ground condemning Arius, the founder of Arianism, a belief stating Jesus Christ was a created being. Athanasius is responsible for grounding the Bible doctrine of the Trinity into the generation of believers he influenced.

Around 400 A.D., Pope Innocent III declared cruel war on all European believers who held to the right that each Christian could read the Bible for himself in his own language. Taking it as a threat to dissolve the power of Rome, it was decreed by Innocent that "to save one-half of Europe from perishing by heresy,...the other half should perish by the sword."

The *Oxford Companion to the Bible* records,

> In Provence, the **followers of Peter Waldo**, who claimed the scriptures as their sole rule of life and faith, **translated** the **Psalms** and other books of the **Old Testament** and the complete **New Testament** into Provencal by the early thirteenth century. **Pope Innocent III attempted to suppress** the movement, but their influence was felt not only in France but also in the Netherlands and Germany and in Italy.[25]

Pope Innocent III thundered forth his pandemonium of squelching all Scripture texts outside the Latin Catholic "Vile"gate, er, "Vulgar"ate, I mean, Latin Vulgate. Countless lives of thousands of Waldenses were permanently censored without formal trials or hearings. The Critical text leaves a bloody legacy wake behind itself in its quest for prominence in religion. Freedoms were suppressed. Innocent Christians died painfully. Religious worship was manhandled by the state of civil authority. Enforced through Catholic-regulated governments, the Critical text was regurgitated back onto the lap of authorities who were forcing it down the public's throat. Meanwhile, inspired Majority Text Scripture surged westward with joyous leap and rush to regions beyond Europe.

By the first few centuries A.D., Christianity had been carried to the Britons (England), the Irish, and the Kelts, out from Jerusalem. Modern historian Lightfoot, strongly suggests that some of St. Paul's converts traveled westward and introduced the Gospel first to Britain. Paul himself, according to Clement (*Ep. ad Corinth.c.5*), carried the story of Christ to "the end of the West", meaning Spain.

Romans 15:28
When therefore I have performed this, and have sealed to them this fruit, I will come by you into **Spain**.

It is indeed probable Paul journeyed northwestward to Britain as well on the assumption of a 2nd Roman captivity. Paul's inspired epistles went with him.

Legendary history ascribes Bran, a British prince, and his son Caradog, became acquainted with Paul in Rome, A.D. 51-58. Bran introduced the Gospel of Christ by early church Scriptures, as well as the inspired epistles of Paul, to his native country upon his return. Included in these legends are Aristobulus (Romans 16:10), and Joseph of Arimathaea (John 19:38), who figures largely in post-Norman legends of Glastonbury Abby.

Wikipedia commonly notes,

> Christianity arrived in Britain in the first or second century (probably via the trade route through Ireland and Iberia), and existed independently of the Church of Rome, as did many other Christian communities of that era.[26]

Historians point as well to the attendance of the 3 British bishops of York, London, and Lincoln at the Council of Arles in 314 A.D. as an early recorded presence of Christians in England. Pelagius (360-420 A.D.) is recognized as a staunch proponent of man's free will as opposed to the forced religion system of his contemporary Augustine.

In Augustine's fourth century writing, *De doctrina Christiana,* he admits to the precision of equal Words in the Majority Text *Itala* Bible to first century inspired Scripture,

> Now among the translations themselves the Italian (Itala) is to be preferred to the others, for it keeps **closer to the words** [of the original books]without prejudice.[27]

British Isles were experiencing revival under other Spirit-filled men of Majority Text Bible preaching: Piranus (325-430), Patrick (approx. 378-493), Servanus (450-543), Drustan (470-540), Columba (521-597), and Columbas (543-615).

Known as the *Apostle of Ireland,* Patrick devoted his life to the conversion of Ireland. He recorded thousands of baptisms from over 300 assemblies which he, himself, started. Although a monk, the Christianity of Patrick was independent of Rome, appealing to the traditional Majority Text Scripture as the final authority in matters of faith. Traces of an original Latin version of Scripture differing from the Catholic Vulgate bible are found especially in Patrick's writings. He quotes from Majority Text-based Latin Scripture 75 times and only 3 times from the Apocrypha (Catholic books). He became known as Saint Patrick. Ireland's name was coined from this period of revival, as it literally means, "Island of the Saints".

> It is during this time period that the *Book of Armagh* appeared. The *Book of Armagh* is the only complete New Testament that has come down to us from the Irish church. The *Book of Armagh* contains a **non-Vulgate New Testament text.** The text was partly in Latin.[28]

The Gothic Bibles of the 4th century also burst forth the inspired Majority Text.

Partial translations out of the Majority Text were communicated in – the Psalms by Aldhelm (709), the Gospels of Egbert (766), the 10 commandments by Alfred the Great, King of England (901), and selections by Aelfric, *The Grammarian* (1020).

The Old English language was ushered in by German invasions of the Anglos, Saxons, and Jutes during the 5th century. This language upgraded to Middle English with the conquest of England by the Danish-French speaking Normans in 1066. When Rome sent out missionaries to extend her power, she found Great Britain and Northern Europe already professing a Christ-centered Christianity. They traced it back through Iona, then Asia Minor, into Antioch.

Iona, on the northwest island of Hy off the coast of Scotland, became a center of Bible knowledge and Christianity. Its most historic figure, Columba, founded a theological school and studied *precious* (Majority Text) *manuscripts*, according to historian of this age, D'Aubigne. From this center, a missionary spirit breathed out over the ocean by British missionaries armed with the Majority Text to Netherlands, France, Switzerland, Germany, and Italy. They did more for the conversion of central Europe than the half-enslaved Roman Church. Iona was justly coined the "Light of the Western World".

In 1100, *LaNobla Leyeon*, "The Noble Lesson", was written to assign official opposition by the Waldensian Christians to the Church of Rome in the days of Constantine the Great and Pope Sylvester. Their Bible was the renowned *Itala,* a Word-equals-Word Majority Text translation into Latin. The very name "Itala" is derived from the Italic region district of Vaudois.

This sparked vehement atrocities inflicted against this peace-loving civilization by Rome. A copy was presented to the Pope at the Lateran Council of 1179. However, the 1229 Council of Toulouse condemned it, and many copies were destroyed. A surviving copy was given in 1658 to Sir Samuel Morland by way of Oliver Cromwell, which now lies in the Cambridge University Library.

This inspired Bible matches exclusively the old Italic of the Majority Text and resists the Critical text Latin Vulgate. The bloodshed that flowed through the serene valleys of Vaudois all the way to a devastating massacre in 1655 ought to still our hearts and chill our conscience towards the Bible-loving Waldenses and their perfectly preserved Majority Text Scripture in Italian text.

Noted Waldensian historian and scholar, Leger, labored exhaustively during the mayhem massacres of 1655 to preserve their ancient records. Admired as the apostle of his people, Leger's assemblage entitled, *General History of the Evangelical Churches of the Piedmontese Valleys,* was published in French in 1669. Leger describes here the Olivetan French Bible, as translated **"entire and pure"** from Majority Text Waldensian Scripture. Waldensian history of its Holy Scripture is ornamented with stories of gripping interest.

Professor at Waldensian Theological College in Florence, Italy, Emilio Comba, wrote *History of the Waldenses of Italy,* in 1889. Comba's direct ancestors were Waldenses. His historical research aroused the attention of the scholarly world by showing the Majority Text Waldensian Bible "corresponds *word for word* with the [Majority Text] German [Tepl] Bible". The Tepl manuscript differs widely from the neo-scripture versions of Rome, adhering to the Majority Text.

Known for his Greek and Latin scholarship, Dr. Frederick Nolan wrote, *The Integrity of the Greek Vulgate,* in 1815. A chronological researcher and lecturer, Nolan spent 28 years tracing back the Waldensian Bible to its apostolic (days of Jesus Christ) origin. Nolan's powerful results proved the Waldensian *Itala Bible* enjoyed "unequivocal testimony of a **truly apostolic** branch...the celebrated **text of the heavenly witnesses**...which prevailed in the Latin [Waldensian] Church" (pgs. xvii, xviii).

Before the Catholic Vulgate bible was ever stamped onto the public by the iron heel of the Roman Papacy, these Divinely inspired manuscripts were perfectly copied and carried from independent churches in Judea to the valleys of Italy and spread by fruit bearing Christianity throughout Asia Minor.

Dr. Henry C. Vedder, authority on church history, said that as the Roman empire was breaking up into modern kingdoms, the groups who suffered the most were the Paulicians, the Bogomiles, the Anabaptists, the Waldenses, and the Albigenses. These curators of Scripture safeguarded the precious Majority Text from extinction, and carefully passed it down through generations without changing a word of it. Their Bibles retained Word-equals-Word translation purity. Tortured deaths of their children, and men and women, are described in John Foxe's *Acts and Monuments* (later titled *Foxe's Book of Martyrs*). While using the Majority Text, they wished to place a perfectly preserved Bible from God into the hands of common men.

To attack truth is to *s p r e a d* the truth,

II Corinthians 13:8
For we can do nothing against the truth, but **for** the truth.

The infamous 1229 Council of Toulous decried orders from the Pope for the most terrible onslaught upon simple Christians of Southern France and Northern Italy. The Church of Rome would no longer tolerate personal possession of any portion of the Catholic-despised Majority Text Word. Destroying Bibles, books, and every sacred document held precious, cruel and relentless war assailed against the Albigenses. They were publicly beaten, tortured while incarcerated, and burnt at the stake, legally.

Catholic and Orthodox historians Obolensky and Knowles both called the Waldenses and Albigenses the proto-Protestants. A Protestant is basically someone who rejected Catholic beliefs, its abuses, and separated from them. Their Bible translations into Old French, Old High German, Slavonic (language of Poland, Russia, Hungary), as well as Middle English in this period, are sometimes called West Saxon Gospels. Since these Scripture texts mirror the Majority Text at 99% (1% obvious slips of the copyist pen - repeating words, misspellings, etc.), it is solid testimony to the inspiring *formal equivalency* method that continued God's inspired Scripture. The inspired New Testament Gospels and Epistles from first century apostles and disciples were accurately copied in Word-equals-Word order without error amidst centuries of time and catastrophic events. Perfect.

Fredrick II became Holy Roman Emperor in 1220. He was King of Sicily, Germany, Italy, and Jerusalem. Boasting of his zeal for the purity of church faith, he abused both the rack and Inquisition to snuff out of his way personal enemies.

His Constitution of 1224 says,

"auctoritate   nostra   ignis   iudicio concernimus"
Heretics convicted by an ecclesiastical court, on imperial authority, suffer death by fire.[29]

"Personal enemies" routinely meant those Christians whose allegiance to God was outside the Roman Catholic Church and its beloved Latin Vulgate bible. It became official. The persecution of conservative, Majority Text believers was now in vogue. European government bureaucracy was puppet-strung to Rome, being overshadowed in the global tentacles of the Papacy. This spawned the Inquisition of the Middle Ages (5th - 16th centuries, between Ancient Age and Modern Age).

The Catholic Church made itself despot over the consciences of men. Truth is, from its beginning the Critical text has been made prominent out of the bile of religious genocide. Separatist believers who endured their abuses were well taught by the Apostle Paul, his inveterate Scripture books, and his ongoing legacy of perseverance, absorbing the aftershock of tyrannical adversity.

Pope Gregory IX followed suit in 1233. The edict of evil was reinforced by an ensuing line of Popes: Alexander (1254-61), Clement IV (1264-68), Nicholas IV (1288-1302), Boniface VIII (1294-1303).

In 1233 a church court, or Inquisition, was set up by Pope Gregory IX to end heresy, or beliefs that the church thought was wrong. It was primarily in response to the Albigenses, a religious sect of southern France. People suspected of heresy had one month to confess; those accused came before the Inquisition until they confessed. They were punished by being whipped or sent to prison.[30]

It is impossible to imagine how many victims were handed over by civic powers for Catholic Inquisition tribunals. "In 1249 Count Raymund VII of Toulouse caused eighty confessed heretics to be burned in his presence without permitting them to recant."[31] The murderous hate and slaughter pummeled true Majority Text Christians. Innocent Bible-loving believers were put into the crosshairs of a legal, yet backward, witchhunt.

The Reverend John Hooper of Gloucester, endured 3 separate attempts to start a fire due to strong winds and green fagots (bundles of sticks). After the second fire had scorched his hair, his skin, and nether parts [extremities], he cried with a loud voice, "For God's love, good people, let me have more fire!" In the third flame, he knocked his breast with his hands until one of his arms fell off, praying, "Lord Jesus, have mercy upon me! Lord Jesus receive my spirit!" Bowing forwards, he yielded up his spirit, being three-quarters of an hour in the fire.

Bishop Hooper was noted for his fervent desire to the love and knowledge of Holy *Scripture*. These and many others are actual abuses by Catholic supremacy oppression and its Inquisition during the Middle Ages. The bloodletting of Majority Text Bible custodians stain forever the every-Word-preserved King James Bible in a permanent way. Because these martyrs were spent for One Lord, One faith, One Book, not one Word was lost.

William Hunter, a teenager, was sentenced to the stake and burnt to death over refusing **one word change**. He quoted Psalm 51:17 *"The sacrifices of God are a broken spirit: a broken and a **contrite** heart, O God, thou wilt not despise."* The inquisition board insisted the word "contrite" is false. The word is "humble", said they. William Hunter refused to admit to the one-word change.

While smoke from the flames choked out his life, he prayed, *"I am not afraid...Lord, Lord, Lord receive my spirit."* The same Word "contrite" sealed by a young martyr's blood is found in the King James Bible, Psalm 51:17. The Good News For Modern Man version, as well as the Catholic New American version chants "humble" along with the Critical text inquisition board.

Conservative estimations suggest 1 out of 30 "examined" by Inquisition courts were burnt for "heresy" during the most active period of its constitution. Hundreds were slaughtered. Thousands were afflicted being permanently traumatized. Unrest due to this civil corruption by the state-sponsored Roman Catholic Church excited skirmishes between princes and peasants between 1378 -1416.

While Majority Text Scripture watered the seedlings of the New Testament church, the blood of Christian martyrs fertilized its pure Gospel fruit.

The severe Catholic Inquisition has been so aptly labeled the Dark Age (5th-8th centuries, Early Middle Ages), and the Medieval Age (Middle Ages, 9th - 16th centuries). The Roman Catholic Church's civic power sponsored widespread examination (torture), imprisonment, and deaths of Majority Text advocates until Martin Luther in 1517 A.D. As the Catholic Church cruelly tortured saints and churches of the Majority Text, was she also the divinely appointed guardian to God's "true" Bible, the Critical text?

This European full-court pressure to suppress independent Scriptures, and its Christianity independent of Roman Catholicism, eventually became a negative thrust which caused American pilgrims to search out a new religious freedom across the ocean in an unfamiliar land. They knew that "separation of church and state" is less about governmental control over Christianity and

more about the Scriptural-based guarantee of religious
and civil liberty with justice for all.

> It was for the love of the truths of this great
> Book that our fathers abandoned their native
> shores for the wilderness.[32]
> **U.S. President Zachary Taylor,** 1850

True freedom is being governed by God's Word
from within. That is why Majority Text Christians
believed this Word, every Word, must be preserved at all
cost. American freedom and independence were
eventually won based on individual *soul liberty.* This
lofty principle was coined by British Baptist Pastor
Samuel Howe, who taught it to the pilgrim Reverend
Roger Williams, passing it next to James Madison, who
penned the United States Constitution.

The King James Bible is the ballast to cultural
human rights reform. Advocates for our national freedom
were birthed out of this Inquisition Era of Majority Text
suppression.

The persecution of the *Anabaptists* were among
the worst victim's of Papal abuses. "They suffered in the
year 1528 when fanatical Catholic emperor, Charles V,
issued an edict making 'rebaptism' a *capital crime.*"[33]

Not to be out-ruled, King Henry VIII issued the
following proclamation in 1538,

> Anabaptists and the like who sell books of false
> doctrine, and all who rebaptize themselves, are
> ordered from the kingdom or shall burn at the
> stake.[34]

Anabaptists, forerunners of today's Independent
Baptist, believe that baptism, whether by sprinkling *or*
immersion, is **not** a necessary or Biblical part of

salvation, as Catholic doctrine dictates. When an individual trusts in Jesus Christ **alone** as a personal Saviour, salvation of one's eternal soul is guaranteed in Scripture. Romans 10:9, *"That if thou shalt confess with thy mouth the **Lord Jesus**, and shalt believe in thine heart that God hath raised him from the dead, thou shalt be saved."* Baptism naturally will <u>follow</u> salvation, as a church ordinance, an act of obedience that Jesus Christ Himself instituted. It is a public picture of what happened privately in the heart of a believer. Ascending from baptismal waters shows an individual's new faith and new life beginning in Christ, just as Christ Jesus raised to new life from the tomb of death. Defeated forever is sin. Heaven awaits. Hell is conquered. Jesus saves. Baptism by immersion personally testimonies this Gospel truth.

Anabaptists, who were converted out of Catholic sprinkling from childhood, were then baptized by immersion later (re-baptized), after leaving Roman Catholic doctrine to trust Jesus Christ alone for salvation. As a matter of vice-grip control over Catholic membership losses, these dissenters of Catholic faith were strung-up to suffer in public view. "The Diet of Speyer (1529) sanctioned the Emperor's decree and ordered that such heretics should be deprived of any judiciary process and killed immediately like 'wild beasts'."[35]

Catholic historians gloss over this and like travesties in the historical record. They would rather you read about a Pope's "generosity and humor", and not focus on the Pope's victims. These inhumane tortures of peaceful, Biblically obedient Christians are explained away as "the spirit of the times" and "unfortunate acts of an unenlightened age", instead of listing those who had holes burnt into their cheeks, others rotted away in malnutrious prisons, some hanged on trees, beheaded by sword, racked and drawn asunder, some roasted on pillars or torn apart by red-hot pincers, and those who escaped were driven to live in caves, rocks, and clefts from one place to another, ALL FOR REFUSING ONE CHANGE TO THE WORDS OF GOD IN TRANSLATION AND PRACTICE OF NEW TESTAMENT CHURCH FAITH.

The Majority Text Bible was at the core of these believer's independence of Rome. This Holy Scripture is the heart of what the tight-fisted Catholic aristocracy were hoping to strike down by usurpations of state authority. The Critical text has always thrived on taking the place of Majority Text Scripture by nature of bully tactics.

> I believe the Scripture to be true, and in the defence of the same I intend to give my life, rather than I will deny any part thereof, God willing.[36]
> **Ralph Allerton**
> Burnt at the stake 1557
> Written in his own blood, because he had no ink in prison

Out of the Protestant Reformation (13th - 16th centuries), and the European Renaissance (14th - 17th centuries) Eras, emerged intellectual titans of Scripture. The Renaissance revival of arts, learning, and culture gave us the painting geniuses DaVinci and Michelangelo. The Reformation gave us "the living library" Erasmus, Wycliffe, and Tyndale, the noted martyr-reformer whose death opened the King of England's eyes to God's Word.

These humbly committed, spiritual giants allied themselves with first century inspired New Testament Majority Text manuscripts. They saw their lives having a purpose - to continue to keep intact the inspired and formally preserved Scriptures. Their translation work in English became part and parcel to the long awaited apex of Holy Writ - the 1611 King James Bible. They risked everything to do so.

OLD AND NEW TESTAMENT JOINED

JOHN WYCLIFFE

This brings us to the age of "The Morning Star of the Reformation", John Wycliffe (1330-1384). Born in a small village called Hipswell in Yorkshire, he grew to achieve recognition as the most able theologian on the faculty at Balliol College in Oxford. Wycliffe was named the King's chaplain in 1366, receiving his doctorate in 1374.

Reformation efforts steadily increased on a wider scale in opposition to government-controlled churches from 1300. By 1500, the apex of this departure from forced religion swung into full view with the Protestant Reformation. It is this movement by which conservative, Christian leaders spoke out against nefarious Roman Catholic and Anglican Church dictatorship.

The Anglican Church of England is sister to the Roman Catholic Church. Beginning in 6th century, it remained under Papal (Roman Catholic) authority until King Henry VIII separated from Rome in 1534. "Bloody" Queen Mary rejoined them in 1555. The Anglican Church has always maintained a preference for traditional Catholic practices.

Reformation advocates came out of these state churches themselves, because the Majority Text Bible was being suppressed from the common man. Rome's control was like a headlock on the culture. Their converts were made from fear of negative reprisals. The Reformation ignited a revival of free will, free thought, and most importantly free access to God's Holy Words. Leaders rallying the masses to embrace these freedoms were titled Reformers.

In this era, religion was controlled by government. For example if someone lived in Spain, he had 3 religious "choices":

1. Roman Catholicism
2. Silence
3. The Inquisition (examination by torture, prison; if guilty of heresy, death).

Someone living in England also had 3 "choices":

1. The Anglican Church
2. Silence
3. The rack, burn at the stake, being drawn and quartered, or some other "persuasion".

The third options were reserved for "heretics", or reformers, who did not think the way the government wanted them to. To governments of this era, heresy and treason were synonymous.

Wycliffe turned his intellectual guns on Rome through his pen, and was named by clergy as the "Damascus blade". He wrote prolifically in Latin and English. As the monks of his day were known for their taste of "good food and bad women", Wycliffe depreciated their monasteries as "a nest of serpents, and houses of devils". Writing sermons and tracts, he emphasized that the true Church is the whole company of believers with Christ alone as its head.

Blasting apart such doctrinal heresies as purgatory, transubstantiation (the juice in communion actually materializes into Christ's blood), the priesthood, and auricular (private) confession, Wycliffe despised false teachings that left the masses in spiritual ignorance and beholden only to Rome for salvation. "He believed that the Scriptures were a sufficient rule of life apart from canon law [politics], and that every man, whether clergyman or layman, had the right to examine the Bible for himself."[37]

Those who followed Wycliffe's teachings were dubbed, "Lollards", meaning, "poor priests", because they suffered persecution for their Bible distribution and street preaching. Of course, the Roman Catholic Church and Wycliffe went back and forth condemning one another. Archbishop Arundel of Canterbury forbade, on penalty of imprisonment, anyone in his jurisdiction to read Wycliffe's works, announcing, "no man shall, hereafter, by his own authority, translate any text of the Scripture into English". The last thing anyone should do to a Christian patriot is to challenge him with the words - "you can't". This prompted Wycliffe to give the rest of his life to complete *the first translation of the entire Bible into the English language.*

Doing so in spite of terrible suffering from rheumatism and partial paralysis due to a stroke, the New Testament was completed in 1382, and the Old Testament in 1384. With little knowledge of Greek or Hebrew, the work was based primarily on Majority Text Latin manuscripts, likely the Itala Bible of 157 A.D. Majority Text manuscripts are purely the source of the first, complete English Bible.

Although modern day scholarship stresses Wycliffe's reliance on the Catholic Latin Vulgate bible of Jerome, one only needs to read the Wycliffe Bible prologue to know otherwise....

> "...[T]he church readeth **not** the Psalms by the last translation of **Jerome** [Vulgate] out of Hebrew into Latin, but another translation of other men..."[38]

Wycliffe's access to the Hebrew Old Testament was found to be in complete agreement with the Itala Bible. This means the Masoretic Text Hebrew Bible is the basis for Wycliffe's English Old Testament. Wycliffe expounds,

> "[T]he Jews were dispersed among the nations, taking with them their Hebrew manuscripts. Now this happened...that we might have recourse to their manuscripts as witnesses to the fact that there is **no difference** in the sense found in our Latin books and those Hebrew ones."[39]

"A later revision of the work done by John Purvey [a secretary of Wycliffe at Lutterworth], which *brought the translation back in tune with Jerome*, makes it evident that Wycliffe had access to some old Latin manuscripts."[40] In other words, Wycliffe translated from the Majority Text (Masoretic Old Testament - Itala and Greek New Testament), and years later his secretary *revised* it to reflect the Critical text using dynamic equivalency techniques. The revised copies never were accepted as inspired Scripture by Wycliffe Bible advocates. Why?

To the Dynamic Equivalency method, translation is not always an exact science. Words are considered *moveable parts*. Most Latin and Greek words have more than one English equivalent. Dynamic Equivalency translates *either* a conservative **or** liberal word choice. Formal Equivalency maintains the purest, conservative word choice that *matches* the word being translated from. Word for word equals Word. Most of Wycliffe's translators after him (Purvey) took his Latin words and gave them a liberal (dynamic equivalent) slant.

John Wycliffe's conservative translation work mirrors the Majority Text. Wycliffe's translators after him gave us the liberal translations of his work. There are in existence today approximately 170 copies of the Wycliffe Bible, most of them being **Purvey's revision**.

Wycliffe Bible, John 17:1,
> These things Jesus spak; and whanne he hadde cast up hise eyen into thi hevene, he seide: Fadir, the our cometh; clarifie thi sone, that thi sone clarifie thee;

King James Bible, John 17:1,
> These words spake Jesus, and lifted up his eyes to heaven, and said, Father, the hour is come; glorify thy Son, that thy Son also may glorify thee:

A *rental* fee was attached for one hour's reading of this precious treasure, an entire load of hay. And, since the Scripture was handwritten (printing press invented 1439) the *purchase* price neared four marks and forty pence, an entire year's salary.

The Wycliffe Bible marks the Middle English language in its transformative years. Written in the 14th century, Modern English would take shape through two succeeding centuries. We may compare something of a difference of antiquated words found in the Wycliffe Bible that are foreign to the Modern English King James Bible. Words such as: spelong (cave), sellis (chairs), sudarie (napkin), gemels (twins), boyschel (bushel), carkeis (carcass), and yuel (evil). These words are *not* indicative of *new* words in the Holy Bible, but simply semantic updates of the Majority Text as the English language was settling.

A Renaissance literary giant was directly influenced by John Wycliffe:

> The Oxford historian, Anthony à Wood, stated that at Canterbury Hall, Wycliffe was Geoffrey Chaucer's teacher. Chaucer wrote *Canterbury Tales,* the work chosen as most exemplary of fine Middle English writing. Chaucer and his teacher Wycliffe were merely students, taught by the Word of God.[41]

Wycliffe's pen was very active all the way to his death by stroke while officiating in his home church at age 64 on December 29, 1384. He died on the last day of the year. Thirty one years after his death, the Catholic-led Council of Constance in 1415, who condemned the Christian leader John Huss to the stake, ordered Wycliffe's writings burned and his decayed body to be exhumed and burned posthumously and released to the Severn River. In 1428, it was so done. As the Swift River carried Wycliffe's ashes, the stream of Majority Text Scripture also continued to flow well into the swelling Protestant Reformation.

Enraged by secret house churches, who worshipped by possession of Wycliffe-translated Scripture, Parliament exploded out the following decree in 1401:

> Our sovereign Lord the King...has granted, established and ordained that no one...shall presume to preach openly and secretly without first seeking and obtaining the license of the   local diocesan [bishop having territorial jurisdiction]....no one shall hold, teach, or instruct, or produce or **write any book, contrary to the Catholic faith** or the

determination of holy Church,...And if any person...is convicted by sentence before the local diocesan, the mayor and sherriffs of the city shall, after such sentence be proclaimed, receive those persons....**and shall cause them to be burned** before the people in a prominent place, in order that such punishment may strike fear into the minds of others, nor their authors and favorers, be sustained...or in any way tolerated.[42]

Among the many burning victims were: John Badby (1410), a tailor; two London merchants, Richard Turming and John Claydon (1415); Joan Broughton, the first woman, perished at Smithfield with her daughter, Lady Young beside her! Foxe adds, In 1519 seven martyrs were burned in one fire at Coventry, 'for having taught their children and servants the Lord's prayer and the 10 commandments in English.' Cardinal Alexander VI (1488) brought Florentine Reformer, Girolamo Savonarola, to the stake, a converted Dominician who wrote of his distain against the standard hypocrisies of Rome. The sweet Joan Clark was obligated to light the fagots (bundles of kindling) that would torch her own father, William Tilfrey, in 1506. A pregnant woman suffering in the flames at Channel Islands delivered her baby, only to have 'the fair man-child' retrieved and cast back to the mother's side to be burned with her.[43]

Religious wars racked Europe. Prisons overflowed with suffering saints. Anglican Church-controlled British Parliament decreed the burning deaths of anyone who read, wrote, copied, taught, or preached from Majority Text Scripture contrary to Catholic Church scripture, the Critical text Latin Vulgate bible.

What maddening, documental abuses of authority! It is directly from this Critical text legacy that today's modern bible versions breed, like it or not. This is a whole world of difference to the every-Word-preserved Scripture that the King James Bible alone secured from this furnace of affliction.

The mere *possession* of a Wycliffe Bible was enough to bring a common charge of heresy by the Roman Catholic Church. We flippantly possess the Wycliffe Bible's likeness today without common regard to the awful human price of Divine Preservation.

From the time Polycarp, disciple of John the Apostle, was burnt at the stake (155 A.D.) for openly advancing the truth of Jesus Christ contrary to the political system of religious beliefs, the written Words of the same inspired Majority Text would also become illegal to possess, read, or copy. While singing hymns, the fire danced in a circle surrounding Polycarp but did not touch him. The order was then given to stab him to death, and afterwards his remains were burned.

Likewise, liberal heat waves aimed at Christian oppression still sizzle today. However, the unique tendency *inside religious circles* to melt down King James Bible perfection is recent to its own history. Contemporary leaders of Critical text Greek New Testament, Wescott and Hort (1870), chose the words "vile" and "villainous" to describe their feelings toward the *Textus Receptus* that flourished through Majority Text Scriptures.

ERASMUS

Because Wycliffe translated from *Latin* (Itala Bible) into English, there arose a need for a single embodiment of the 1st century inspired *Greek* New Testament manuscripts. Its acceptance by conservative spiritual leaders, as well as doctrinally sound New Testament churches, earned its label, Received Text, or *Textus Receptus*.

The one to collate (collect) and copy this text was the highly sought after intellectual giant, Desiderius Erasmus (1466-1536). His contribution to producing *the first printed Greek New Testament*, and his 5 editions (esp. his 3rd ed.), would pioneer and set the standard high for wholly preserved Scripture. He is revered as the "Father of the Received Greek Text".

D.A. Carson sheds light on the historical backdrop,

> The only major area where Greek was spoken as a living language from about the end of the 3rd century on, was the eastern part of the empire, which came to be known as the Byzantine Empire...With the fall of Constantinople (AD 1453), the Byzantine Empire, or what was left of it, collapsed, and many of its scholars fled west, **bringing their manuscripts with them**. The Renaissance more or less coincided with their arrival; and the new thirst for knowledge of the languages in which the Scriptures had been given, gave impetus to the Reformation and to the early textual work of Desiderius Erasmus.[44]

Erasmus' 2nd edition would be used by Martin Luther in 1534, to give Germany its first complete German Bible. Government heads courted his citizenship. He declined professorships at the leading universities, such as Leipzig and Ingolstadt. Enticing him were King Francis I of France, Pope John Paul III of Italy, King Charles of Netherlands, and the King of England.

Henry VIII implored Erasmus,

> I propose therefore that you abandon all thought
> of settling elsewhere. Come to England, and
> assure yourself of a hearty welcome. We shall
> regard your presence among us as the precious
> possession that we have. You shall name your
> own terms; they shall be as liberal and honorable
> as you please.... We ask nothing of you save to
> make our realm your home.... Come to me,
> therefore, my dear Erasmus, and let your
> presence be your answer to my invitation.[45]

In his childhood, an uncle sent Erasmus and his
brother to a Catholic monastery after plague-related
deaths of both his parents. This early grounding in
Catholicism gave him later authority to speak out against
the Church's manifold abuses. Erasmus manifested a non-
Catholic attitude of puting God's Word into the hands of
every common man.

Erasmus traveled extensively throughout Europe.
He was welcomed as a precious commodity everywhere.
His collation (collection) of Scripture manuscripts from
hundreds of sources, libraries, and schools of learning in
every crack and crevice of the Eastern peninsula, earned
him the reputation as a "living library". In eight years, his
collection of Greek manuscripts stacked up to 5000.

Erasmus' *rejection* of the Latin Vulgate bible was
evidenced by his division of documents into two
categories – the Received (Majority) Text, and those few
not in agreement, namely the Critical text Codex
Vaticanus. Vaticanus is a Catholic Greek text of
"unknown origin" (resides in the Vatican since 1475).
Erasmus recognized it as conforming to the Latin Vulgate
bible of Rome, because of an ancient written agreement,
the *Bulla aurea*.

This document explains the condition of a union between 1st century Greek and Roman churches in Florence. These churches gave in to Roman Catholic pressure, much **unlike** the Waldenses and the Albigenses. It said that the <u>Greeks</u> must *conform their readings* of Scripture to those of the Latin Vulgate in order to join together. This is why Latin Vulgate manuscripts match only a handful of Greek manuscripts (44), such as the Codex Vaticanus and Codex Sinaiticus (discovered 1844), of which virtually all new bible versions are translated from (see Life and Letters X, p. 355 / Cambridge Volume III, p. 203-4).

Erasmus was acutely aware of these intertwined "scripture" readings and attributes them to Origen (Father of Critical text Alexandrian manuscripts). Erasmus himself said in the Preface of his Majority Text Greek New Testament, that he consulted, not the Latin Vulgate, but the ancient Italic Bibles (the Itala) during his several tours to Italy's libraries (see Nov. Test. Praef. Basil: Froeben, 1546, p. xi).

Let us rummage through Erasmus' library to uncover an important manuscript collection. At age 35, Erasmus came across the manuscript of Lorenzo Valla's annotations from 3 Greek New Testament manuscripts in the library of Premonstration abbey at Pare. Valla had noted many errors in the Latin Vulgate. Erasmus, then, devoted much of his career to the task of developing, refining, and extending Valla's study methods.

He devoured and exhausted entire books, book shelves, and libraries from city to city. He wrote in his *Life and Letters* how two assistants helped him to carry the heavy manuscript load and arrange them. While spending time in Venice, Italy, because it had the world's only native Greek-speaking teachers, Erasmus wrote a book on the proper pronunciation of ancient Greek. By age 40, he was the world's leading authority in Greek, and because of all his study and scholarly research, Greek scholars became obligated to Erasmus and inundated him with GREEK manuscripts.

While teaching at Cambridge for 4 years, he spoke of his collation of over 5000 ancient Greek manuscripts. They were enough to represent the entire New Testament many years before the translation work began on the text (Life and Letters, p.92).

Erasmus knew the inspired Scripture of God is equally and obviously patterned in the Majority Text documents. His life mission was purposed in pulling all of the known Greek Majority Text documents together into a single Greek New Testament. Critics of Erasmus attempt to make his real accomplishments seem blown out of proportion, or of lesser value. Why? It's the difference between the life mission of a realist and a critic. Realists serve fact-finding missions for truth. Critics aid fault-finding missions on truth. A critic's opinion should never be allowed to trump fact.

Available to Erasmus was the 1383 Psalms and New Testament by Johan Schutkenin, the Ferrar Bible of 1417, the Bible of Alba, the 1477 Delft Bible, which circulated widely in the Netherlands, and the Spanish Bible of Alphonso II, translated from the vernacular French into Spanish in 1287. None of these Bibles were of Latin Vulgate Catholic origin. These Majority Text Bibles, stolen from their owners during the Inquisition, "lie hidden in manuscripts scattered in many different libraries, awaiting those who will study them" (*Erasmus*, Cambridge, p. 491).

Today we have copies of Italian Bibles that would have been very familiar to Erasmus: the Tuscan version of the early 1200's, a Venetian dialect Bible of the 1300's, the Riccardiani Bible of 1252, the Malermi Bible of 1420, and the Jenson Italian Bible. Erasmus would have no problem determining what readings were accepted by the *real* body of Christ in Italy.[46]

The names associated with all of these Bibles are not indicative of *different translations*, but of the *different men* who edited (reissued; to prepare for publication) the same Majority "Received" Text of the Bible in their native language.

Erasmus verified his Greek text with Majority Text Scripture quotations directly from early church writers. He spent almost 15 years formally translating just the works of the Patristic (church fathers) writings. These represent the oldest inspired Scripture readings from the 2nd, 3rd, and 4th centuries, predating by several hundred years the Critical text Vaticanus and Sinaiticus manuscripts. His impeccable translation work was the capstone that peaked 50 years of his devoted life work.

To his credit, Erasmus masterfully completed the *first, complete, printed Greek New Testament* in 1515 at the zenith of Renaissance literacy (Life and Letters, p. 119). This printed Majority Text Greek New Testament (*Textus Receptus)* is validated by, and in equal word agreement with the inspired *hand-written* Majority Text Greek manuscripts that were already received by followers of Christ Jesus in the historical record.

The remainder of his life up to his death in 1536 would be spent overseeing 5 revisions (1516, 1522, 1527, & 1535) of *misprinted* errors and spelling adjustments, as the printing press was then an advancing invention from 1439. It is his 3rd edition that is the basis of the New Testament for the King James Bible committee in 1611.

Erasmus was fabled for his exacting care of the transcription of Scripture. This is because Erasmus knew the Majority Text Words he was translating from were God-breathed. While lifting each Word of inspired Scripture from one text into another, he believed the exact same Word should remain. He perfectly copied. There was not one Word change from its original form. Word for word equals Word. His intellectual might did not trump his sense that God's Words, as witnessed by manuscripts predating him back to the day of Christ, should never be tampered with or altered. Perfection? It is more than possible, yeah probable, with Erasmus.

God is in every syllable.
Erasmus[47]

Critics of Erasmus ludicrously assert that he did not have access to all manuscript copies we have today when, in fact, he did. He exhaustively reviewed *every* current Majority and Critical text Scripture reading, including the Vaticanus in Rome. His acquaintance, Professor Paulus Bombasius at Rome, checked it frequently against the true Old Itala reading. That Bombasius also sent Erasmus the readings he requested is obviously noted by his two-fold division of manuscript evidence.

Critic extreme, Kutilek, flabs to his readers in pamphlet form, "The work on the Greek text was hastily and carelessly done...in great haste."[48] Uhmm...Question - how is a 50 year project "great haste"? Also popular King James Bible critic James White calmly states in his *King James Only Controversy,* that Erasmus did not even know Hebrew (p.54); he "created and guessed" at words he wasn't sure of (p. 58, 59), and translated the last 6 verses of Revelation from the Latin Vulgate, because there was no Majority Text readings of the same. Whew boy.

Well, first of all, it was not necessary to know Hebrew, since he was translating from **Latin to Greek, and handwritten Greek to printed Greek,** to copy the **New Testament** *only.* Mr. White correctly notes a brilliant associate of Erasmus, Oecolampadius, a leader in later Reformation efforts, looked up references in the Masoretic Hebrew for verifications in the Old Testament. Secondly, a "created and guessed at" approach is necessary *only* if one believes Erasmus' resources were limited. This we have already shown is opposite of antiquity (relating to history).

Erasmus *only* **copied**, not created, the Divine Text from the "solidly based Greek originals", as pointed out in *The Collected Works of Erasmus*, Epistle 384, 3:222-223. And finally, the **seven** manuscripts for the last six verses of Revelation Erasmus availed himself to, from the **Latin Old Itala Bible**, are as follows: c(6), dem (59), g(51), h (55), m (PS-Auspe), reg (T), t (56), and z (65). Even Critical text advocate Bruce Metzger admits in his Appendix to his third edition of *The Text of the New Testament*, that White and his own book categorically misrepresent Erasmus (p. 291). White's book is a best seller in Christian circles today.

Unfortunately, the standard fraud perpetrated against Erasmus' work stems from a popular, yet distorted, 1899 *Life and Letters of Erasmus,* by J.A. Froude. The *Dictionary of National Biography* assesses Froude's methods,

> Froude was charged with misrepresenting the views of many persons...He was accused of misreading his documents and even manipulating them in order to justify his preconceived ideas...Professor Norton says, Almost every letter in the Life...which I have

collated with the original is incorrectly printed, some of them grossly so.[49]

Froude's father, who knew him best said that his son "was little better than a common swindler". His own biographer, Lytton Strachey, writes that Froude's work was seen as "a mass of inaccuracies" by one of Oxford's greatest history professors, Edward Freeman.[50]

In Froude's own words,
I have...compressed the flow of Erasmus' eloquence, and have omitted some parts of it.[51]

There were thousands of manuscripts for Erasmus to examine, and he did. The inspired Majority Text had an outstanding history in Greek manuscript orthodoxy, Syrian and Waldenesian church acceptance, Spanish utilization, Latin profundity, and Italian-rich representation. Internal evidence of these documents constitute an overwhelming argument for the proof of God's providence to provide Word-equals-Word exact preservation. At last, after a harsh millennia and a half, the New Testament was completely printed in the original Greek tongue (1515).

The fog was rolling away, and strains of new gladness were heard in a crescendo from the whole choir of inspired textual voices that broke forth into this Text Divine. As the poet so aptly coined, *"Truth that was crushed to Earth shall rise again"*.

Erasmus' feat inspired other Majority Text native translations that followed: French versions LeFevre and Olivetan (1534, 1535); the Swedish Uppsala Bible (1541); a Spanish translation of Reyna (1569); the Danish Christian III Bible (1550); Biestkens' Dutch work (1558);

the Czech Bible (1602); and Diodati's Italian version (1607).

    As a result of revival coming from the 1558 Dutch Bible, the Dutch declared religious freedom for everyone. The Dutch nation fought for the Reformation and religious freedom. Amsterdam, capital of Netherlands, became an open city, and English Puritans arrived by the boatload.

    These list a few of several vernacular (native tongue) Bibles harmonious with the printed Greek New Testament of Erasmus. This westbound movement of the inspired Majority Text Word was destined for the ultimate manifestation in another expanding language – Modern English.

WILLIAM TYNDALE

The era of William Tyndale came due (1494-1536). He became acquainted with Erasmus at Cambridge and experienced a spiritual enlightenment there, similar to that of Martin Luther, that released him from the dogma of priesthood.

Herman Bushchius, a friend of Erasmus and pen pal, described Tyndale as "so skilled in 7 languages, Hebrew, Greek, Latin, Italian, Spanish, English, French, that whichever he spoke, you would suppose it his native tongue." While Wycliffe translated from Latin, Tyndale eluded to the original language of the Greek New Testament. Tyndale had among his study helps Erasmus' 2nd and 3rd editions of the Greek New Testaments, and Luther's German Bible. Tyndale did not utilize Wycliffe's Bible because the revisions of Purvey upon it were stilted and mechanically discordant from more accurate Majority Text Bibles.

Capturing the daring spirit from Wycliffe to "put the Word of God into the hand of the ploughboy", his sole motivation was to translate the Majority Text Greek New Testament into English from the Textus Receptus of Erasmus' 2nd, and 3rd editions.

Due to Anglican Church religious oppression in England, Tyndale fled to Germany to complete his work. This British scholar gave his beloved countrymen their *first ever* _printed_ *English New Testament* in 1525.

This first printed English New Testament is formally translated from the Majority Greek Text of Erasmus, who precisely copied and printed inspired Greek handwritten manuscripts of the 2nd-4th century apostles, and early church leaders. Word for word equals Word.

Indicative of the fear that common people would neglect the Catholic Vulgate bible, authorities in Parliament passed an act in 1543 prohibiting the reading of Tyndale's New Testament. It became punishable by law.

> **No manner of persons**, after the first of October, should take upon them to **read** openly to others in any church or open assembly...**the Bible or any part of Scripture** in English, unless he was thereunto appointed by the king...on pain of suffering **100 months imprisonment**...**no woman**, except noblewoman and gentlewoman, **might read to themselves** alone...the New Testament or to any other, privately or openly, on pain of **one month's imprisonment.**[52]

Compatriots of the Tyndale Bible were equally excised with unimaginable grief,

> Thomas Curson was martyred in 1530 for 'having the New Testament of **Tyndale's translation**, and another book containing certain books of the Old Testament, translated **in English**...'

> Lawrence Staple was martyred in 1531, 'For having the Testament **in English**, the five books of Moses...'

> Christopher, a Dutchman from Antwerp, was martyred in 1531, '[F]or selling certain New Testaments **in English**.

> Walter Kiry was martyred in 1531, because he 'had and used...The Testament **in English**.

> John Mel was martyred in 1532, 'For having and reading the New Testament **in English**, the Psalter **in English**...'

William Plaine was martyred in 1541 for 'loud reading the **English Bible**' to expose false Catholic practices.

Stile was burned at the stake and a copy of the book of Revelation was 'fastened unto the stake, to be burned with him'.[53]

Betrayed months later by an undercover Catholic agent, Henry Phillips, who had gained the reformer's confidence, Tyndale was arrested and imprisoned for 18 months. Oddly, as his New Testament was being smuggled and secretly spread throughout England, the King's own patent printer, Thomas Berthelet, was printing a folio-edition of Tyndale's New Testament in London with his name on the title page. This became the *first copy of New Testament Scripture ever printed on English ground.*

What an ultimate price Tyndale paid on October 6, 1536, in Vilvorde, Belgium. Despite the efforts of Thomas Cromwell, vicegerent in ecclesiastical affairs for King Henry VIII, Tyndale was convicted of heresy and sentenced to burn at the stake. After being strangled by the hangman and burning in flames, his last words of zeal were these: "Lord! Open the King of England's eyes". This request was granted as King Henry himself sanctioned two English Bibles within a year of Tyndale's martyrdom. Tyndale is commonly hailed as "Father of the English Bible". Foxe labeled him the "Apostle of England".

Chapter Three

The 1611
King James Bible

*The Authorized Version translators have taken care to
reproduce the syntactic details of the original.*

The Literary Guide to the Bible
Harvard University

*...Authorized Version, the one that came into being when
the England of King James was scoured for translators
and scholars. It was the time when the English language
had reached its peak of richness and beauty. It has
already been gotten right.*

Ronald Reagan
(1911-2004)
40th President of the United States of America
Cold War Victor

*Thank God for this precious Book, divinely written
and divinely given to save the world*

Sam Jones
(1847-1906)
Renowned Methodist Evangelist, Revivalist

COVERDALE, MATTHEWS, GREAT, GENEVA, BISHOPS - MAJORITY TEXT BIBLES

The first of England's two sanctioned Bibles is named after Tyndale's former proof reader, Miles Coverdale (1488-1569), called the **Coverdale Bible**. Using Tyndale's New Testament, and Luther's German Bible with minimal aid from the Swiss Zurich Bible, as well as Tyndale's formal translation of the Pentateuch (Genesis - Deuteronomy), this translation became *the first* **complete** *English Bible ever <u>printed</u>* in 1536.

Coverdale was converted out of the monastery to evangelical preaching from the influence of William Tyndale. He became an outspoken opponent of Romanist liberal teachings. *Encyclopedia Britannica* states of Coverdale that he "began to preach against confession and the   worship   of images."[4]   His book, *The Old God and the Newe*, marks a line in the religious sand distinguishing the clear teachings of Christ. Tyndale and Coverdale began to polish an English Majority Text Old Testament while in refuge from Britain's persecutions in Hamburg. Having both recanted the Catholic faith, they knew how to distinguish the pure Majority Text from the Catholic Vulgate Critical text. Coverdale was hired by Jacob van Meteren, an Antwerp merchant, to oversee this first-ever PRINTED English Bible.

He prudently dedicated the Holy Bible to the King of England, Henry VIII, as the "defender of the faith" with a drawing of him seated, crowned, and a drawn sword in hand on the cover page. The King personally licensed it, perhaps after feeling the sting of Tyndale's death.

Coverdale specifically addresses the omission of the Apocryphal (Catholic) books from the Old Testament. They were placed *in between* the Old and New

Testaments for historical record of the intertestamental period. Coverdale prefaces them with distinct intent:

> ...[Apocryphal books] are **not to be reckoned to be of like authority with the other books of the Bible** neither are they found in the Canon of the Hebrew...[and] are not judged among the doctors to be of like reputation with the other scripture...
> And the chief cause thereof is this: there may be many places in them, that seem to be repugnant unto the open and manifest truth in the other books of the Bible.[5]

Attractive wood-block illustrations surround the title page. Six pictorial woodcuts of the 6 days of creation introduce the reader to Genesis. Pictures and 188 visual aids enhance the Bible throughout. Historical geography was orientated by an aerial map of Bible lands. The original imprint on the cover gave the title as *BIBLIA*. The inside Introduction to the Reader signifies,

> The Bible, that is, the holy scripture of the Olde and New Testament, **faithfully and truly translated** out of the Douche and Latyn in to Englishe.

There is in existence today approximately 120 copies of the Coverdale Bible. Kenneth Connolly's *The Indestructible Book*, quotes Coverdale verifying that the Holy Bible in English is just as much the Words of God as the originally inspired books:

...the Holy Ghost is as much the **author** of it in Hebrew, Greek, French, Dutch, and **English**, as in Latin.

Coverdale refers to the English Bible to be inspired Scripture in the *Prologue*,

> Finally, who so ever thou be, take these **words of scripture** in to thy heart...to the worship of the **author** thereof, which is even **God himself**:[6]

It bears repeating. Remember, the name-titles associated with all of these Bibles are <u>not</u> indicative of *different or new Bibles*, but of the *different men* who edited (to direct for publication; reissued) the <u>same</u> Majority "Received" Bible Text in *their* native language.

Middle to Modern English language was still in formation. Correct spelling would come into play during the mid 1700's. So, the Holy Bible needed certain edits as the English language was settling down. HOWEVER, the <u>*words*</u> **of Majority Text Scripture have never evolved.** The Words of God are what they *always have been* in the Majority Text.

Many King James Bible critics attempt to discredit Scripture perfection by saying that the Majority Text went through "several thousands changes", even after 1611 A.D. This assertion is patently ludicrous.

The straight truth is, the Majority Text was Divinely Inspired and Divinely Preserved word-by-word beginning with Moses (1400 B.C.) through 3000 years of exact transcription into the 1611 King James Bible. The "changes" that critics distort are the *orthographic* and *lithographic* edits. Orthographic means **spelling**. Lithographic means **printing**. There have been updated edits for both as needed, due to the *formation of the*

English language over centuries of time into its present and complete state.

Examples of orthographic (spelling) changes: The Middle English alphabet (established 15th -16th centuries) was not finalized when the entire Bible was first printed in English. The letter "v" was used in place of the letter "u". The letter "f" was used in place of the letter "s". The letter "i" was used in the place of the letter "y", "ch" for "g". The rules for the "silent e" at the end of a word had not arrived yet.

As the English language was being sorted out, these letters, and like grammatical rules, were applied to reflect correct spelling, and correct alphabet usage for the inspired, unaltered Scripture already in existence. I realize it overstates the obvious, but the ***text*** of inspired Holy Scripture REMAINS THE SAME throughout. Thanks to Word-equals-Word formal equivalency translation of Majority Text Bibles.

Examples of lithographic (printing press) changes: For several decades following the invention of the printing press (1439), each character on the press was changed by hand (and by candle light!). Each character. Each letter. Each period. Each number. It was dull, monotonous work. Sometimes words were repeated. Phrases were repeated. Or, a word, phrase, or an entire verse was inadvertently omitted. **These were not errors of the text**. They were simply copyists errors. When they were discovered, the printing mistake was corrected under the next printed edition.

Each reissued printing took on a new name to distinguish it from the previously one, yet ALWAYS contained the same Majority Text Scripture. Remember, different names of the same Majority Text Scripture only represent the men who edited it for spelling (orthographic) and printing (lithographic) typos. Different names never means different Bibles in the succession of Majority Text Holy Scripture.

Don't be fooled by "Professor Dum-bum", or some other armchair theolog who gleefully tirades that the Majority Text, Textus Receptus, or the 1611 King James Bible (all one in the same) have gone through "several thousand changes", "just like all other English versions". Not the way critics mean it. Spelling, printing press, and linguistic adjustments are not "Scripture text changes".

Again, although there have been edits for spelling and printing press errors, THE HOLY **TEXT** OF INSPIRED SCRIPTURE HAS NOT CHANGED. People unaware of this phenomenon see nothing wrong in changing the <u>text</u> of Scripture. Most using Critical text bibles have been misled to believe that all scripture versions go through changes in the text. All, **with one exception**. The history of the King James Bible definitively proves itself unique to this fact.

The primary purpose of this book is to magnify perfectly *continued original inspiration* within Divine Majority Text Scripture from its original source, the Words of God. The King James Bible IS THE ONE AND ONLY BIBLE that embodies **preserved Words of original inspiration** cascading from the pristine reservoir of God-breathed Scripture into Word-equals-Word formal translation through epochs of history.

The second Bible gaining official sanction in 1537 by King Henry within a year after Tyndale's death is known as the **Matthews Bible**. The translation work was done by the renowned Reformationist, John Rogers (1500-1555), taking the pen name Thomas Matthew, because of his well known association with Tyndale.

John Rogers matriculated at Cambridge and graduated in 1525. He became a chaplain in Antwerp. There, he met William Tyndale, who led him to receive

Christ as a personal Saviour. Under Tyndale's discipleship, Rogers became an energetic reformer. He settled down in marriage with Andriana Pratt who mothered their 11 children. Rogers took Pastorate of a church in Wittenberg.

The fundamental improvement in the Matthews Bible is the inclusion of Tyndale's "dungeon works" of Joshua through II Chronicles while in prison. The Pentateuch emanates from Tyndale's Bible. Also, Rogers secured some assistance from the Majority Text French LeFevre and Olivetan Bibles to fill in the needed Old Testament gaps. The New Testament exclusively mirrors the Majority Text of the Tyndale Bible and the French Olivetan Bible.

Olivetan, a relative of John Calvin and Pastoral leader of the Waldensian valley, translated a Waldensian Majority Text Bible into French. The Preface of the Olivetan French Bible acknowledges the direct connection of Christ's apostles to Waldenses Scripture, "*since the time of the apostles*...the torch of the Gospel has been lit among the Vaudois [dwellers of the Waldensian valley]... and **has never been extinguished.**"

Leger, notable scholar and historian of Waldensian persecutions in 1655 labeled Olivetan's French Bible "**entire and pure**". This means that the Majority Text Bible sanctioned by the Waldensian Church directly descends from the same God-breathed Scripture set forth by the apostles of Jesus Christ, who ministered personally within their communities. It was formally translated *with purity* into the French dialect by way of the Olivetan Bible, and arrived in perfect Word-equals-Word order on the desk of the future 1611 King James Bible committee.

Along with chapter summaries, the Matthews Bible is filled with woodcut illustrations, marginal notes, as well as a first ever alphabetical concordance-dictionary at the beginning. It was dedicated to,

Prynce Kyng Henry the Eyght and Queen Jane

The Matthews Bible licensed by the King made it legal to buy, read, reprint or sell. A royal proclamation gave the Matthews Bible ecclesiastical and royal recognition, decreeing it to be "openly laid forth in every parish."[7]

Rogers, too, separated the Catholic Apocryphal books from the canon of Scripture, saying,

...the books called Apocrypha...are not found in the Hebrew or in the Chaldee.[8]

Rogers himself died victim to a martyr's death. Two throne changes after Henry, Queen "Bloody Mary", a vehement Catholic, condemned Rogers to death as a heretic. On his way to death by fire, Rogers met his lovely wife and 11 children who comforted him by repeating Psalm 51. Foxe records that he took his death with wonderful patience, bathing his hands in the flames as if it had been cold water.

Wycliffe, Tyndale, Rogers. These men were not only preservers of God's sacred Words by ink, but were spear catchers of hell's fury. They are heroic legends. Giants in history. Men of intellectual gifts. Public servants, preachers, champions for truth. They shielded a perfect Bible with their quills, and literally with their bodies. Religious and political landscape took shape through their devotion. Released now was a native English copy of God's Word, as pure as the original inspired books, into the hands of common culture. Will we yawn our way through Scripture reading in church again? Will men "tap out" over the suffering that spiritual warfare yields? How can we, when so much blood-soaked courage have gone into the sacrificially preserved Holy Bible?

1538 brought about a work of exceptional size, 16½ x 11 inches, called the **Great Bible**. Miles Coverdale oversaw this re-editing of the Matthews Bible. The work was overseen by Thomas Cranmer, Archbishop of Canterbury. It is sometimes called Cranmer's Bible. Cranmer died in Queen Mary's fires of martyrdom in 1556.

Non-textual changes were sparse, such as the excising of Roger's controversial marginal notes, (I Peter 3 notation said if a wife was disobedient and not helpful, she should have the fear of God beat into her head, to learn her duty, and do it, hence, the nickname "Wife-Beater's Bible" was synonymous to the Matthews Bible).

The Great Bible was officially issued in 1539. The title page boasted of a remarkable woodcut picture of King Henry handing a Bible to Archbishop Cranmer, who represents a clergy group, and also handing a Bible to Thomas Cromwell, who represents the nobility. The picture dramatizes the King's hopefulness of loyalties to him, from both religious and patriotic realms, which may result from making the Holy Bible accessible to common people in the church house.

The title page issued the following proclamation
from King Henry VIII,

> This is the Byble apoynted to the use of the
> churches... The **Bible in English** in the largest
> and greatest Volume, authorized...to be
> frequented and used in every church.[9]

Being the first Bible authorized officially for
public use in England's churches, it was fastened by a
chain to the piece of furniture where the parishioner read
it. The people were allowed to read the Bible in groups,
even during church services.

A 1543 Act of Parliament spewed across England
a blast from the past. It took away the right to use any
other Bible except the Great Bible, specifically
criminalizing the beloved Tyndale Bible.

The Psalms from the Great Bible are used today in
the Book of Common Prayer in the Church of England. It
never became "great" in the eyes of public sentiment and
publication for it ceased in 30 years. Still, the craving for
a Bible that the average Englishman could hold in his
hands and read at home was met with the Bible that
followed.

The six year horrific reign of Catholic fanatic,
Queen Mary, began in 1553. Hundreds of peace-loving
saints were brutalized by sword and fire after being found
heretics for holding against her the only sword she feared
– the Holy Bible of the Protestants. Hundreds of
Englishmen fled the country to a safe haven in Geneva,
Switzerland. These religious refugees all came together to
assemble in one place the greatest minds of the Protestant
Reformation.

It was there the very first *committee* to attempt a
translation work was fortuned to include such leaders and

intellectual giants as Theodore Beza, John Knox, William Whittingham (brother-in-law of reformer John Calvin), William Cole, Christopher Goodman, Anthony Gilby, and Miles Coverdale. The Olivetan French Bible formed a solid Majority Text guideline to pilot the formal translation committee. Laboring for 6 years in the original language as indicated in the title, "translated according to the Ebrue and Greke", the **Geneva Bible** represented *the first English Bible translated entirely out of the original languages*.

Ezra through Malachi completed the Old Testament from the Hebrew Masoretic Text where Tyndale left off. The New Testament was consulted in Beza's Greek *Textus Receptus* and commentary. It was published from April 1560 through 1644. There were 200 editions printed between 1560-1630 to update spelling and to edit printing mistakes. Meeting the need of the hour, this Holy Bible enjoyed circulation in several countries. It was the first Bible published in Scotland, and its parliament required every household to possess a copy.

The front cover read,

THE BIBLE
and
HOLY SCRIPTVRES
Contetned in
The Olde and Newe
Teftament

The Introduction read,

Translated according to the Ebrue and Greke, and conferred with the best [Majority Text] *translations in divers languages.*

The popularity of the Geneva Bible was increased by the fact of annotations (marginal notes) at difficult places or obscure words, and "principal matters" passages most profitable to memorize. There were "certyne mappes of Cosmosgraphie" (world maps). Two index tables gave interpretations of Hebrew names and alphabetically arranged Bible topics.

Easier reading included a smaller Roman type letter style, a **feature-first numbered verses**, and *italicized* words. Words italicized simply means that there is no English term or tense to represent the word type in the original Hebrew or Greek, so the English <u>verbal</u> <u>equivalent</u> was used and *put in italics*. Verbal equivalent means verbal equal. The translators made the strictest, conservative word choice by rule of grammar. The *italicized word* was either understood or silent in the language being translated from.

This is an oversimplified example:

Let's translate "the blue house" from English into Spanish.
English: the blue house
Spanish: the house *of* blue (el casa de azul)

Can you see how the Spanish dialect picked up the extra word (*of*) in the translation? Notice that it was placed in italics. The same principle applies when translating from Hebrew or Greek into English. Rules of grammar must apply necessary words to the sentence structure in order for it to make sense in the language being translated to. *Italicized* words are understood or silent words that must become **visible** in another language.

It is my humble opinion that italicized words in Majority Text Scripture are as inspired and divinely preserved equal to all other words. Why? They are a grammatical necessity when translating from Hebrew or Greek into English. We know *how* they were translated in the Majority Text Holy Scripture. Word equals Word purity. Verbal (formal) equivalency does not allow for any deviation of word choice from the original word. Although the King James Bible honestly lets us know which *italicized words* in English were invisible in the original Hebrew or Greek language, new bible versions sloppily include them as actual **words of the text** without being italicized at all. There is more in-depth explanation of italicized words in Chapter 4.

William Shakespeare quoted all Scripture citations in his plays from the Geneva Bible. It was the Bible read by John Bunyan, author of *Pilgrim's Progress.* Such literary giants during this period, as John Donne, famous poet known for his inventiveness of metaphor and his Holy Sonnets, relied heavily on the Geneva Bible. His passionate lines in poetry and sermons influenced Earnest Hemmingway's *For Whom The Bell Tolls*, and Thomas Merton's *No Man is an Island.* It was also the cherished volume aboard the Mayflower and was the Holy Bible of our Puritan forefathers.

It has been stated by historical experts that the Geneva Bible was the Bible present at the signing of the Declaration of Independence and the United States Constitution. Regardless of whether it was the Geneva Bible or the King James Bible, America owes its foundational authority to Divine Majority Text Scripture that bolstered national faith in the superpower of religious freedom. The earliest known "Soldiers Pocket Bible", containing 125 verses, is taken from the Geneva Bible. The lowest estimate, at the time of its completion, for a copy of the Geneva *New Testament* would be just under one week's wages. 1560 Geneva Bible featured a number of study aids. Included were woodcut illustrations, maps, explanatory "tables", indexes of names and topics, and the notorious marginal notes by the Reformers. The front cover depicts the Israelites standing at the brink of the Red Sea. Larger editions added pictorial illustrations such as one showing Adam and Eve, with Adam sporting a typical Elizabethan-style beard and moustache.

Because of the anti-Catholic stance of its translators, the marginal notes were found offensive by Catholic church leadership, expressing allegiance ultimately to the Lord Jesus Christ, not to any venerated man. Succeeding Mary on the throne in 1558, the benevolent Queen Elizabeth had this Bible affectionately dedicated to her, when the exiles returned home to a more friendly government.

The remaining predecessor to the King James Bible would be the highly promoted **Bishop's Bible** of 1568. Archbishop of Canterbury, Matthew Parker, desired an official, standard Bible of the clergy, since no bishop had a hand in the origin of the Geneva Bible. This lovely revision of the Great Bible featured 123 engravings of maps, pictures, a coat of arms, and a general cosmetic makeover with thicker paper, more color, and a hieroglyphic writing style.

The Majority Text readings of the Great Bible were retained in the Bishop's Bible. It is considered an "authorized" Bible, even though no royal confirmation was given to it, as a copy was presented to Queen

Elizabeth. It was "set forth by authoritie" of the bishops in the prologue. "Convocation made enactments on behalf of the translation, and each bishop and archbishop was ordered to have in his house a copy of the Bible 'of the largest volume, as lately printed in London', placed in the hall or dining room where it would be useful to servants or to strangers."[10]   Perhaps this is where our tradition of a "coffee table Bible" was passed down from. However, it was the Geneva Bible that remained the people's Bible for 43 more years until 1611.

It is thrilling to note the seven-fold "polished rub" given to the **English language** Majority Text Scripture beginning with Wycliffe, Tyndale, Coverdale, Matthew, Great, Geneva, and Bishop Bibles (1384-1568). Psalm 12:6 radiates more clearer than ever, *"The words of the Lord are pure words, as silver tried in a furnace of earth,* **purified seven times.**"

King James Bible historian, Bill Grady, lends the meaning of these numbers,

> With the numbers seven and eight representing **'perfection'** and 'new beginnings' respectively, we marvel at the King James Bible being erected upon the **sevenfold** foundation.[11]

It has been duly noted in Grady's, *Final Authority,* that a consensus of textual authorities concede approximately 90 percent of Tyndale's Scripture Text is left intact all the way leading up to the King James Bible (p.161). The remaining 10 percent were mostly Old Testament portions where Tyndale lacked the *purest* in Majority Text documents to translate from.

This accounts for 86 years of scrutinizing copy (Tyndale Bible 1525 - 1611 KJB), or 229 years if we include Wycliffe (1382 Wycliffe Bible – 1611 KJB). As more Majority Text manuscripts became available, the formal equivalent method was expertly followed for each subsequent Scripture translation, ensuring each Word is exactly as the original inspired Word being translated from. Word equals Word perfection guaranteed.

Strains of modern lower criticism scholarship barely acknowledge Majority Text Word-equals-Word purity. The *Reformed Reader* almost mumbles,

> In their New Testament translation, the King James "translators" didn't even revise and compare. What they did was simply **copy** - almost **word for word** - William Tyndale's 1525 New Testament.[12]

STEPHENS, BEZA, ELZIVIR - MAJORITY TEXT GREEK NEW TESTAMENTS

There were provisionary works of Erasmus' Greek New Testament before 1611 that reflected more Majority Text manuscript finds. The first revisions were that of French printer Robert Stephanus, known as Stephens (1503-1559). He was the royal printer of Paris. His four editions (1546, 1549, 1550, 1557) were popular throughout England (esp. 1550 ed.). During his last edition, he professed his conversion and fully immersed himself into Protestantism.

Stephanus used the 16 Majority Text Greek manuscripts in the library of King Francis I and son Henry II. These were all identical, even down to the letter, according to textual scholar Scrivener (1813), who quoted Stephanus (see Scrivener Vol. 2, p. 188). The funding of the project came from the King to the chagrin of the Catholic Church. "The Stephanus Greek Text of 1550 was surprisingly identical to that of Erasmus, except in nine inconsequential places (some of these were typographical errors). Stephanus does not mention ever seeing or using Erasmus' text!"[13] Perfection begets perfection.

It was said of Theodore Beza (1519-1605), that he "astonished and confounded the world" with the Greek manuscripts he unearthed. A contemporary of John Calvin, Beza took additional, decidedly Majority Text manuscripts and upgraded the existing Textus Receptus of Stephanus. Of his 9 editions, 5 were smaller-sized reprints, 4 were edited revisions (1565, 1582, 1589, 1598). He was a Swiss reformer who accomplished his work in Geneva. Beza surrounded himself with an illustrious group of scholars such as John Calvin, Henry Stephanus (son of Robert, collator of additional Greek Majority Text manuscripts), and other leading textual scholars. We begin to understand how the Textus Receptus was the unhampered thread of *union* which great, historic leaders wove into the Protestant movements.

Beza included various notes on every page that provided additional textual information and insight. These were invaluable to the King James Bible committee who primarily utilized the 1598 edition, and also the 1589 edition. Beza also gleamed from the pro-Majority Text Syriac and Aramaic Scripture. This caused his text to differ from Stephanus in only 38 insignificant places, which followed Erasmus' Greek New Testament.

A 3rd provisionary work of the Greek Textus Receptus was completed by Bonaventure, and nephew Abraham, Elzevir (1546-1617). They are mistakenly, but commonly called the Elzevir brothers. They followed the texts of Erasmus and Beza. His Dutch Leiden Publishing House propelled 7 editions of the Greek New Testament from 1624-1787. "His 1633 second edition introduced the term *Textus Receptus* in the preface words, "Textum Ab

Omnibus receiptum", meaning, "You have therefore the *text* now *received* by all." [14]

1890 conservative Anglican scholar Scrivener notes that there is no material difference between any of the Stephens, Beza, or Elzevir Greek texts (Scrivener Vol. 2, p. 193, 195). He further pinpoints the 287 microscopic differences (word order, spelling, printing hiccups, etc.) are often errors of the press. Each one built upon the other a finished, shining hue as more supportive Majority Text manuscripts poured in. This perfection of the Greek Textus Receptus served to be a mirror to the 1611 Holy Bible New Testament.

The King James Bible committee availed themselves to all 18 total editions of the Majority Text Greek New Testament printed by Erasmus, Stephens, and Beza. This is what "Translated out of the Originall Greeke" means on the title page of the 1611 King James Bible. These Greek texts also served as textual parents of beloved Majority Text Scriptures in the Italian, French, and Spanish Bibles as well. Every one of these agree in harmony with the one another. Word equals Word perfection.

1611 KING JAMES BIBLE

The dawning of 1558 sighed with relief at Queen "Bloody" Mary's passing. Having spilt more innocent blood of Christians than any of her predecessors, her guilt-laden mind was left nearly deranged according to medical records. The filthiest word in England's language was attributed to her memory – bloody. Next, heirless Elizabeth's 45 yr. reign would be followed by James VI, King of Scotland (1567-1603).

As a searing backdrop, King James Bible committee members personally witnessed firsthand during childhood, Queen Mary's lust to burn Catholicresistant Christians at the stake. They loathed the holocaust of their peers being tortured to death, refusing to retract faith and practice to Holy Majority Text Scripture.

Hadrian Saravia, born in 1530 at Hedin Artois (Northern France)observed as a teen the Inquisition killing Christians in Europe and Henry VIII burning them in England. In his twenties, he saw the torch carried again by Bloody Mary.

KJB translator, Lawrence Chaderton, born in 1537, would have been 16-21 years of age when the burning of Bibles and martyrs was a weekly occurrence in Lancashire, where he was reared.

KJB translator, Thomas Holland, born in 1539, would have been 14-19 years of age during the holocaust he testimonied in Ludlow, Shropshire.

KJB "chief overseer", Richard Bancroft, born in 1544, was a 9-14 year old bystander, as the fires burned people in public squares.

KJB translator, Henry Savile, born in 1549 at Bradley in Yorkshire, watched at the tender ages of 4-9, men and women burn at the stake.

KJB translator, John Rainolds, born at Devonshire in 1549, too would have seen saints burn for half of his young life at ages 4-9.

KJB translator Giles Tomson, born in 1553, lived in London, where burnings of Bibles, men, women, AND children were frequent occurrences, when he was 5 years old.

KJB translators Miles Smith, Lancelot Andrew, Richard Eeded, and Thomas Bilson, born 1554-1555, residing in London, Hereford, Sewella, and Bedfordshire, never forgot the horror stories of heroism when the last years of persecution ceased at ages 3-5.

KJB translator George Abbott's parents had been **"sufferers for the truth in times of popish cruelty"**. [15]

The King James Bible committee members felt the inhuman impact of genocide aimed squarely at squelching this particular group of Majority Text Scripture advocates. Their mission to equally duplicate Majority Text Scripture was fueled by an indomitable spirit. At all cost, every word of the Word would remain as it was delivered to them by heroic sacrifice.

How does this compare by stark contrast to what today's new bible version committee members watched as they were growing up - *Breakfast at Tiffany's, Tom and Jerry, 3's Company, Three Stooges, Pac Man, M.A.S.H.?*

KING JAMES

His title would change from James VI, King of Scotland (1567), to James I, King of England (1603). His theological beliefs remain unflappable in a serious commentary on the Book of Revelation, and his devotional entitled "Meditations on the Lord's Prayer". He was able to master Latin, Greek, and French, all by the **age of eight**. James was schooled as well in Italian and Spanish. He once authored a tract entitled "Counterblast to Tobacco", to discourage the use of tobacco in England.

> James was a man of extraordinary talents...his astounding knowledge of Scripture is reflected in his writings on political theory, poetry, theology, and the Bible. While not yet twenty years old he wrote a *"Paraphrase on the Revelation of St. John"*. [16]

Perhaps one of the greatest, if not the greatest monarch England ever saw, King James I was a uniter and up-builder of his country. First, in Scotland, he united the warring tribes of Scotland into a solidified nation. He later joined England and Scotland together forming what is now known as the British Empire.

When James became England's ruler, the Anglican churches and clergy were the only ones privy to handle the Holy Scripture. People-first King James desired common folks to have a copy of the Holy Bible in their native tongue, as the English language had reached its zenith.

Because he would open the final floodgate of God's inspired and preserved written Word with the 1611 King James Bible, James was destined for satanic opposition. Critics firing away at his physical features described him as rough, his voice loud, with nimble legs, a bury tongue, knobby nose, and lacking common sense. Even though the *Dictionary of National Biography* and all Encyclopedias (Americana, Britannica, Collier's, World Book, New Standard, Academic America, and Catholic Home and School) do not give even a slight hint of this. More exacerbating critics assail James as a homosexual.

Sir Anthony Weldon, politician and courtier, was dismissed from King James' court in reaction to a negative treatise he wrote about Scotland entitled, "A Description of Scotland". Weldon swore his revenge. More than **twenty years after** the death of King James, Weldon wrote a paper calling James a homosexual. This would appease years of Weldon's skulking rage toward the King. The report was largely ignored, since there were still enough people alive who knew it to be fallacy. Weldon's paper lay dormant for years, but was later published in a book, "The Court and Character of King James I", after Weldon's death.

Weldon's false account is still perpetuated today by those who further vilify King James in hopeful audacity of turning Christians away from the King James Bible to modernistic neo-versions.

A flagrant example resurfaced in a tabloid-flavor article by a female informant. Writer Karen Ann Wojahn, from the July/Aug. 1985 issue of the Moody Monthly, released this report with ZERO documentation, entitled, "The Real King James". She quotes James as admitting to homosexuality with his statement, *"I am neither a god nor an angel, but a man like any other. Therefore, I act like a man and confess to loving those dear to me more than other men."*[17] Of course, this parades perfectly how modern textual critics translate written words, as loosely as possible.

Not seeing her own blunder coming, she goes on to blast this "power-crazed King" for being so eager to claim his throne that he left his **pregnant wife** in Edinburgh and mounted a horse for London. So, Karen, are we to deduce that James is bi-sexual now? Her article is silent of this faux-pas.

1605 brought out the worst in satan's attack against the inevitable Holy Bible-to-be. Guy Fawkes, a Roman Catholic under direction of Jesuit priest, Henry Garnet, schemed a plan to "off the king". They were discovered in the basement of Parliament with 36 kegs of gunpowder and every intention to blow up the king and Parliament with him. These two knuckleheads and eight other conspirators were tried, convicted, and hanged for treason.

It seems almost providential doesn't it? Those who try the hardest to discredit King James and his tri-millennial preservation of the inspired Holy Scripture, end up taking the fall themselves.

The documental **truth** is at King James' death in 1625, he embellished a Christian throne to his son and heir:

If then you would enjoy a happy reign, observe the statutes of your Heavenly King.[18]

MILLENARY PETITION

Four days after Queen Elizabeth's death, as the new King was traveling to London, he was met by a band of Puritan ministers. They sought out his attention over a statement of grievances against the Church of England with a thousand signatures to boot, known as the *Millenary Petition*. The King politely responded by scheduling a conference together with them on Jan. 14, 16, and 18, 1604. It was held at the largest of the royal palaces, Hampton Court, located 15 miles southwest of London on the Thames River.

Leading the delegation was President of Corpus Christi College at Oxford, Dr. John Rainolds. Dr. Rainolds and 3 other Puritan leaders were led to the King's private chamber to face 50 high church officials, led by Richard Bancroft of London, and the Archbishop of Canterbury.

Dr. Rainolds explained the proposals. Lastly, he addressed the need for a Bible to be translated from the original languages with current English Majority Text Bibles to be used as a guideline. This was meant to bring together all English Bibles, especially the rivalry between the Geneva Bible that the people used, and the Bishop's Bible that the church officials used.

King James expressed his dissatisfaction with the Calvinistic marginal notes of the Geneva Bible, which negated his philosophy of the Divine Right of Kings. James also recognized the lasting potential to provide his subjects with a Bible that would be truly English, being translated on English soil, as the Geneva Bible was not. Ladies and Gentlemen, we owe a serious debt of gratitude to the Hampton Court of 1604. With prudent motive to unify his nation behind a single English Bible, James placed his official sanction on the proposal:

> That a translation be made of the whole Bible, as consonant as can be to the original Hebrew and Greek; and this to be sent out and printed, without any marginal notes, only to be used in all churches of England, in time of Divine service.[19]

Dr. Rainolds became a Fellow of Corpus Christi College, where he served as President, at the astounding age of 17. He was well received for his accomplishments, "prodigiously seen in all kinds of learning, most excellent in all tongues,…reading, famous in doctrine, and the very treasure of erudition [knowledge]."[20] Rainolds was known as "the human library, a third university". Although Dr. Rainolds would not live to see the project through that he initiated, he worked on the Old Testament formal translation of the prophets until his death in 1607. The 1611 King James Bible took off on the right track following his steps from the beginning. Expiring in May 1607, the providence of God took his soul to flight in the Heavens. His purpose was served. Dr. John Rainolds laid the initial foundation for the King James Bible you hold in your hands today.

KING JAMES HOLY BIBLE PREPARATION
     King James made public his selection of 54 of the kingdom's brightest intellects. Their crowning academic

achievements are bountiful. We will notice a few in due course.

> This committee prayed and fasted for a period of 3 years (1604-1607) before the actual work began in 1607. [21]

The project would be a formal revision of the 1602 Bishop's Bible. However, all English Majority Texts, and vernacular (Chaldee, Hebrew, Syrian, Latin, French, Italian, Dutch) Majority Text Bibles, and a great host of over 5,000 ancient and recent witnesses of both the Hebrew *Masoretic Text* and the Greek *Textus Receptus* lay before them.

These would ensure an exact *copy* of the Majority Text in English. Of course, *formal equivalency* translation was employed to assure that each English word translated to, mirrored the original word being translated from. Word for word equals Word.

The Majority Text Old Testament **Masoretic Text** are the 1st and 2nd Rabbinic Bibles of 1516 and 1524 A.D., respectfully, as edited together by Daniel Bomberg and Ben Chayyim. These represent the God-breathed, preserved Holy Scriptures of the Old Testament from 1400 B.C. (Moses) through 200 B.C. The Rabbinic Bible is often referred to as the "Old Testament Textus Receptus" (Received Text). Inherent within this Old Testament Scripture is the following:

- Torah of Moses (Genesis - Deuteronomy) that the Sopherim and Masoretes transmitted with letter by letter, word by word accuracy and perfect precision from approximately 1400 B.C through 1000 A.D. (2400 years)! This is the same Torah that was canonized by King

Josiah, the Samaritans, and Ezra from 627-250 B.C.

- Tenach, 3-fold divisions of the Old Testament - the Law, Prophets, and the Writings or Psalms. This Tenach was verified by the Maccabees, *Ecclesiasticus*, Jaffa Jewish Synod, Josephus, the *Mishnah*, and the *Talmud* from 180 B.C. - 1000 A.D.
- 1st Rabbinic Bible 1516
- 2nd Rabbinic Bible 1524

Recent witness of the Dead Sea Scrolls in 1947 verify the Word-equals-Word pure translation of the Masoretic Text Hebrew Rabbinic Bible. See Chapter 4 for more detail on the Dead Sea Scroll's validation of Majority Text preservation perfection.

The Majority Text New Testament is the direct lineage of Holy Scripture manuscripts descending straight from the original Scripture books initially inspired 30-100 A.D. The inspired Gospels of Jesus Christ's disciples, the inspired epistles of the apostles, John's Book of Revelation, all were *formally* copied (Word equals Word order) and spread out across Asia minor during the sonic boom of early church missionary work. These Scriptures mirror each other amazingly in 5000+ manuscripts available to the King James Bible committee. These 5000+ equal Majority Text manuscripts are represented in the Greek *Textus Receptus*, and vernacular (native language) Bibles. Exclusive to these documents rest ***preserved Words of original inspiration.***

- 60 A.D - P64 world's oldest New Testament fragment, *Magdalen Papyrus*. This Scripture corrects several modern English bible versions, and reaffirms the Majority Text King James Bible exclusively.

- 66 A.D. - Matthew 26:22 fragment reading, *"hekastos auton"* - "every one of them". Mirrors perfectly the King James Bible. Proves wrong the NIV and NASV bible readings.
- 116 A.D. - Ignatius, martyred Bishop of Antioch, wrote *To The Romans IV.* His quotes from 18 books of the Majority Text New Testament verifies them as inspired and authoritatively Holy Scripture.
- 120 A.D. - P66 perfectly copies the apostles inspired epistles personally bestowed upon the earliest Waldenesian Church by Word-equals-Word translation.
- 120 A.D. - *Peshitta Bible* served the Syrian Christian Church where the apostles of Jesus and their inspired books frequented. Written in Aramaic, this Bible exclusively mirrors Majority Text Scripture.
- 157 A.D. - *Itala Bible* is the first Latin translation of the Majority Text Scripture for the young churches established in the Italian Alps. It enjoyed broad circulation across Europe and Asia. 50 manuscripts exist today. *Itala* authenticates the Majority Text, matching Erasmus' Greek New Testament and the King James Bible.
- 193 A.D. - Irenaeus, grand pupil of the Apostle John, in his writings of the Christian faith, he quotes from Majority Text Gospels, Acts, the Pauline Epistles, and Revelation. He verifies and defends them as inspired Scripture. He also notes the title "New Testament" is first used by an unknown writer.

- 200 A.D. - Church Father, Tertullian, verified the early church guarded purity of Scriptural Words to be the Majority Text.
- 398 A.D. - John *"Golden Mouth"* Chrysostom, renowned Bible expositor of the Church of Antioch. His homilies on the Sermon on the Mount utilize and verifies Majority Text New Testament Scripture.
- *The Cappodocian Fathers* quote Majority Text New Testament Scripture in their writings: (379) Basil, (389) Nazianzus, (395) Gregory.
- 4th Century - St. Augustine's *De doctrina Christiana* affirms Word-equals-Word preserved Scripture in the *Itala Bible*.
- 461 A.D. - Saint Patrick represents 75 Latin Bible Majority Text Scriptures in his writings.
- Majority Text Scriptures are exclusively communicated in Psalms by Aldhelm (709), Gospels of Egbert (766), 10 Commandments of Alfred the Great, King of England (901), Aelfric's *The Grammarian* (1020).
- 1100 - *LaNobla Leyeon.* This is an official opposition document by the Waldenesian Church to the Church of Rome (Catholic). Their Scripture quotations are the renowned *Itala Bible* of Majority Text lore.
- 1229 - West Saxon Gospels. These Bibles are Majority Text Word-equals-Word translations into Poland, Russia, and Hungary.
- 1287 - The Spanish Bible of Alphonso II was translated by formal equivalency from the Majority Text French Bible into Spanish.
- 1330 - John Wycliffe first translated the English Bible from Majority Text Latin and Greek

Scripture. It mirrors exactly the *Itala Bible* of 157 A.D.

- 1417 - Ferrar Bible and the Bible of Alba exclusively mirror the Majority Text.
- 1466 - Mentel Bible. First printed Bible in any vernacular language. Translated from the Majority Text Nuremberg Bible in Germany from the 1300's.
- 1466 - Erasmus first printed the Majority Text Greek New Testament (printing press invented 1439). He collected over 5000 Majority Text handwritten Greek and vernacular (native) manuscripts to make the first printed **copy** of them.
- Erasmus' Greek New Testament Scripture was the New Testament basis for other Majority Text Bibles that lay before the King James Bible committee: French LeFevre and Olivetan (1534, 1535), Swedish Uppsala Bible (1541), Danish Christian III Bible (1550), Dutch Brestkens Bible (1558), Spanish Reyna Bible (1569), Czech Bible (1602), Italian Diodati Bible (1607).
- *Textus Receptus* - Erasmus (1466-1536, 5 editions), Stephens (1546-1557, 4 editions), Beza (1565-1598, 9 editions). These printed Greek Majority Text New Testaments mirror the 2nd-4th century handwritten copies of the inspired Greek Gospels and Epistles from 1st century Patristic Fathers (Jesus' disciples and apostles). There is no material difference in Erasmus, Stephens, and Beza's *Textus Receptus.*
- 1522 - Complutensian Polyglot Bible. Oddly enough, Catholic Cardinal Ximenes, edited this Bible based on the Majority Text, not the standard Roman Catholic Vulgate bible.

- 1525 - William Tyndale's first **printed** Majority Text *English* New Testament.
- 1534 - Martin Luther's German Bible. Luther gave Germany its first complete, native Bible translated from Erasmus' *Textus Receptus*, and the German Tepl Bible (an equal translation of the Waldensian Bible into German named after Tepl, Bohemia).
- 1535 - French Olivetan Bible. Waldensian Majority Text Bible copied into French.
- 1536 - Coverdale Bible. The first complete Bible printed in English.
- 1537 - Matthews Bible. Update of the Coverdale Bible to include Tyndale's Old Testament dungeon works of the Masoretic Text Joshua-II Chronicles.
- 1538 - Great Bible. Update of the Matthews Bible. 16½ x 11 size, chained to church pulpits, minus marginal notes. First Majority Text Bible authorized for use in England's churches.
- 1560 - Geneva Bible. First complete Majority Text English Bible formally translated from the original Hebrew and Greek languages. Bible of the people.
- 1568 - Bishops Bible. Update of the Great Bible. Added maps, engravings, pictures, coat of arms, and featured hieroglyphic printing style. Primarily utilized by the clergy.
- 1569 - Reina Spanish Bible. Nicknamed "Bear Bible". Outlawed by the Roman Church. The title page featured an engraving of a bear seizing honey from a tree.
- 1602 - Reina-Valera Spanish Bible. Renowned "King James Bible of the Spanish world". Exclusively translated from Hebrew and Greek Majority Text Scripture.

- 1602 - Czech Bible. Exclusively translated from the Textus Receptus.
- 1607 - Diodati Italian Bible. Based solely on Majority Text Scriptural documents.

Laying before the King James Bible committee were these and more Majority Text Scripture witnesses, including: Zwingli's German Bible, Latin Bibles by Pagninus (1518), and Sebastian Münster (1535 - a German monk who became a Protestant Christian), Sebastian Castalio (1545 - French Bible), Plantin "Nuremberg" Polygot (Syriac New Testament 1572 - polygot: side by side versions of the same text in different languages), as well as the Aramaic Targums (Aramaic translation of the Hebrew Bible used in the early New Testament Syriac Church through the first millennium).

The "King James Bible of the Spanish world" is the 1602 Reina-Valera Spanish Bible. Catholic monk, Casidoro de Reina, converted to Protestantism (Christianity) through lectures by Dr. Blanco Arias, was influenced by the preaching of the Albigenses. Being a proponent of free conscience and thought, he moved to London from Seville to escape the blood-thirsty Catholic Inquisition. Reina was endeared to the Old Latin (*Itala*) Bible of the Waldenses, as well as writings of the Reformers. He worked 12 years to complete the Majority Text formal translation into Spanish by 1569. It was formally edited from 1582-1602 by Cipriano de Valera, whose ministries to seamen and inmates motivated his work. They both believed the Majority Text Spanish Bible was the *perfect* Word of God for Spaniards.

One authoritative Spanish-language work on Bible translation in this language, *Versiones Castellanas De La Biblia*, states: "The authors [Reina and Valera] claim to have penetrated to the depths of Holy Scriptures and have translated **with perfection** the Greek and Hebrew languages."[22]

All of these vernacular (native language) formal translations of the Majority Text were alluded to in the 1611 King James Bible *"Introduction to the Reader"*. Why? To let each reader know the character and direction of this committee. They were not bringing "back to the anvil" the inspired Text, which had already been hammered out. They were simply duplicating preserved Words of original inspiration into English. That is, **they were not creating a *new* bible** from these, but reproducing the *perfect* Bible already validated in history.

Lest we forget, the names associated with all of these Bibles are not indicative of *different Bibles*, but of the *different men* who edited (to reproduce; direct for publication; reissued) the same Majority "Received" Text of the Bible in their native tongue. These are all the same inspired Scripture! Their word-by-word agreement with each other 99%, with the minute exception of spelling differences, printing omissions and errors, and linguistic variants, announce a shockwave of conformity that documents sustained and continuous Words of original inspiration.

The King James Bible committee had access to all of these Majority Text Bibles and TONS more that was afterward purchased or immortalized in museums scattered around the globe. This is why we do not possess every manuscript today that were available to the King James Bible committee.

Vintage Majority Text Scripture retained **exact** word copy of both Old and New Testament books. These 5000+ manuscripts were NOT for the purpose of creating a *new* text, or so the translators could "pick-n-choose" words from a "bible smorgasbord buffet". On the contrary, they copied what had already been released from Heaven, to perfectly preserve His WORDS with exact conformity. Word for word equals Word.

They even had the Critical Alexandrian text manuscripts before them as represented in the Latin Vulgate. These line of documents deviated wildly from the Majority Text of Scripture. Therefore, it was not followed on purpose by the King James Bible committee, as their objective was not to create neo-scripture. The King James Bible committee specifically mentioned their non usage of the Critical text Latin Vulgate bible on this basis alone.

The formal equivalent, Word-equals-Word, method was strictly adhered to by every King James translation committee member. Even the "out of date" and "archaic" words *of that time* would not be changed remaining in Scripture, because the committee understood that even though these words would need to be looked up in a dictionary at that time, they could not call their translation pure if the text were altered in any way.

They took the high road to follow **Aristotle's dictum:**

> The benefit of the doubt is to be given to the document itself, and not arrogated by the critic to himself. [23]

The 95% Anglo-Saxon English words used in the King James Bible were capable of containing in themselves not only their central thoughts, but also the different shades of meaning which were attached to the central thought in Greek. This is the King James Bible's unique power of inflection. The usage of more "Latinized" words in modern English versions have more difficult-to-understand prefixes and suffixes, due to the derivative copyright law changes placed upon them.

Complaints that the King James Bible is too hard to understand must square with the fact that 80% of its text are one-syllable words. 95% of its text are one or two-syllable words. Flesch-Kincaid Grade Level Formula reveals the King James Bible is at 5th grade reading level. The reading level average in America is 6th grade. A 5th grader can read the King James Bible and comprehend what it means.

Because there were no changes placed upon the Majority Text, magnificent lingual aids were intricately maintained within the King James Bible itself. These are already built into Holy Scripture. The King James Bible has always earned an A+ in English.

1. The King James Bible contains its own *built-in dictionary*, defining each word, in its context. When difficult words are first used, there is a definition in the same passage or verse!
2. The King James Bible has a vocabulary and reading level which slowly builds progressively from Genesis to Revelation.
3. The King James Bible uses words with the appropriate sound symbolism (phonaesthesia) to communicate meaning.
4. The King James Bible has a sentence structure which enhances **accurate doctrinal interpretation**.
5. The King James Bible gives a transparent view of the Hebrew and Greek vocabulary, grammar, and syntax. It is the only pure language lexicon we have of the 16th and 17th centuries.
6. The King James Bible's words are *cognitive scaffolding* words. Sentences are woven by words that build the meaning in a consistent form and pattern by its fabric content. Ex: Philippians 4:6

"Be careful for nothing" (Do not be full of care about things you should turn over to the Lord.) New versions *"Be anxious for nothing"* lacks cognitive scaffolding.

7. The King James Bible has an internationally recognizable vocabulary and spelling.

8. The King James Bible is a historically accurate, one-volume library of the age, events, and future of the earth.[24]

Although the King endorsed this project, it was funded by Puritan, Anglican, and independent churches of England. "…the historical truth is that payment did not come from the Crown but from the Church, and Church funds were very limited. Funds were raised and received for the purpose of sustaining the translators during their work on the translation, but they were not given financial reward."[25]

How unlike today's modern bible committees is this? New version committee members who receive royalties from marketed bibles have a conflict of interest. Who are they being true to? God, or public consumers?

The King James Bible committee enjoyed pure motive, pure impetus, and a perfectly pure canon to reproduce the greatest assemblage of world-wide Majority Text manuscripts. The inspired Holy Scripture in English would come to rest at last in the year 1611.

KING JAMES BIBLE COMMITTEE MEMBERS

*There were many chosen that were greater in other men's eyes than their own, and that **sought the truth** rather than their own praise.*
Miles Smith
1611 King James Bible "The Translators to the Reader"

An accurate, historical account of King James Bible committee members is available through the exhaustive work of Alexander McClure, author of *"Translators Revived"*. It is a concise history of the individual scholars who regarded superior the Words of the Majority Text. These scholastic executives had as their goal to preserve, by identical detail, Divine Scripture in English.

The original committee of 54 was reduced by 7 to 47 due to deaths and health reasons (Richard Eedes, Edward Lively, Ralph Hutchinson, William Dakins, John Rainolds, Thomas Ravis). They were divided into 6 companies at tri-hub locations. In **Westminster**, a group of 10, under the leadership of Lancelot Andrews, translated Genesis-II Kings. Edward Lively's group of 8 rendered I Chronicles-Song of Solomon. In **Oxford**, John Harding led a group of seven to labor upon Isaiah-Malachi. The Oxford Greek committee of 8 completed the Gospels, Acts, and Revelation under chairmanship of Thomas Ravis. A second Westminster company of seven, led by William Berlow, worked on Romans-Jude. The two **Cambridge** groups toiled in the Hebrew.

The remaining John Bois-led group worked on the translation of the Apocrypha (Catholic books). The issue made of the Apocrypha books being included in the 1611 King James Bible Scripture is a **common misnomer** among King James Bible critics. These event books were routinely placed INBETWEEN the Old and New Testaments to appease Catholic tension and ONLY for historical record of this "inter-testament" 400 year period. Like Martin Luther, the King James committee drew a line of distinction between the inspired Hebrew and Greek canon and the uninspired Catholic Apocryphal books.

.....the translators were careful to set these spurious books apart from the inspired text by inserting them between the Testaments. And to ensure that there was no misunderstanding, they listed **7 reasons why the apocryphal books were to be categorically rejected as part of the inspired canon**. The only reason for their inclusion at all was due to their accepted historical value. Whereas our Scofield Reference Bible divides the testaments with an informative article entitled, 'From Malachi to Matthew', the King James translators inserted **the actual literature of that nebulous intertestamental period.**[26]

Within 40 years, the Apocryphal books were left out of the space in between the testaments.

Dr. Lancelot Andrews, director of the Genesis-II Kings Westminster group, was skilled in 15 languages, especially the oriental. His manual of private devotions, prepared by himself, is entirely in the Greek language. He was known to pray 5 hours every day. Dr. Andrews was a man of such piety that he was appointed Chaplain to the previous Queen and later Bishop of Winchester by King James. He was deemed as the potential interpreter-general at Babel, had he been present at the confusion of tongues. At his funeral, Dr. Buckeridge, Bishop of Rochester, regaled the audience with a fact Andrews kept to himself, that he was conversant in **15 different languages.**

Geoffry King hailed from Cambridge University as the Regius Professor of Hebrew. Dr. John Richardson was such an excellent linguist that he publicly debated *entirely in the Latin language*. He later became Vice Chairman of Cambridge University. Dr. Richardson's Fellowship was held at Emmanuel College. Leonard Hutton excelled as an "excellent Grecian and scholar" among his peers. He was impeccably versed in the learned languages, and his encompassing knowledge of the early church fathers gave him a "floating" position to the translation groups. Richard Kiley was appointed by the King as Professor of Hebrew literature at Oxford. He was personally appointed by King James to be on the committee. Dr. John Duport was four times Vice Chancellor of his alma mater, Jesus University, and made Fellow in 1580.

Dr. William Bedwell of the same Westminster group is reputed as an eminent Oriental, Arabic, and Persian language authority. In 1612, he published the Gospel of John in Arabic from a Latin Version. He was engaged for many years in compiling a 3-volume Arabic lexicon (dictionary). The beginnings of Dr. Bedwell's Persian dictionary are nestled away and preserved in the Bodlenian Library at Oxford. Cognate (similar) languages, such as these, as related to Hebrew, are like brother and sister. If a word in Hebrew used only one time in the text is unclear in English, cognate versions were there to fall back on to understand the clear word represented in the text.

The translators of the King James committee knew firsthand these cognate languages – Arabic, Persian, Aramaic, Coptic, Syrian, and Italian. They could go to these words and translate exclusively by Word-equals-Word without losing any parts, gaining any parts, and without any doubt of each word's intended equal.

Dr. William Teigh, Archdeacon of Middlesex, and Rector of All Hallows, was hailed to be "an excellent textuary and profound linguist". Dr. F. Burleigh was Fellow at none other than King James College. World shaker Richard Thomas, Fellow of Clare College was hailed as "a most admirable philologer" (disciple of literature). His credentials so expanded that he was better known in Italy, France and Germany than at home. Not much is heard of Richard Eedes. He was Chaplain to both Queen Elizabeth and King James. Eedes died shortly after the translation work began.

Dr. Miles Smith, who wrote the *Translators to the Readers* preface, was a member of the Oxford group responsible for Isaiah-Malachi. He notated and commented on every Greek and Latin church father manuscript (300 Majority Text documents from 100-600 A.D.). He was well acquainted with the Rabbinical Hebrew glosses in the marginal comments. He was as familiar with his native tongue as Chaldee (sister of Hebrew), Syriac, and Arabic. Hebrew was said to be at his fingertips. He was labeled as "a walking library". Dr. Smith was one of the twelve members on the final examination committee.

Professor Andrew Downes enjoyed a full forty year tenure as Regius Professor of Greek at St. John's College, Cambridge, before being asked to the King James Bible committee. He was on the final checking committee of 12. Dr. John Harding doubled as Royal Professor of Hebrew for 13 years at Cambridge University and President of Magdalen College. Francis Dillingham carried on debates *entirely in the Greek language* just for sport. Due to his discernible skill and expertise in this language, he was dubbed the "Great Grecian". Dillingham, Fellow of Christ College, wrote *"A Disswasive from Poperie"*. Contained therein were twelve effectual reasons which challenged every Papist, not willfully blinded, to be brought to truth. Dr. Hadrian Savaria was educated in several languages. His primary skill in the Hebrew earned him his Doctor's Degree. Dr. Savaria's many published Latin treatises gained wide spread recognition.

Sir Henry Savile contributed in the Oxford group of the Gospels, Acts, and Revelation. He enjoyed Fellowships at both Merton and Warden College. Sir Henry was Provost (high ranking university dignitary) at Eton. He enjoyed tutoring Queen Elizabeth in Greek and math. He was a scientist as well as a Bible scholar. Savile translated Latin historian Tacitus' work into English. He became the 1st to edit Chrysostom's complete work, the most famous Greek early church father of his day, into 8 full volumes. This portfolio was the size of a large dictionary or encyclopedia. His knowledge of Greek is incomparable as a critical scholar. Savile's pioneer work in many branches of scholarships founded the Savillian Professorships of Mathematics and Astronomy at Oxford.

Dr. Laurence Chaderton, Fellow of Christ College, was a powerhouse of Reformation doctrines and Majority Text advocacy. He was a noted Puritan, and one of four original clergy represented at the Hampton Court Conference with King James in 1604. For fifty years he was Afternoon Lecturer at Cambridge. Forty clergyman later said they owed their conversion to his preaching. His doctrinally conservative convictions were tested and cemented in his young adulthood through a most difficult proposal. He had been brought up Roman Catholic. Facing inconceivable temptation, his own father offered him an allowance of thirty pounds if he would leave Cambridge and renounce Protestantism. His father's ultimatum, "Otherwise I enclose a shilling to buy a wallet - go and beg."

John Bois, chair of the Apocrypha committee, was taught by his father to read Hebrew by age 5. It would probably be safe to say that he did not play Nintendo or Playstation all day to exercise his mind. Nevertheless, he was skilled in classical Greek, studying as a student at St. John's College Library from 4am-8pm, as a common practice, **at age 14**. Bois became the chief Greek lecturer at his college for 10 years. He was later elected Fellow of St. John's College. Classical Greek encompasses 3 branches: Ionic, Doric, and Attic (Koine) with each one a little different in spelling, dialect, rules, and grammar. Boise utilized all of these, especially the Koine Greek of the New Testament. His library was one of the largest collections of Greek literature ever. He was of the 12 on the final examination committee. He was also the secretary, taking notes of all proceedings. His notes are some of the only evidences we have for letting us know how the proceedings were professionally conducted. "He was so familiar with the Greek New Testament that he could, at any time, turn to any word that it contained."[27] Dr. Bois became Dean of Canterbury in 1619.

Edward Lively was the King's Professor of Hebrew at Cambridge University. He was elected Fellow of Trinity College at Cambridge in 1572. His reputation as an oriental linguist was unequaled in this period. Hailed as "one of the best linguists in the world", Lively was grounded by 11 children at home whom he raised on his own after the death of his wife. He authored a Bible Chronology book as well as a commentary of the five minor prophets.

Dr. John Overall was celebrated for the appropriateness of his quotations of early church fathers. He had spoken Latin so fluently for so long, it was troublesome to him to speak English in a continued oration. Dr. Overall was Fellow of Trinity College, Master of St. Catherine's, Bishop of Coventry, and Regius Professor of Divinity at Cambridge.

Thomas Harrison was expert in Hebrew and Greek *idioms* (descriptive narrative phrases). For example, how would you translate "step on the gas" or "I have a frog in my throat" from English into another language? Harrison was well versed in Hebrew and Greek idioms. Dr. Harrison was Fellow of St. John's College, and chief Hebraist examiner of those who sought to be professors of Hebrew and Greek at Trinity College in Cambridge.

Dr. Thomas Holland is described in his day as "mighty in the Scriptures; and so familiarly acquainted with the fathers, as if he himself had been one of them". Richard Killey was so accurate in Hebrew that he was appointed the King's Professor in that branch of literature at Oxford University. It is recorded that he was also so perfect a Grecian, that he was personally appointed by King James to be one of the translators.

Dr. George Abbot was known for his strong Puritanism from his studies at Balliol College. In 1593, he became Master of University College at age 35. A few years later he was selected among his peers as Vice Chancellor. Although holding high office in the Anglican Church as Archbishop of Canterbury, he severely opposed the "Romanizing" influence on the culture. He vigorously challenged the King's declaration permitting sports and pastimes on the Lord's Day. He was hailed as the "Voice of Puritans" within the Church of England.

A final editor committee member, Thomas Bilson, was aptly labeled "commander in chief in spiritual warfare", because of his unwavering defense of the literal interpretation sense of the Bible. He was an avid poet, distinguished theologian, and Bishop. His expertise in poetry and theology became an excellent guardian of straight theology, as well as a skill in word-for-word editing that characterizes the King James Bible.

Dr. Richard Brett published a number of erudite (instructive) books in Latin. Skilled and versed in Latin was he, as well as Hebrew, Greek, Chaldee, Arabic, and the Ethiopic tongues. Dr. Brett was Fellow of Lincoln College at Oxford. Dr. John Peryn was known as the

"King's Professor of Greek" in Oxford University. Of course, the list of these men's superior language skills could go on into volumes of more documented background history.

Dr. Richard Kilbye was Regius Professor of Hebrew at Lincoln College. This author of a commentary on Exodus was expert in both Hebrew and Greek formal translation. Dr. John Layfield, Fellow of Trinity, Cambridge, was a Greek lecturer who was specially skilled in architecture. The King James Committee consulted his expertise in passages describing the Tabernacle of God and the Jewish Temple. John Spencer astounded his childhood peers by becoming a lecturer of Greek at Corpus Christi College, Oxford, **at age nineteen**. "His wife was the great niece of Thomas Cranmer, the archbishop of Canterbury, who was burnt at the stake by bloody Queen Mary"[28]

Dr. Richard Clarke was highly regarded as an exemplar Christian and well known preacher. He was Fellow of Christ College at Cambridge. Clarke was one of six preachers at Canterbury Cathedral. He was revered as being an eminent scholar, as well as Vicar of Anglican Churches in Minster and Monkton. A large folio of his sermons were published by London's Charles White in 1637.

In our day, it is a remarkable feat for a professor or linguistic translator to be thoroughly comfortable in only one or two vernacular languages. Each King James committee member was expert in *several* key, Scripture languages and passages. How great were the Renaissance and Reformation tides of learning awash with art, religion, language, and literature, as the waves rolled into the shore of 1611 and its translation committee! The purpose of this era was served, as the crowning jewel of the English alphabet had reached its zenith. It was polished by the most trained and noble human minds ever assembled together for one Divine Book – The 1611 King James Bible.

KJB COMMITTEE CHECKS AND BALANCES

A series of checks and balances were employed to safeguard a perfect product. There were 15 rules governing the committee members. Although it was not a rule, several committee members **stood** while studying the Holy Bible, out of respect for the Word of God.

Each translator had to translate the books of his particular group **on his own** (Rule #8). This is key! They each had to be independently proficient in the necessary skills and languages of their own particular task. They couldn't fake it.

Next, each translator brought in their own work to their own company. The whole work was compared by the company and destined into one copy that would be agreed upon by all and stand (Rule #9). For example, if a particular company had seven members, that was **seven different times** the portion of Scripture was looked over. Then, as they met together as a group to go over it once more to finalize Word-equals-Word translation, that would be the **eighth time**.

The company would then send their completed work to the other companies (2,3,4,5,6). They interchanged their work to be reviewed. This makes five more times it was gleaned over, rising to the total of **13 times overall**. If any unsatisfactory or doubtful places were found, Rule #10 says these are to be noted and sent back to the original company from whence it came. If the original company should not concur with the suggestions made, the matter was finally addressed and decided upon at the final review committee (of 12 translators). Rule #11 stated that letters were also sent out to outside learned men of intellectual authority for processing any special place of obscurity in the text. Altogether, this makes a **total of 14 times** the Bible from Genesis to Revelation was translated, analyzed, and scrutinized by the best scholars ever unified on a textual committee.

This is a team technique unequalled by any modern day translation committee. This harmony could *only* be accomplished through Word-equals-Word *formal equivalency* method of translation that was fully employed by each member. They committed to translate without error from the original language. That is, chiefly the *Ben Chayyim Masoretic Text* for the Old Testament, and Beza's *Textus Receptus* for the New Testament.

A great resource which details the exhaustive checks on Scripture translation employed by the King James committee is Gustavus Swift Paine's, *The Men Behind the King James Version*. This book also sketches a vivid biographical portrait of individual committee members. Clearly, no group of Bible scholars before or since have ever been as thoroughly fit for their task as was the 1611 King James Bible committee team.

Modern day translation committees can't even come close to conformity, translating by *dynamic equivalency* as a group, with carefreeness in word choice, and without any overriding rules to govern them, and without each member having to translate by themselves. Of course, it would be chaos if the dynamic method was employed together with the rules of the King James committee. When, suppose, the individual members came back together as a group to review, each version would be completely different from one another! All bible versions since 1885 have been translated by *dynamic equivalency* (Word equals...whatever).

The King James Bible translators were a team. Each highly skilled member was unaided by anyone else.

Seven separate times the original book was formally
translated by word equals word. One time together was as
a group. The other 5 companies scrutinized an objective
review. Two men of each group (12 total) made a final
edit. No less than 14 times was each book, each chapter,
each verse, each line, each word checked, and re-checked,
from rich Majority Text manuscript body evidence.
Perfect.

The title read:

> *The Holy Bible,*
> *Conteyning the Old Testament and the New:*
> *Newly Translated out of the Originall tongues &*
> *with the former translations diligently compared*
> *and reuised by his Maiesties speciall*
> *Commandement.*
> *Appointed to be read in Churches.*
> *Imprinted at London by Robert Baker, Printer to*
> *the Kings most Excellent Maiestie. Anno Dom.*
> *1611.*

The prefatory *"Translators To The Reader"*
signifies the completion of their work as a perfect
representation of God's Words. The phrase "...nothing is
begun and perfected at the same time...", meant to the
translators that **human** perfection in translation is
impossible from the get-go. The phrase goes on to say,
"...and the later thoughts are thought to be the wiser...",
meaning succeeding Majority Text translations "worked
out the kinks", until the present copy represents purely
God's PERFECT Word. The 1611 King James Bible
checkmated any future move by transcribers to "update"
Holy Scripture.

And this is the word of God, which we translate...we do not deny, nay, we affirm and avow...the Bible in English set forth by men of our profession...containeth the word of God, nay **is the word of God**. Truly, good Christian Reader, **we never thought** from the beginning that we should need to **make a new translation**.[29]

THE KING JAMES BIBLE SINCE 1611

It is not surprising that certain word spellings and linguistic structure of the 1611 King James Bible are no longer in existence. In 1611, Middle English still lingered while developing into Modern English. Just as the English language would settle itself, until correct spelling was established in the mid 1700's, five basic revisions of the 1611 King James Bible were necessary to enhance punctuation, linguistic adjustments (inadvertent word omissions, grammatical word order), printing press errors, and spelling mistakes.

It is extremely noteworthy to express the UNALTERED TEXT of Divine Scripture. God's eternal Words have historically never been sullied away from its provenance (original source). Holy Writ is only updated by word spellings, sentence structure, and printing errors! These conscientious editions - NOT new versions - kept the same Divine Text intact and appeared in 1612, 1629, 1638, 1762, and 1769.

- 1612 - Lithographical adjustment from 𝕲𝖔𝖙𝖍𝖎𝖈 to **Roman** type
- 1629 - Lithographic adjustments (typographic corrections begun)
- 1638 - Lithographic adjustments (typographic corrections continued)

- 1762 - Orthographic adjustments (correct spelling begun)
- 1769 - Orthographic adjustments (correct spelling and typographics complete)

The 1769 edition by Dr. Benjamin Blayney has become the standard by which modern texts of the 1611 King James Bible are printed today. The more technically correct label of the 1611 King James Bible most have in possession today is the 1769 King James Bible. However, we all know what it means to say, the 1611 King James Bible.

The mere **136** actual word <u>adjustments</u> from the 1611 KJB to the 1769 KJB *were not word changes*, but the settling of the English language into its current form.

Examples: The 1611 reading is first, then the edited reading with date.

1. requite good – requite me good (1629)
    this book of the Covenant – the book of this covenant (1629)
    chief ruler – chief rulers (1629)
    which was a Jew – which was a Jewess (1629)
2. this thing – this thing also (1638)
    And Parbar – At Parbar (1638)
    For this cause – And for this cause (1638)
    a fiery furnace – a burning fiery furnace (1638)
    now and ever – both now and ever (1638)
3. shalt have remained – ye shall have remained (1638)
    Achzib, nor Helbath, nor Aphik – of Achzib, nor of Helbath, Nor of Aphik (1762)
4. returned – turned (1769)

1611 King James Bible, Psalm 23,

PSAL. XXIII
Dauids confidence in God's Grace
A Psalm of Dauid
The LORD *is* my shepheard, I shall not want.

2 He maketh me to lie downe in greene pastures: he leadeth mee beside the still waters.

3 He restoreth my soule: he leadeth me in the pathes of righteousness, for his names sake.

4 Yea, though I walke through the valley of the shadowe of death, I will feare no euill: for thou *art* with me, thy rod and thy staffe, they comfort me.

5 Thou preparest a table before me, in the presence of mine enemies: thou anointest my head with oyle, my cuppe runneth ouer.

6 Surely goodnes and mercie shall followe me all the daies of my life: and I will dwell in the house of the LORD for euer.

While co-author critics Geisler and Nix denounce 75,000 detailed "deviations" of the 1769 from the 1611 version, Dr. Scrivener (Bible scholar, 1885) alludes to less than 200 even noteworthy to mention. Legitimate human errors of the press, diction shortcomings, and misspellings should not be ascribed as hundreds and thousands of "errors" to the King James Bible-loving community.

In 1985, Dr. D.A. Waite published a comparison of the 1611 KJB to the 1917 Old Scofield Reference Bible, which represents the 1769 KJB edition. He catalogued only 136 actual word variants between the two out of 791,328 words. These were, again, linguistic modifications of spellings, and adjustments to semantical rules of the English language, as it was settling down into its final formation, complete with correct spelling in force since the mid 18th century.

The first edition of the King James Bible is often referred to as the "He Bible", because a *printing* error occurred in Ruth 3:15, which reads, "he went into the city" instead of, "she went into the city". The corrected edition is logically referred to as the "She Bible".

The royal printer was Robert Baker, who printed with *Cum Privilegio* (with privilege) under authority of the Crown. Some critics consider this a "copyright" that barred anyone else from printing copies the first 100 years before 1711. Yet, royal historian, John Dore, has dated a 1642 folio edition of the King James Bible printed in Amsterdam, a Geneva printing, a 1628 Scotland edition, various editions published outside of England in 1642, 1672, 1683, 1708, and in England itself in 1649. A special dispensation was granted to the University of Oxford edition of 1628, and the University of Cambridge edition of 1675; all of these without the *Cum Privilegio*. Thus, this assault is unwarranted.

Of course, the King James Bible is the only Bible in existence today that has never been copyrighted. Why? The King James Bible is not a vested part of the derivative copyright law's $400-million-dollar-a-year market of today's new bible versions.

The uniqueness of the King James Bible is felt in the tone of Oxford's Alister McGrath:

> Our culture has been enriched by...the King
> James Bible. Sadly, we shall never see its equal–
> or its like - again.[30]

The 1611 King James committee foresaw the need to loathe future tampering with the perfect Bible in English. *The Translator to the Reader* preface chides ancient heretics and warned their own generation of future divergent translations:

> If every man's humor should be followed, there would be **no end of translating**. Neither was their this **chopping and changing** in the more ancient times only, but also of late...**Satan** taking occasion by them...did strive he could, out of so uncertain and manifold **a variety of translations**, so to mingle all things that nothing might seem to be left certain and firm in them...[O]ur adversaries do make so many and so **various editions** themselves and **do error so much** about the worth and authority of them.

Chapter Four

Common Questions, Accurate Answers

There is not one word in our Bible that should not be there and no word is omitted that should be included. Through the ages - yea, from everlasting - God has protected His Word.

Oliver B. Greene
(1915-1976)
Evangelist, Renowned Radio Broadcaster, Author

1. Do the earliest Scripture manuscripts in existence today support the King James Bible?
Yes.

The *oldest* **Old Testament** manuscripts <u>existing in present day</u> are from the caves of Qumran, where the Dead Sea Scrolls were found. "Scholar Solomon A. Birnbaum ventures to date them as far back as the fifth century B.C. Many other scholars date the fragments in the 4th to 3rd centuries B.C."[2] Dr. Thomas Holland dates the scrolls from 168 B.C. to about 68 A.D.

Of the 830 documents discovered, roughly one-fourth of them (202) were Biblical texts. They contained fragments of the Pentateuch (Genesis - Deuteronomy), the Minor Prophets, Psalms, and the complete book of Isaiah. These reflect exclusively none other than the text of the King James Bible Old Testament, or the Masoretic Text.

By contrast, an embarrassed Mr. Burroughs, Revised bible version committee Chairman, said he was wrong when he made at least 13 changes in the Old Testament, after the discovery of the Dead Sea Scrolls in 1947.

> Old Testament scholar Gleason Archer concluded that the Dead Sea Scrolls 'proved to be **word for word identical** with our standard Hebrew Bible [Masoretic Text] in more than 95% of the text. The 5% of variation consisted chiefly of obvious slips of the pen and variations in   spelling.'
> F.F. Bruce states that 'the consonantal text of the Hebrew Bible which the Masoretes edited has been handed down to their time with conspicuous fidelity [exactness] over a period of nearly 1,000 years.[3]

The *oldest* **New Testament** manuscripts and fragments <u>existing in present day</u> are the following:

- 60 A.D - P64 world's oldest New Testament fragment, *Magdalen Papyrus*. This Scripture corrects several of the new English bible versions, and reaffirms the Majority Text King James Bible exclusively.
- 66 A.D. - Matthew 26:22 fragment reading, *"hekastos auton"* - "every one of them". Mirrors perfectly the King James Bible. Proves wrong the NIV and NASV bible readings.
- 120 A.D. - *Peshitta Bible* served the Syrian Christian Church where the apostles of Jesus and their inspired books frequented. Its roots are within the Semitic (Jewish) culture of Upper Mesopotamia and Syria. Translated in Aramaic, it exclusively mirrors the English Majority Text King James Bible.
- 157 A.D. - *Itala Bible* is the first Latin translation of the Majority Text Scripture for the young churches established in the Italian Alps. It enjoyed broad circulation across Europe and Asia. 50 manuscripts exist today. *Itala* perfectly mirrors the English Majority Text King James Bible.

Christopher De Hamel is an impartial manuscript expert. He does not avow allegiance to either the Majority or Critical text. His conclusion is drawn to the Majority (Received) Text outliving the Critical text. Equal Bibles listed above make the King James Bible a pure and continuous copy of the *original* inspired books of Holy Scripture. De Hamel agrees,

> Protestant Christianity found its cause allied to a Bible text which was **older than the Church of Rome**...[T]he Hexapla of Origen...was the famous long-lost **third century compilation**

which Saint Jerome is reputed to have brought back to Bethlehem to use for his own preparation of the Vulgate text.[4]

2.   What about the original Scripture books? What happened to them?

Psalm 12:6,7
The words of the LORD *are* **pure words**: *as* silver **tried in a furnace of earth**, purified seven times. Thou shalt keep them, O LORD, **thou shalt preserve them** from this generation **for ever**.

God's promise for eternal preservation of Holy Writ extends to every word, not the paper upon which they were written. His Words are unending. This exacts confidence that every *word* in the 1611 King James Bible are the pure, inspired Words of God.

Koine Greek died as a spoken language around 800 A.D. So, God is finished with the original Koine` Greek Scripture. Also, there is no civilization in the world who speaks the language. What would Jesus do? Inspire and preserve a Bible people can read today, or inspire original books in a language that is nonexistent today, then loose them?

Historic reasons for the "missing, original Scripture books" are as simple as A-B-C :

A) The materials they were originally composed upon, papyrus, were extremely perishable. Can you name **any** piece of paper that is 1,500 years old?

Papyrus is made from papyrus plants that grew abundantly in Egypt. The inner bark of the plant was cut into thin strips, which were laid side by side and crossed with other strips. They were then pressed together and sun-dried. The papyrus was, for the most part, written only on one side and bound together in rolls. The custom was to write in very narrow columns that had no separation of words, accent marks, or punctuation. Paragraphs were marked with a line in the margin of the text. The papyrus manuscripts are very fragile, and most of what we have are fragments.[5]

J. Harold Greene observes, "The autographs of the New Testament books were probably on papyrus and could hardly have survived except possibly in the dry sand of Egypt or in those conditions similar to the caves where the Dead Sea Scrolls have been found."[6] As a side note, animal skins (vellum) became the background material for parchment writings in the 3rd century. Paper was invented in the 14th century.

B) The early scribes who copied the manuscripts observed the Jewish practice of destroying old, worn-out copies when new ones were made. Kirsopp Lake of Harvard University comments, "It is hard to resist the conclusion that the scribes usually destroyed their exemplars when they copied the Sacred Books."[7]

Fredric Kenyon explains the destruction of older copies:

> The same extreme care which was devoted to the transmission of manuscripts is also at the bottom of the disappearance of the earlier copies. When a manuscript had been copied with the exactitude prescribed by the Talmud, and had been duly verified, it was accepted as authentic and regarded as being equal value with any other copy. If all were equally correct, *age gave no advantage to the manuscript*; on the contrary, age was a positive *disadvantage*, since a manuscript was liable to become defaced or damaged in the lapse of time. A damaged or

imperfect copy was at once condemned as unfit
for use.[8]

C) If the originals were still around, religious
souls everywhere would venerate (revere) these objects as
deity. The manuscripts would, in effect, be more
important than the message. The tendency to venerate
relics above what they stand for is always with us.
Centuries ago, when the Israelites were going through the
temple, the brazen serpent of Moses was found. The
people in turn began to worship the object. If the original
manuscripts in Hebrew and Greek were found today,
would we respond in more loving favor to our English
Holy Bible? It is the author's humble opinion that way too
much emphasis is placed upon the non-existent, and
unnecessary, "original" Scripture books.

Davidson adds,
...the rolls in which these regulations are not
observed [defective copies] are condemned to be
buried in the ground or burned; or they are
banished to the schools, to be used as reading
books.[9]

Cathedral schools did **NOT** possess pure copies of
inspired Scripture, it seems. What does this say about
ancient Scriptural discoveries made at ancient school
sights? The Critical Greek text *Sinaiticus Manuscript*
underscores virtually all New Testament modern versions
today. This manuscript was discovered at a monastery
(**school** for monks) of Saint Catherine at Mount Sinai in
1844. It contains 199 pages of an Old Testament, the
Epistle of Barnabas, and the Shepherd of Hermas
(Catholic books). It was recovered out of a trash basket
and from being burned as wastepaper. It influenced the
production of the failed English Revised version in 1885,

which would later be combined with the King James Bible to form the American Standard version in 1901.

In Mark 12:10, Jesus connects Himself to Old Testament prophecy for His audience. He implores them to read the **Scripture**, Psalm 118:22, *"...the stone which the builders rejected."* Philip is asked by an Ethiopian eunuch to explain the **Scripture** in Acts 8:32. He was reading from Isaiah 53:7, *"...he is brought as a lamb to the slaughter, and as a sheep before her shearers is dumb, so he openeth not his mouth."* In I Timothy 5:18, Paul says that he quotes **Scripture** out of Deuteronomy 25:4, *"Thou shalt not muzzle the ox when he treadeth out the corn."*

The **Scripture** referred to in these passages are not the original books. They are inspired and preserved *copies.* If Jesus Christ labels *copies* of His Word, **Scripture**, then rest assured, perfectly preserved *copies* of Holy Scripture are just as inspired as the original manuscripts.

Erickson's theological textbook, *Christian Theology*, though discordant from true Scripture, admits,

> ...undoubtedly the **Scripture** [II Timothy 3:16] that he was referring to **was a copy** and probably also a translation...[10]

The first to disparage inspiration of current Scripture to claim that only the *original books* were truly inspired in the mid to late 1800's, are the likes of Charles Hodge and Benjamin Warfield of Princeton University. This author suggests perhaps a "Tomb of the Unknown Bible" in Washington DC would represent all the "lost original books" in the War on Scriptures, if this is the only true Word of God.

Here is the bottom line. The real ORIGINAL Scriptures are located in Heaven. No one is guaranteed to observe the original source of the Holy Bible, until an individual receives Jesus Christ as a personal Saviour. This act of faith assures salvation of the soul, and a home in Heaven after this life. God would love to escort you there at the end of life's journey. To view a perfect _copy_ of the inspired books of Holy Scripture in English, simply open up your 1611 King James Bible.

Psalm 119:89
For ever, O LORD, thy word is settled **in heaven**.

3.   Were the King James Bible translators inspired like Moses?
No. The translators were great scholars. From their work on the King James Bible, many of them sparked other notable linguistic studies. King James called them _"our principal learned men within this our kingdom."_[11] "Gustavus S. Paine [author, _The Men Behind the King James Version_] noted that the king's translators were not superb writers doing scholarly work, but were superb scholars doing superb writing."[12] The translators were _not_ inspired themselves, since they were merely **copying** the inspired Scripture that already lay before them. They did not need to be inspired like Moses. Why? The WORD is already inspired. Their job was to respect the perfectly inspired Word while copying it and locking it into English. Word for word equals Word.
Paine makes the following assessment:

Though we may challenge the idea of word-for-word inspiration, we must surely conclude that these were men....filled with the Holy Ghost.....they so adjusted themselves to each other and to the work as to achieve a unique coordination and balance, functioning thereafter as an organic entity - no mere mechanism equal to the sum of its parts, but a whole greater than all of them.[13]

4. Where did the Dead Sea Scrolls come from and when were they written?

An Arab lad, herding his flock on the northwest corner of the Dead Sea in 1947, threw a rock into a cave and heard a cracking noise that would break open the attention of the religious world. Manuscript support abundantly poured forth in advocacy for the Hebrew Masoretic Text underlining the King James Bible Old Testament. "Scholar Solomon A. Birnbaum ventures to date them as far back as the fifth century B.C. Many other scholars date the fragments in the 4th to 3rd centuries B.C."[14]

In Jesus' day there were 3 sects of Judaism: Sadducees (the more liberal group), Pharisees (the more conservative group), and the Essenes (the more cultish group). As perhaps a cultic spin-off of the Pharisees, the Essenes are not mentioned in the Christian Bible or Jewish Talmud. Historians Josephus (95 A.D.), Philo (50 A.D.), and Pliny (79 A.D.) verify Essene existence.

This religious sect left Damascus for Jerusalem (perhaps driven out as heretics) to form communities of holiness by extreme abstinence. One group settled in Qumran on a flat hilltop. Caves rested a few hundred yards behind them, a quarter mile above the Dead Sea Coast. Believing sexual intercourse is a sin, they remained celibate and without women. Because of no private property, material possessions were cast into a common pool, supplying the needs of all. Jews tired of the busy, competitive lifestyle in Judea, and desirous to return to the simple lifestyle of their ancestors, resorted to the Essene community. The community was governed by 3 priests and 12 laymen. Their main function was performed in the scriptorium where scribes copied sacred Jewish Scripture, commentaries, and a Manual of Discipline.

> It was this scroll library that was placed in large clay jars and hidden in caves around Quram above the Dead Sea just before the destruction of the community around A.D. 70 [by the Roman Empire]. The Essenes had planned to return to their ruined abode and hidden library after the heat of war settled down. They never returned. The scrolls remained hidden nearly 1900 years. The Essenes have disappeared, but we have their library of writings [in "The Shrine of the Book" at Jerusalem]. Among the thousands of scroll fragments discovered, scholars have found excerpts of every book in the O.T., except Esther [the only book of the Bible that does not mention God]. Secular scrolls unique to the Essene community were also found.[15]

Through the years, these scrolls and fragments have been gradually translated. Many of the manuscripts remained unpublished until the 1990's. That the scrolls survived at all for two millennia is a slow-motion miracle.

A Jewish Revolt (66-73 A.D.) prompted the Essenes to hide the scrolls in the caves in preparation for Roman attack. It was a wise move. The Roman legions burned and leveled Qumran in 68 A.D.

To eliminate any question, as to whether the Masoretes had altered even to some very small extent the original text, the Essene book of Isaiah was found in healthy shape and showed virtually 100% perfect conformity to the Masoretic Text.

> Of the 166 words in Isaiah 53, there are only 17 letters in question. Ten of these letters are simply a matter of spelling, which does not affect the sense. Four more letters are minor stylistic changes, such as conjunctions. The remaining 3 letters comprise the word 'light' which is added in verse 11, and does not affect the meaning...Thus, in one chapter of 166 words, there is only one word (3 letters) in question after a thousand years of transmission.[16]

The impact of this discovery found the closeness of the Essene Isaiah scroll, written in the 1st century, with the Masoretic Isaiah Text written almost a thousand years later (900 A.D.). Out of 11 caves, around 830 distinct documents were salvaged. Roughly one fourth (202) are biblical texts. The biblical manuscripts represent the Masoretic Traditional Text (65%), the Septuagint Text (5%), the Samaritan Text (5%), and a non-aligned category (25%).

Where the Dead Sea Scrolls slightly differ from the Masoretic Text, let us remember that the Essenes were a socialist, religious cult, who did not agree with all the teachings of Christ by choice. They remained an extreme off-shoot of the Pharisees (imagine they *out-Phariseed* the Pharisees) obscured from mainstream society. Being then unavailable to the Masoretes, some of their texts could have started out in error (corrupt). Nonetheless, the similarities of the Majority Text to the Dead Sea Scrolls are staggering.

Old Testament scholar Gleason Archer concluded that the Dead Sea Scrolls 'proved to be **word for word**

identical with our standard Hebrew Bible in more than 95% of the text.

> The 5% of variation consisted chiefly of obvious slips of the pen and variations in spelling.' F.F. Bruce states that 'the consonantal text of the Hebrew Bible which the Masoretes edited has been handed down to their time with conspicuous fidelity [exactness] over a period of nearly 1,000 years.[17]

> One manuscript , 1QIsa b [Isaiah], is called by W.F. Albright 'virtually **identical'** to the Masoretic Text.[18]

Today the scrolls reside at the Shrine of the Book in Jerusalem. The evidence pours out from Qumran, demonstrating the Traditional Hebrew Masoretic Text existed long before Daniel Bomberg's *First Rabbinic Bible* in 1516. Once again, the overall Biblical principle of Word-equals-Word Divine Preservation of the King James Bible is forever marked in history, nestled in ancient religious scrolls. The perfect King James Bible is authenticated by matching Scripture texts dated well before the days of Christ.

5.   What is the Septuagint?
        A Greek version of the Hebrew Bible is called the Septuagint. Alexander the Great founded Alexandria, Egypt, in 332 B.C. with a colony of Jews. It became the central hub of Hellenistic learning (Greek religious mythology) mixed with Jewish culture. Many of the Greek-speaking Jews were unable to read Hebrew. These non-Christian Jews desired a translation of the Hebrew Bible in Greek language.

According to a Letter of Aristeas, who lived about 100 B.C., the King of Egypt from 285-246 B.C., Ptolemy II, brought 72 elders (six from each of the 12 tribes of Israel) to Alexandria, because he wanted a copy of the Pentateuch to be added to his famous library there. "This story may be almost entirely legendary, and was perhaps told to give authority to a revised standard Greek translation of the Pentateuch about 100 B.C. It may, however, reflect the actual making of a complete translation of the Pentateuch about 250 B.C. for the Jewish community by Alexandrian Jews."[19]

The legend is told how the 72 translators were confined each one or two in a cell, while they each worked separately on the translation. Lo and behold, when they each finished equally in 70 days, their translations agreed word for word. Such a story was told to prop up the translation with divine authority. The Pentateuch (Genesis - Deuteronomy) was translated first into Greek. Then, gradually, the other books followed, and by 132 B.C., the Septuagint (meaning "Version of the Seventy") was complete. The Koine` Greek period 300 B.C - 300 A.D. provided the lingual backdrop.

The Septuagint (LXX - Roman numeral for 70) did not follow or match the inspired Masoretic Text. Award winning author Jeffrey Sheler writes,

> The Greek bible [Septuagint] included several books that the Hebrew Bible did not, as well as shorter and longer versions of some of the books in the Hebrew text. Those disagreements would go largely unresolved; they account for the differences that exist today between the Bibles of Protestantism and Catholicism.[20]

Historical author Hershel Hobbs adds,

> When the Alexandrian canon [Septuagint] was established, they also included the 14 books of the Apocrypha which means 'hidden' [their origin is unknown], reflecting the **anonymous** character of these books. The Roman Catholics included these books in their Bible. However, the Protestant canon followed the Hebrew canon and so **omitted** them.[21]

Father of the Catholic Latin Vulgate bible, Jerome, extensively used the Septuagint. It also remains the official, natural Old Testament of the Greek Orthodox Church, since it is in Greek. The most noted copy of the Septuagint was later produced by Origen (250 B.C.), called the Hexapla. A few limited fragments exist today of Origen's Hexapla. Origen's Hexapla was revised by two students, Pamphilus and Eusebius. The Aquila, Symmachus, and Theodotion Greek versions replace certain Bible books (Ex: Daniel in Theodotion) with their own readings.

Sir Fredric Kenyon brilliantly established that Biblical guardians, the Jews (Romans 3:1-2) of the Old Testament, have categorically not accepted the Septuagint throughout history. The great Jewish historian, Josephus, refused the Septuagint (LXX) as well, because of its additions to the Hebrew canon of Scripture (Masoretic Text).

Dr. Ernst Wurthwein clears the air by pointing out,

> ...the LXX does not shed light on the text of the original Hebrew, but only on how some *interpreted* the Hebrew text.[22]

The Septuagint failed the inspired Scriptures many times, departing from the Hebrew Masoretic Text wildly, causing the King James Bible committee to depart from the Septuagint. It is interesting to note how the King James Bible committee viewed Septuagint translators as *interpreters* in their "Translator to the Reader",

> ...the Seventy were interpreters...they may be noted to add to the original, and sometimes to take from it: which made **the Apostles to leave them many times** when they left the Hebrew...This may suffice touching the Greek translation of the Old Testament.
> The translation of the Seventy dissenteth from the Original in many places...Origen, **urch of God for certain hundred years, were of another mind: for theywere so far from treading under foot,...the translation of** Aquila, **that is, one that had turned Jew; of** Symmachus, **and** Theodotion, **both** Ebionites, **that is,** one vile hereticks, **that they joined them together with the Hebrew original,...and set them forth openly to be considered of and persuaded by all.**[23]

The 3-fold division of the Greek Septuagint are Law, Psalms, and Prophets, contrary to the Hebrew Masoretic Text order Law, Prophets, and Psalms, notarized by Jesus in Luke 24:44. The Lord Jesus, Himself, authorized the traditional Masoretic text, not the Septuagint, in Luke 24:44,

> And He said unto them, These *are* the words which I spake unto you, while I was yet with you, that all things must be fulfilled, which were **written**, in the **law** of Moses, and *in* the **prophets**, and *in* the **psalms**, concerning me.

This order describes the entire Hebrew Old Testament to the Jew. Contrary to the Septuagint order, Jesus put His hand on the entire Masoretic Hebrew Old Testament Text that existed then and AUTHORIZED it. The King James Bible is a perfect word mirror in English of the Majority Text that Jesus Christ authorized.

6.   Why are there italicized words in the Bible?

Words *italicized* simply means that there was no English term or tense to represent the word type in the original Hebrew or Greek language, so the English <u>verbal equivalent</u> was used and put in *italics*. Verbal equivalent means verbal equal. The translators made the most strict, conservative word choice by rules of grammar. The *italicized word* was silent or understood in the language being translated from (Ex: Greek).

This is an oversimplified example:

Let's translate "the blue house" from English into Spanish.
English: the blue house
Spanish: the house *of* blue (el casa de azul)

Can you see how the Spanish dialect picked up an extra word - *of* - in the translation? Notice that it was also placed in *italics*. The same principle applies when translating from Hebrew or Greek into English. Rules of grammar must apply necessary words to the sentence structure in order for it to retain sense in the language being translated to. *Italicized* words are understood or silent words that must become **visible** in another language.

It is my humble opinion that italicized words in Majority Text Scripture are as inspired and divinely preserved equal to all other words. Why?

1) When Jesus quoted the Old Testament, the italicized words in the Old Testament were not italicized in the New Testament after Jesus spoke them.

Examples: Deuteronomy 8:3 & Matthew 4:4; Isaiah 65:1 & Romans 10:20; Psalm 94:11 & I Corinthians 9:9; Deuteronomy 25:4 & I Corinthians 9:9.

2) Italics are a grammatical necessity when translating from Hebrew or Greek into English. We know *how* they were translated in the Majority Text Holy Scripture. Word for word equals Word. Verbal (formal) equivalency does not allow for any deviation of word choice from the original word. Although the King James Bible lets us visibly see which *italicized words* in English were <u>invisible</u> in the original Hebrew or Greek language, new bible versions sloppily insert "understood" words from the Critical text **without being italicized** at all.

In Acts 2:25, Peter quotes Psalm 16:8. Notice the italicized words "*he is*" in Psalm 16:8. They are not italicized in the New Testament Acts 2:25. Why? God VALIDATED the correct usage of the italicized words "*he is*" in the Old Testament Majority Text Scripture.

Psalm 16:8
I have set the LORD always before me: because *he is* at my right hand, I shall not be moved.

Acts 2:25
For David speaketh concerning him, I foresaw the Lord always before my face, for he is on my right hand, that I should not be moved:

Our friends of the more popular bible versions today, (New King James, New American Standard, New International versions) may appreciate clarification that the text of modern bible versions **do not necessarily come from inspired Scripture**. Based upon the Ben Asher's Critical Hebrew text (1270 A.D.), Rudolf Kittel's *Biblical Hebraica* (Hebrew Bible, 1909) makes over 20,000-30,000 footnoted changes throughout its entire old testament. New versions are based squarely on Kittel's old testament *Biblical Hebraica*. The NKJV and NASV keep the footnotes in place. The NIV inserts Kittel's footnotes as the **TEXT ITSELF** <u>without being italicized</u>. A devout Masorete Jew would never even do such a thing.

7.   **What are Apocrypha books?**

apoc ♦ ry ♦ pha
ə-'pä-krə-fə
Greek apokryphos (obscure)
apokryptein(to hide away)

1: writings or statements of dubious authenticity
2: a: books included in the Septuagint and Vulgate but excluded from the Jewish and Protestant canons of the Old Testament
b: early Christian writings not included in the New Testament

Merriam-Webster's Dictionary
11th Collegiate Version 3.0, 2003 ©

The term *apocrypha* refers to a collection of Catholic books that fall outside the canon of inspired Scripture. The enigma of the Apocrypha book's origin will always render them empty of Biblical authority. Using the Critical Alexandrian Greek text, St. Jerome translated a bible for the Roman Catholic Church with full financial backing and a full staff of copiers in 405 A.D. It is known today as the Latin Vulgate Roman Catholic bible. Jerome added the Apocryphal books (means "hidden" – their origin is unknown to this day) to his Latin Vulgate Catholic bible translation in 405 B.C.

They are as follows:

I & II Esdras	The Wisdom of Solomon
Susanna	Tobit
Ecclesiasticus	Bel and the Dragon
Judith	Baruch
Prayer of Manasses	The rest of Esther
The Song of the Three Holy Children	I & II Maccabees

These questionable books have never been accepted as part of the historical lineage of inspired Majority Text Scripture by religious conservatives. No one knows how or where they originated. The author remains anonymous. Divine credibility can not be pinpointed. Therefore, the verdict of history is against them.

King James Bible critics categorically confuse the truth by claiming the Apocryphal books were included in the Holy Bible by the King James Bible committee of 1611. Is it true? Not how they mean it.

In between the Old and New Testaments is an "Intertestamental Period". In many English Bibles there is a "Summary for the Reader" detailing this 400 year period between the testaments. However, when the 1611 King James Bible was first printed, the committee put the *actual historical record of events* during this 400 year period (Apocrypha books) in between the testaments. The Apocryphal books were used as a historical reference of this age, since the events and characters of these books are set at this time. The King James Bible committee then listed 7 reasons why the Apocrypha books were **NOT** to be accepted as part of inspired Scripture.

The King James translators inserted **the actual literature of that nebulous intertestamental period** in between the testaments. Within 40 years after 1611, the Apocryphal books were left out of the space in between the testaments.

The Apocrypha books are included as actual <u>words of scripture text</u> in the Jerome's Catholic Vulgate bible. This apocryphal "scripture" mother text gave birth to the NIV, NASV, ESV, and the TNIV, via *Codex Vaticanus*. The inspired Majority Text Scripture remains foreignly separated from these dubious apocryphal books.

Bible journalist expert Bill Grady explains,

> .....the translators were careful to set these spurious books apart from the inspired text by inserting them between the Testaments. And to ensure that there was no misunderstanding, they listed 7 reasons why the apocryphal books were to be *categorically rejected as part of the inspired canon.* The only reason for their inclusion at all was due to their accepted historical value. Whereas our Scofield Reference Bible divides the testaments with an informative article entitled, 'From Malachi to Matthew', the King James translators inserted **the actual literature of that nebulous intertestamental period.** [24]

Historical author Hershel Hobbs adds,

> When the Alexandrian canon was established, they also included the 14 books of the Apocrypha which means 'hidden' [their origin is unknown], reflecting the **anonymous** character of these books. The Roman Catholics included these books in their Bible. However, the Protestant canon followed the Hebrew canon and so **omitted** them.[25]

8.   What is "canon" and "codex" of Scripture?

The *canon* is a listing of books that are the standard, or rule, finalizing a written body of work. It is the accepted standard by which to measure all similar books. The canon of inspired Holy Scripture, for example, are the 66 books listed in the 1611 King James Bible. This is the complete measure of inspired writings that we accept as inspired Divine Scripture. The canon of Scripture represents *God's* Words.

Codex means "book". The canon of New Testament Scripture has been divinely preserved in writings on Papyrus (plant leaves), to vellum (animal skins), to codex (paper bindings in book form). The writings of early Christianity fathers from the 1st and 2nd centuries A.D. (in all 3 forms) testify to the canon of the Majority Text New Testament Scripture.

Biblical scholar Hershel Hobbs assesses,

> Irenaeus was a pupil of Polycarp who, in turn, was one of the Apostle John's disciples. In his defense of the Christian faith he quotes from the four Gospels, Acts, the Pauline epistles, several of the general epistles and the Revelation; he regarded all these as inspired Scripture. Tertullian in Northern Africa does virtually the same…By the end of the 2nd century the **canon** of the Gospels was settled. The same is true also of the Pauline epistles.' He notes that the title 'New Testament' is first used by an unknown writer about 193 A.D.[26]

9. What is the Latin Vulgate?

By 2nd century A.D., the traditional Majority Text had established itself. An adverse Latin form of scripture would establish the Roman Catholic version of their bible, called the Latin Vulgate in the 4th century. The Latin word *vulgatus*, meaning "common", has no uniqueness other than the shortening and lengthening of the existing books, and the adding of other non-canonical books to form new "scripture".

St. Jerome of the early Catholic Church was among the first noted scholars to be versed in both languages of the Bible (Hebrew and Greek). In 383 A.D., Pope Damasus commissioned Jerome to "revive and revise" the Old Latin *Itala* Bible (157 A.D.), which is allied to the Majority Text.

Reluctantly agreeing, because he knew this new version would not be welcomed by early New Testament Christianity who had already begun to divide itself over which line of manuscripts and translations best reflect the original autographs, Jerome translated the Greek into the "mother tongue" of Latin.

Jerome completed the new version of the Latin Vulgate bible in 405 A.D. Jerome was influenced by church father Eusebius (260-340 A.D.), who was commissioned by semi-Christian Emperor Constantine to procure 50 new Bibles in the wake of Diocletian's decade-long persecution (302-312 A.D.). (Many believe Codices *Vaticanus* and *Sinaiticus* are two of these 50 copies, representing the Critical text Alexandrian manuscripts that virtually all new bible versions are based upon.)

Traveling to Bethlehem to do his work in native surroundings to the Bible, Jerome translated from a Greek manuscript closely resembling the Critical text (Codex

Sinaiticus). This manuscript conspicuously agrees with Jerome's Vulgate, demonstrating the influence of the Critical "Alexandrian" textual line upon it. Although Christ and the apostles never referred to them, and the 1st century Christians did not include them into Scripture, Jerome added the Apocryphal books into the Latin Vulgate Catholic bible.

We sense the quiet panic of Jerome in the Preface to the Latin Vulgate bible, that his translation was a mistake,

> You [Pope Damascus] urge me to revise...copies of Scripture which are scattered throughout the world...is there not a man, learned or unlearned, who will not...call me a forger and a profane person for having had the audacity **to add anything to the ancient books**, or **to make changes**.[27]

Volume 9 (p. 732) edition of the *Encyclopedia Britannica* verifies the feign scripture of Jerome's Latin Vulgate.

> [I]t revealed the fact that the Vulgate [whose readings can be seen today in the new versions]...was not only a second-hand document, but in places **an erroneous document**.[28]

10. What would be the harm in updating "thee, thou, ye" archaic words?

> As a rule, whenever we encounter a syntactic oddness or aberration in the Authorized Version [KJB] - the kind of thing the word 'archaic' is used unthinkingly to describe - **we ought to assume** that it reflects an attempt to reproduce **the original's word.**[29]
> The Literary Guide to the Bible
> **Harvard University**

It is worthy to note the marked difference between the text of the 1611 King James Bible and its Preface. The Preface verifies the text of Scripture was *not* translated into the language of that period, but rather **copied** the inspired words of *original* Scripture. While new versions paraphrase the archaic words "ye and thee" to "who and you", the King James Bible proudly leaves them in the sacred text. It shows the faulty understanding of the new versions mindset to these purposeful words.

Ordinary Englishmen did not use the "archaic" Scripture words in everyday language back in 1611, either. Why leave them in the sacred text then? There are times when the reader of the Holy Bible can properly understand the meaning of a passage by its personal pronoun. The personal pronouns that begin with the letter "T" are singular (*thee, thy, thou, thine*), and personal pronouns beginning with the letter "Y" signify a plural meaning or audience (*ye, you, your*).

Dr. Thomas Holland clarifies,

> In Greek one can tell if the personal pronoun is singular or plural by the ending of the Greek word. The same is true of the English found in the KJV. The words "thou", "thee", "thy", and "thine" are all singular, allowing the reader to understand that personal pronouns beginning with the letter "t" are singular. The words "ye", "you", and "your" are all plural, allowing the reader to know that personal pronouns beginning with "y" are plural. Luke 22:31-32 provides a good illustration: *And the Lord said, Simon, Simon, behold, Satan hath desired to have you, that he may sift You as wheat.(32) But I have prayed for thee, that thy faith fail not: and when thou art converted, strengthen thy brethren.* The Greek reader would understand from the words used that Christ is at first speaking to Peter about the disciples collectively, while in vs. 32 Christ is speaking to Peter about him singularly. The same is conveyed in English with the words "you", "thy", and "thee". This is lost however, when all these words are changed to a generic "you". Thus the reader cannot tell if the "you" is singular or plural.[30]

By using the appropriate pronoun, the King James Bible gives an exact representation of the audience being spoken to as well as **the original interpretation**. If Christ were speaking for an audience and said, *"Ye are of your father the devil"*, one person could not look at another person and say, "He is referring to you". Why? Because *"ye"* is plural.

Matthew 11:28 correctly reads in the King James Bible, *"Come unto me, **all ye** that labour and are heavy laden, and I will give you rest"*. The Revised Standard version incorrectly reads, *"Come to me, **all who** labor and are heavy laden, and I will give you rest"*. The words "all who" in the Revised version grammatically conflict with each other and the original intent of its meaning, "all" is plural, and "who" is primarily singular. The *new* Revised version words lack *cognitive scaffolding*. Sentences in the King James Bible are woven by *cognitive scaffolding* words that build the meaning in a consistent form and pattern by the fabric of its content.

John 3:7 says, *"Marvel not that I say unto **thee**, ye must be born again."* Jesus uses both the singular "thee" and the plural "ye", one right after the other, in the same verse. A reader can immediately pick up on both the individual and community audience. The King James Bible does a great service of conveying the accurate need of man's salvation ***without having to know Hebrew or Greek***. Modern versions replacing the word "thee" with "you" in all cases obscures the precise and correct meaning of this great verse.

Suffixes "eth" and "est" are significant to correct verbal inflections of Holy Scripture. They distinguish between **first person** (the speaker), **second person** (the one spoken to), and **third person** (the one spoken about). The "s" in "est" reminds the reader of the second person. The "t" in "eth" reminds the reader of third person.

KJB Verb Inflections:

I write	first person
Thou writest	second person
He writeth	third person

New versions completely lose verbal inflections by merely changing the l e t t e r i n g of the words. Doing so shows a lack of appreciation to understand the original intent of a verse or passage.

The MAIN reason why *"thee, thou, thy, thine, and ye"* words should be left alone is because they are each inspired as God's specific word choice. If you believe in an every-word-preserved text of Holy Scripture that mirrors exactly the original source, then you believe *"thee, thou, thine, and ye"* are God's word choices. Didn't He know what He was doing the first time? Doesn't He get it right the first time?

> Either the whole Bible is inspired, the Words as well as the sentences, the syllables as well as the Words, the letters as well as the syllables, every 'jot' and every 'tittle' of it, or the whole of it must be abandoned, since no part of it can be certainly depended upon as an infallible guide. [31]
>
> **Dean JOHN WILLIAM BURGON**
> (1813-1888)
> Venerated Conservative Anglican Church Scholar

11.   What are "Alexandrian" manuscripts: Codex Sinaiticus,   Codex   Vaticanus,   and   Codex Alexandrinus?

Critical text evolution trickles through a divergent stream of "Alexandrian" manuscripts. Alexander the Great founded Alexandria, Egypt, with a colony a Jews. It became a great center of Hellenistic learning (Greek religious mythology). Many of the Greek-speaking Jews there were unable to read Hebrew. Hence, the inspired Hebrew Masoretic Scriptures became a foreign commodity inside Alexandrian culture. According to the Letter of Aristeas, who lived about 100 B.C., the King of Egypt, Ptolemy II (285-246 B.C.), wanted a copy of the Pentateuch (Genesis - Deuteronomy) to be added to his famous library there.

Headmaster at the Catechetical School in Alexandria, Egypt, was Origen (185-254 A.D.). Origen was the first to fully enact the *allegorical* (dynamic equivalency) freestyle interpretation and translation of Scripture. This Critical text Greek translation from the Hebrew Old Testament is the Septuagint. The Pentateuch was translated first into Greek. Then, gradually, the other books followed, and by 132 B.C., the Septuagint ("Version of the Seventy") was complete. The Septuagint **did not follow the inspired Masoretic Text.** "Two such manuscripts that reflect the text of Origen are *Codex Vaticanus* and *Codex Siniaticus* of the Alexandrian line of manuscripts."[32] This *allegorical* interpretation mode of Alexandria pales in stark contrast to the *literalist* mode (Word-equals-Word) of Antioch and the first century New Testament church there.

> The manuscripts which challenge the established text of the Byzantine world, and hence, the KJB, are *Alexandrian* in geographic origin. They are named after Egypt's capital city of Alexandria…while Alexandria pioneered the **allegorical** or figurative style, Antioch maintained the strict **literalist** mode of orthodoxy which would naturally demand a greater regard for precise word-for-word copying.[33]

> The Church of Antioch has a noteworthy position in Scripture as the first place believers were called Christians (Acts 11:26). It is also interesting that where both Antioch and Alexandria are mentioned in the same passage, Antioch is listed as a place of service and Alexandria as a place of disruption (Acts 6:5-10). Could it be that God, Who foreknows all things, provides for us our starting point in

searching for the original text? If so, the
direction would not be in Alexandria, Egypt.
Instead, it would be in the cradle of New
Testament Christianity at Antioch of Syria,
where the Traditional text originated.[34]

Origen is commonly heralded as "Father of the
Alexandrian text." The **Critical Text** is comprised almost
solely upon *Alexandrian* documents, with a pinch of
Western and Cesarean texts sprinkled in.

Adds historical author Hershel Hobbs,
When the Alexandrian canon was established,
they also included the 14 books of the
Apocrypha which means 'hidden' [their origin is
unknown], reflecting the **anonymous** character
of these books. The Roman Catholics included
these books in their Bible. However, the
Protestant canon followed the Hebrew canon
and so **omitted** them.[35]

In 405 A.D., St. Jerome, "Father of the Catholic
Latin Vulgate bible", was commissioned by semi-
Christian Emperor Constantine to procure 50 new Bibles
in the wake of Diocletian's decade-long persecution (302-
312 A.D.). Many believe Codices *Vaticanus* and
Siniaticus are two of these 50 copies. Virtually all English
bible versions today are the repository of Critical text
Alexandrian manuscripts.
    Two such documents startled the scriptural text
community in the mid 1880's with the discovery of 4th
century Greek manuscripts - *Codex Sinaiticus* and *Codex
Vaticanus*. At this time, both documents were predated
before the known Greek manuscripts of the King James
Bible Committee of 1611. Almost instantaneously they
received textual preeminence. Both of these Alexandrian-

line manuscripts account for most passages of contemporary bible versions and date approximately 300-350 A.D.

Constantine Tischendorf was a German evolutionist theologian and editor of several Greek New Testaments. His penchant for Alexandrian manuscripts caused him to be in constant search for ancient documents supporting his work. In 1844, he happened upon *Codex Sinaiticus* (also listed as Codex Aleph) while rummaging through a wastepaper basket in the Monastery of St. Catherine at Mount Sinai. The monks would burn these faulty copies of discarded vellum (dried animal skins) leaves to warm themselves.

Tischendorf assumed that it came from the 4th century, but never found any proof that it dated earlier than the 12th century. He was interested in procuring these wastebasket Greek Septuagint manuscripts. After Tischendorf's third failed attempt in 1859 to secure the manuscripts, he went to Cairo to be granted his request by the Superior. After paying a hefty sum, he was given 43 leaves of the document nine months later.

Codex Sinaiticus contains over half of an Old Testament, and most of a New Testament. Both testaments contained Catholic apocryphal books within the scripture text, such as the *Epistle of Barnabas* and the *Shepherd of Hermas.* "In the 1700's there was a controversy surrounding the *Sinaiticus* that has since died down. A monk claimed to have written it then in the 1700's."[36]   It now resides at the British museum in London.

It seems the mesmerizing lure of ancient manuscripts invokes an irresistible seduction for Critical text scholars to heap merit upon them at all cost. It began with Tischendorf's lie. His discovery of Codex Aleph [Sinaiticus] clouded his judgment. Previous to that,

Tischendorf milled out seven different Greek New Testaments of his own, declaring the seventh to be *perfect* and *could not be superseded.* Then, in scandalous fashion, after locating the Sinaiticus Manuscript, he churned out an eighth Greek New Testament, which was **different from his seventh in 3,572 places!**

Sinaiticus has 1,460 disastrous readings affecting 2,640 word changes that are not found anywhere on Earth but in itself. Why? Scribbled, scratched-through, smudged-out corrections are carelessly fraught throughout the entire manuscript by **10 different revisers** at **10 different periods.**

An interesting question begs, "Should ten different scribes spread their corrections piecemeal over every page through centuries of changes to the Sinaiticus...unless they considered the original Greek draft was <u>not genuinely inspired</u> and needed correcting?"

Codex Vaticanus (also listed as Codex B) is a Catholic Greek text of "unknown origin". It was officially catalogued in the Vatican library in 1475 and remains there to this day.

Erasmus recognized it as conforming to the Latin Vulgate of Rome, because of an ancient written agreement, the *Bulla aurea.* This document explains the condition of the union between 1st century Greek and Roman churches in Florence. It says that to join together, the Greeks must *conform their readings* to those of the Latin Vulgate. THIS IS WHY LATIN VULGATE MANUSCRIPTS MATCH ONLY A HANDFULL OF CRITICAL TEXT GREEK MANUSCRIPTS (44), such as the *Codex Vaticanus* and *Codex Sinaiticus* OF WHICH ALL NEW BIBLE VERSIONS ARE BASED Erasmus knew of these intertwined (corrupted) readings and attributes them to Origen (Father of the Alexandrian line manuscripts). *See Life and Letters X, p. 355 / Cambridge Volume III, p. 203-4.

Vaticanus places uninspired books Tobit, Judith, and I&II Maccabees after Nehemiah. Inserted after Song of Solomon is Wisdom and Ecclesiasticus, as well as Baruch following Lamentations. **Inside** the book of Daniel is found the Song of Azariah, Susanna, and Bel and the Dragon. Modern bibles such as the *New International version, New American Standard version, English Standard version, and Today's New International version* are translated from the readings of the *Codex Vaticanus.*

It has been humorously stated that the blind adherence of scripture revisionists to the *Vaticanus* manuscript is treated as "the second infallible voice from the Vatican".

As a side note, *Codex Alexandrinus*, the least known of these 3 Critical text uncials (ALL CAPS - NOSPACEBETWEENWORDS), is alleged to originate in the 5th Century A.D. It contains a complete copy of the Septuagint. This manuscript also adds 5 more apocryphal (Catholic) books to its Old Testament "scripture" than the *Vaticanus* and *Sinaiticus* (III & IV Maccabees, Psalm 151, 14 Odes, & Epistle to Marcellinus). It also adds to the New Testament, I & II Clement. Although *Alexandrinus* flaunts the addition of uninspired books to its text, it goes missing Mark 16:9-20, even though this passage is found in almost all Critical text Latin manuscripts.

The document's birthplace and domicile was Alexandria, Egypt, until 1621, when patriarch of Alexandria, Cyril Lucar, presented it to Constantinople, who then presented it in 1627 to Charles I, King of England. It rests next to the *Sinaiticus* in the British Museum and Library. The original writer of the manuscript has always been obscured in clouded mystery. Want a Bible without any known author?

Tischendorf would later become one of 2 people allowed to view the *Codex Vaticanus* in the Vatican library between 1845-1866. It was edited by Cardinal Angelo Mai in the 1850's. A Greek New Testament based on Tischendorf's findings was produced by Cambridge professor F. Hort and liberal Anglican scholar B. Wescott in 1881. This Critical Greek text is parent to the 1898 creation of the first edition *Nestle/Aland Greek New Testament* which underscores the majority of all modern Bible degree education and seminary training. It is the text of new version committees. And, virtually all contemporary English versions of the Bible are predicated upon it.

Dr. D.A. Waite's meticulous word study of the most popular 26th edition of the 1979 *Nestle/Aland Greek Testament* calculated **15 word changes per page** from the inspired Greek Majority Text, *Textus Receptus*.

Codex Sinaiticus and *Codex Vaticanus* not only wildly disagree with the majority of all 5,000+ Greek manuscripts, but they also disagree largely with each other. Over **3,000 stark disagreements** in the Gospels alone conflict Codices *Vaticanus* and *Sinaiticus*. It makes one wonder if these are honestly meant to be highly touted as credible in the diluted world of Critical text biblical manuscripts.

The *Vaticanus* has 589 readings affecting 858 word changes that are not found anywhere on Earth but in itself.

Dean of Chichester, John W. Burgon (1813-1888), made a scholarly point that the reason why B (Vaticanus) and Aleph (Sinaiticus) and other non-Byzantine manuscripts have survived to the present day is because they were *rejected by the early Greek Church as faulty* and thus not used. Their survival is due to this neglect.

The discovery of *Codex Sinaiticus* (1856), and the 1475 *Codex Vaticanus*, embodying the primary Alexandrian textual line, gave credence to the first revision committee of 1881 to formulate the failed English Revised Version in 1885, which would later be combined with the Holy Bible to create the American Standard version of 1901.

The existence of these two Alexandrian codices lend the most impressive sounding challenges and the most frequently used objections against the superiority of the inspired 1611 King James Bible. Why? Critics claim Alexandrian manuscripts predate the *Textus Receptus* by roughly 100 years. However, the voice of a conservative scholar on the 1881 Revision Committee gives us a clearer picture.

We are informed by Dr. Scrivener that there were 2,864 cursive and uncial manuscripts of the New Testament available to the committee. Although these represent many different countries and different periods of time, **the majority of the Revisers ignored these** and pinned their admiration and confidence practically to **two** – the *Vaticanus* and *Sinaiticus*.

Dr. John Charles Ellicott, in submitting the Revised Version to the Southern Convocation in 1881, reported they had made between 8 & 9 changes in every 5 verses. In an average of every 10 verses, 3 of these were made for critical purposes.[37] For the most part, the *Vaticanus* and *Sinaiticus* are responsible, but the *Vaticanus* readings, sometimes chosen on its own, but generally in accord with the Sinaitic, is responsible for 9/10 of word replacements in the Revised Version.

12. Who were Wescott and Hort?

A groundswell of pressure from liberal scholars descended on the Church of England for a revision of the 1611 King James Bible at the completion of Wescott and Hort's Critical Greek text in 1870. Historian Dr. Gibbs sets the stage,

> In 1870, the Convention of the Church of England commissioned a revision of the Authorized Version...Although it was meant to correct a few supposed 'errors' in the Authorized Version, the textual critics of the day assured themselves that they would never again have to submit to the Divine authority of the Universal text.[38]

Several key British scholars dismissed their invitations to join the Revised committee being totally opposed to the prospect of any revision. Dr. F.C. Cook, editor of *Speaker's Commentary*, was Chaplain to Queen Victoria of England. He refused to sit on the Revision Committee after being invited, stating,

> That Textus Receptus...its readings are maintained... with the **best** ancient versions, with the **earliest and best** Greek and Latin Fathers, and with the vast **majority** of uncial and cursive manuscripts.[39]

Consider Revised committee Chairman Bishop Charles Ellicott's own lament,

It is my honest conviction that for any authoritative REVISION, **we are not yet mature**; either **in Biblical learning** or Hellenistic scholarship...it has certainly not been directed...to render any national attempt at REVISION either hopeful or lastingly profitable.

Ellicott adds further,

What course would revisers have us follow?...Would it be well for them to agree on a **Critical Greek Text**? To this question we venture to answer very hesitantly **in the negative**...Nothing is more satisfactory at the present time than the evident feelings of veneration for our Authorized Version, [King James Bible] and the very generally-felt desire for as **little changes as possible.**[40]

In other words, "if something ain't broke, don't fix it". Prior to being Chairman of the English Revised version bible, Bishop Ellicott, delivers an earth-shattering lack of confidence of 1850's translation scholarship,

Even critical editors of the stamp of Tischendorf have apparently not acquired even a rudimentary knowledge of several leading versions... in many instances they have **positively misrepresented the readings** which they have followed...as my notes will testify, are often sadly, and even **perversely, incorrect.**[41]

Enter, Drs. Fenton John Anthony Hort (1828-1892) and Brooke Foss Wescott (1825-1901), the leading anti-Majority Text King James Bible critics of the past 130 years. Their inherent prejudice against the inspired

Majority Text led the first bible revision committee from 1871-1881.

Dubious enough are the doctrinal misgivings of these two opportunists as well. *Crowned With Glory* author Dr. Thomas Holland lays it out in plain view,

> Wescott denied biblical infallibility. Hort stated those that believe in biblical authority were perverted. Hort taught that Revelation 3:14 proclaimed Christ was the first thing created, agreeing with the Gnostic teaching that Christ was a begotten god. Wescott denied that Saint John ever claimed Christ to be God. Hort stated that the ransom for our sin was paid to satan.
> Both men denied the doctrine of eternal damnation, stating hell is not a place of punishment.
> These beliefs stand in direct opposition to the teachings of the New Testament and should be carefully considered when those who hold to such beliefs suggests changes in the New Testament. No matter how careful or unbiased a scholar may be, it is the nature of man to slant Scripture toward his understanding.[42]

Dr. Bill Grady blows the lid on Hort's shocking rant on the United States of America,

> I...cannot say that I see much as yet to soften my deep **hatred of democracy** in all its forms. I care more for England and Europe than for America...the **American Empire is a standing menace** to the whole civilization of Europe...it can not be wrong to desire and pray from the bottom of one's heart that **the American Union may be shivered to pieces.**[43]

Hort writes John Ellerton, July 6, 1848:

> The pure Romish view seems to me nearer, and more likely to lead to, the truth than the Evangelical...We **dare not forsake the sacraments** or God will forsake us...I am inclined to think that no such state as **'Eden' ever existed.**

1851 - Wescott and Hort helped found the *Cambridge University Ghost Society,* precursor to the Society For Psychical Research.

> Among my father's diversions at Cambridge was the foundation of a 'Ghost Society', the forerunner of the Psychical Society for the investigation of the supernatural. Lightfoot, Wescott, and Hort were among the members.[44]

Hort writes to Wescott, October 15, 1860:

> ...the popular doctrine of substitution is an immoral and material counterfeit...Certainly nothing could be more **unscriptural than** the modern limiting of **Christ's bearing our sins** and sufferings to his death; but indeed that is only one aspect of an almost **universal heresy.**

Hort writes to Wescott , October 17, 1865:

I have been persuaded for many years that
Mary-worship and 'Jesus'-worship have **very
much in common** in their causes and their
results.

Wescott writes to the Archbishop of Canterbury,
March 4, 1890:

No one now, I suppose, holds that **the first
three chapters of Genesis,** for example, give a
literal history - I could never understand how
any one reading them with open eyes could
think they did.

Wescott and Hort kept their true beliefs incognito
from the public, yet leaked them all over the new bible
version. A Greek New Testament based on Critical texts
Vaticanus and *Sinaiticus* was produced by Cambridge
professor F. Hort and liberal Anglican scholar B. Wescott
in 1870. What began in 1853 as their own rendition of the
Catholic Douay-Rheims version of the bible morphed into
a outright Critical Greek text overhaul. It was propped up
by Hort's now defunked "Lucian Recension" (a fabled
claim that *"true"* scripture - Critical text Alexandrian
manuscripts - were suppressed by a Council of Churches
in Antioch during the second century). It was proven a
hoax.

Even by Hort's own admission in his *Introduction*
(p. 92), the Received (Majority) Text had for 1,400 years
been the dominant Greek New Testament. Were Wescott
and Hort breed to a superior race of beings, which entitled
them to cast aside as trite, the work of centuries? Yet, the
Wescott-and-Hort-led Revision Committee of 1881
swerved into aligning themselves to the Alexandrian

manuscripts, thanks to Dr. Hort's freakish control. We must remember these Critical text documents of Romanish decent were exalted by injuring believers who disagreed with Catholic abhorrence to the common Holy Bible as supreme final authority.

It can easily be proven the revision committee's agenda was forced, unharmonious, and deceitful. Wescott and Hort secretly corroborated, well before the committee began translation, a scheme to unveil their own (anti - Textus Receptus) Critical Greek text.

Plotting an immediate takeover of the proceedings, Wescott and Hort drew even the turncoat Chairman Ellicott into these unethical maneuvers. Governing rules over the committee were completely ignored from the beginning by Wescott and Hort over the ten-year revision of the Holy Bible. Their own Wescott and Hort Critical Greek text would gradually spearhead the conflicted translation.

Systematically, the Majority Text was removed by vote counts bullied by Dr. Hort. Many members of the Revised committee relinquished their positions. Original committee Chairman Samuel Wilberforce, Bishop of Oxford, resigned his illustrious position after only *one* meeting, deploring, "What can be done in this most miserable business?"[45]

Ellicott once again spotlights Wescott and Hort's true lack of protocol,

> The new Greek New Testament upon which Wescott and Hort had been working for twenty years was, portion by portion, secretly committed into the hands of the Revision Committee. Their Greek Text was strongly radical and revolutionary.[46]

In 1906, Samuel Hemphill, gave us his eyewitness account,

> The Revisers followed... Wescott and Hort, who were constantly at their elbow, and whose radical Greek New Testament, **deviating the furthest possible from the Received [Majority] Text**...And this Greek text, in the main, follows the Vatican and Sinaiticus Manuscripts.[47]

Those who remained attended sporadically. The Archbishop of Dublin, Richard Trench, attended only 63 sessions within the ten years of committee, describing the translation work was "pushed to a faulty excess".[48] Revision after revision altered over 5,000 changes contrary to the Greek Majority Textus Receptus and nearly 36,000 words were made contrary to the English Majority Text King James Bible. Before it was all said and done they had made between eight and nine changes in every five verses.   Not a single one was noted in the margins, as required by committee rules.

Wescott, and especially Hort's, deviant dominance over the committee was not received well by a minority of outstanding conservative scholars on the translation committee. Nine-tenths of the countless divisions and textual struggles arose over Hort's agenda to base the New Testament of the Revision on primarily Greek Vatican manuscripts.

The conservative purists, however, were NOT committed to fabricate a *new* bible, but to satisfy the **original** mission of the committee - to enhance the Holy Bible already enjoyed and received by all. The conservatives stood their ground hoping to salvage a project that was likely to end up trending a future path into mangling Holy Scriptures inside the free-for-all commercial bible market. Their objective in resisting Wescott and Hort was an attempt to valiantly keep a perfect Bible already in existence pure. They saw the handwriting on the wall and resisted.

In Hort's 1871 words by letter to his wife,

> We have had some stiff battles today in Revision...usually with good success.

Westcott's own words echo from 1875,

> We have had hard fighting during these last two days... Our work yesterday was positively distressing.... Today our work has been a little better - only a little, but just enough to be endurable.

In God's own Words through apostles of the 1st century,

I Corinthians 14:33
For God is not *the author* of confusion, but of peace, as in all churches of the saints.

Those committee members who aligned themselves with Wescott and Hort were of the same theological sort. Three clergymen on the committee (Ellicott, Moberly, and Humphrey) previously belonged to a 5-member committee in 1857, who put out a *Revised Version of John's Gospel*. These three brought their Scripture-altering experience to the table.

Of course, the public was kept ignorant of the actual translators and the proceedings throughout the ten years of translation. Otherwise, the project would never have taken root. It would scandalize the committee later for the churches to learn the presence of G. Vance Smith was a major influence on the committee. This Unitarian scholar denied the Divinity of Christ.

The revision committee was sworn to a vow of secrecy. Wonder why. Wescott and Hort's Critical Greek text was purposefully withheld from the publishers only *5 days before* the English Revised bible was unveiled. No one knew the textual duels between the liberal, eclectic methods of Dr. Hort vs. the conservative methods of Dr. Scrivener, until it was over. Dr. Scrivener's ten-year frustration grew more and more as the committee succumbed to Wescott and Hort's overbearing dominance. His writings today reveal the battle-royal over the theological disarray throughout the entire project.

> …they totally ignored **rule one** as well, which enjoined the members, *"to introduce as few alterations as possible* into the Text of the Authorized [King James] Version consistently with faithfulness"….it was determined that the committee had changed the Authorized Version in some **36,191** places.[49]

The stark difference between the 1611 King James Bible committee and the 1881 Revised version committee is telling. The method employed by the Revisers of 1881 was anything but coherent. The Old Testament Committee met together and sat as one body secretly for ten years. The New Testament Committee did the same in separate location. This arrangement left the committee at the mercy of a duel leadership (Wescott & Hort), to lead the weak and divide the rest. The public was kept totally unawares during the long, weary, ten years of translation. Only after elaborate plans had been made to catapult the Revised Version all at once upon the market to effect a tremendous sale, did the world know what had gone on.

These "esteemed" revisers (Westcott and Hort) forsook the sacred trust of religious integrity. The fanfare release of the English Revised New Testament version in 1881, then the Old Testament in 1885 was hopelessly self-condemned. It would fail as a bible, and would later need to be combined with the Holy King James Bible to succeed as the American Standard bible version in 1901. Two wrongs make a right?

Yet, inconceivably, Wescott and Hort's Critical Greek text is exonerated and molds the modern 1979 26th edition *Nestle/Aland Greek New Testament* that supports the majority of all Bible College degree education and seminary training. It is the predominant Greek (Critical) text of new version committees. And, <u>virtually all</u> contemporary English translations of the Bible are predicated upon it. Pastor Jack Moorman catalogued **356** doctrinal passages negatively affected in the revised Greek text of Wescott and Hort. They are clearly laid out in his *Early Manuscripts and the Authorized Version--A Closer Look.*

Dr. D.A. Waite's meticulous count gives us even a closer look,

<u>Wescott and Hort Greek New Testament word changes</u>:

Changes in the New Testament - 5,604
Changes include 9,970 Greek words
Changes 15.4 Greek words per page
Changes 7% of the Greek words
Changes total an equivalent of 45.9 pages in
the Greek text[50]

The Majority Text was shamefully handled by the first revision committee led by Wescott and Hort. The King James Bible became an object of malice and restless assaults by both men. The project was confused through misapprehension of Holy Scripture. There is one glaring "success" due to Wescott and Hort's work. Beginning with the Revised version, new versions thereafter have bewitched millions to believe there is no perfect Bible. This is their ultimate "success".

Wescott and Hort's documented spirit of extreme prejudice against the 1611 King James Bible did not die with them. Kurt Aland is at the head of the West German Institute for New Testament Textual Research in Munster, Germany. Get this ---- In his listing of Greek New Testament documents Kurt Aland is quoted as saying,

> Why should we list the other ones? They are just going to support the King James.[51]

Dr. Hort's own son sheepishly admits,

> Wescott and Hort are therein treated as the chief authors of all the mischief of the Revision, and their text is throughout regarded as the work of a picturesque imagination.[52]

The ripple effects on the church at large are seemingly etched in stone within our current culture. Because of seed changes which sunk into nineteenth century scripture, there sprouted a new type of Protestantism and a new offshoot version of the Protestant Bible. This new brand of Protestantism was, in fact, hostile to the fundamental doctrines of the Reformation. Previously, there were two class of Bibles in the world - Protestant and Catholic. Now, non-Catholic Christians are subjected to a choice between the **true Protestant Bible**, and newer versions which represent **readings rejected by the Reformers.**

13.   What motivated Dr. Clark to write this book?
First and foremost, this book was not published to impress critics of any religious circle. In my over 20 years of research on this subject, I allow facts to lead me to truth.

The initial desire of this author was to pass down invaluable information about our trustworthy, inspired Holy Bible to the following generation of family and friends. *The Perfect Bible* was first and foremost a gift to my supportive family of relatives and friends. This is the primary motivation. However, the reason *why* the author wants to pass down this knowledge to the generation following, has a lot to do with a certain encounter I experienced during my formative years of Bible college education.

I'll never forget it. 1987. As a sophomore student at a large, world-renowned Christian University in middle eastern America, I sat in a Creation Studies class, of all places, and heard the professor make this discordant statement. *"I do not believe that the King James version of the Bible is inspired word-for-word. It may have been 'guided', but I do not believe it was inspired."* I wrote down the statement. I asked two people sitting beside me (who I did not know) to sign it as witnesses (I have the signatures today). I scheduled a meeting with the Creation Studies professor after class.

Sure enough, the professor agreed with the statement that I wrote down. I asked the professor would he mind if I made inquiry to the Founder of the University about the school's beliefs on the King James Bible's word-for-word inspiration. The professor said, *"Sure"*. So, I wrote a cordial letter to the University's founder explaining the circumstances of my inquiry to the school's beliefs about the Bible. The letter was answered two weeks later by the Vice President of Spiritual Affairs at the college, who called my dorm room requesting an appointment. I made the appointment with the Vice President's secretary.

I arrived a few days afterward at the Vice President's office. My letter was in his hand with a hand-written note from the Chancellor on it that read, *"Please help this young man"*. For 2 hours, I was chided by the Vice President of a leading CHRISTIAN University, in the privacy of his own office, about my beliefs that the King James Bible is inspired by God word-for-word. I listened. He scolded. For 2 solid hours. It wasn't exactly the "help" I was looking for. He vehemently disagreed with my beliefs about the 1611 King James Bible. I just listened to him rant without saying a word, dumbfounded, for approximately two hours. After he had exhausted himself, I asked him a simple question, *"Do you mean to tell me that the King James Bible I hold in my hands is not really the Bible?"* His emphatic answer, *"Yes"*.

I then asked the Vice President, *"Is this what (Founder and Chancellor of the Christian University) also believes?"* His answer, *"Yes"*.

I left his office devastated, dumbfounded, and indescribably discouraged. Could I believe what I was hearing with my own two ears? I felt for sure that if there was any place in the world where you ought to have your faith in the Bible stabilized, it would be in a Christian college, or a Christian institution. Truth is, this is where I got my faith shaken.

For the next 20 years, this single incident ignited a fire within my belly to know exactly if the words in the 1611 King James Bible equally mirror the original, inspired words God breathed through the quill of His anointed writers. I have found the 1611 King James Holy Bible true and the Christian University Vice President's opinion false.

The same Vice President is today an aging, nationally-recognized, itinerant speaker on soul winning across America. By authoritative historical fact, may I say to the Vice President who chided and dispirited me about my correct position on the Holy Scripture, *"Get your facts straight. You discouraged a potential Champion for Christ who will one day follow you in service to God. It is a shame that you were willing to scold a 19 year old BIBLE COLLEGE student, because his scriptural beliefs about the Holy Bible checked yours. Only an insecure bully-type would ludicrously tell a teenager the Holy Bible is not really the Bible - in a Bible college. I pray for your soul."*

Chapter Five

Misconceptions

*Remember this: any man who wonders if the
Bible is the Word of God has not been born again.
All born again Christians believe
the Word and love the Word.*

Dr. Bob Jones, Sr.
(1883-1968)
Bob Jones University, Founder
Pioneer Religious Broadcaster

1.   1611 King James Bible and the New King James versions are all the same Scripture.
    False. The *New* King James bible version (NKJV) was initially advertised to identically match the 1611 King James Bible with minor word updates. Nothing could be further from the actual truth. The NJKV New Testament was completed in 1979. The entire bible with both Old and New Testaments were completed in 1982. Minor word changes were supposed to be the "thee, thou, ye" words, as well as 1000 additional "out-of-date words". * We know now that The King James Bible contains its own *built-in dictionary*, defining the 1,000 difficult words, within its context. When a difficult word is first mentioned, its definition is in the same passage (see *In Awe of Thy Word* by Gail Riplinger).
    However, the NKJV was first marketed with a claim that its New Testament followed the (Majority Text) *Textus Receptus* exclusively. Yet 2,000 word changes in the New Testament alone deviate wildly by employing dynamic equivalency translation (NOT Word-equals-Word). For example, in Titus 2:3,4 " *The aged women likewise,... That they may teach the young women to be **sober**, to love their husbands, to love their children"*. The inspired Greek Textus Receptus word for sober is *sobron*. The NKJV left out the English word sober, even though the Textus Receptus said *sobron*. They did not even try to re-translate this word!
    The word sober was arbitrarily left out. Hiccup indeed.
    Likewise, for its Old Testament, the NKJV was not translated from the inspired Masoretic (Majority Text) Hebrew Old Testament, as the 1611 King James Bible. The NKJV's divergence stems from the *1967/1977 edition*

of the Stuttgart [German] *bible,* which has as its basis an Old Testament Critical text 1909 Hebrew Bible (*Biblia Hebraica*) by Kittel. Liberal German theologian Rudolf Kittel combined the Masoretic text with a 1008 A.D. Leningrad Ms B19a (ben Asher Critical text). His alterations are highly suspect due to his family's conviction for the anti Semitic death of millions of Jews during Hitler's holocaust. Rudolf Kittel was High Priest to Hitler during World War II. Therefore, the NKJV **completely omits** JEVOVAH out of the Old Testament. To omit JEHOVAH (God Almighty) completely out of Jewish history would be like leaving out the word liberty from America's Declaration of Independence. Unconscionable.

Misleading readers is the "critical apparatus" accompanying the NKJV. The letter "M" indicates a word change reading, causing readers to believe that the "word update" is according to the inspired **M**ajority Text of 5000+ Greek New Testament documents. Oh, contraire. The misnomer is NKJV word changes are actually supported by the Hodges-Farstad *Greek New Testament According to the Majority Text.* This so-called "Majority Text" is based on von Soden's collation (collection) of **414** of the 5000+ Greek documents. This is less than 9% of all available Greek *Textus Receptus* New Testament documents. Even 76 out-of-thin-air word changes were not found to even follow von Soden. The following words are also omitted in the NKJV: GOD 53 times, BLOOD 23 times, HEAVEN 50 times, LORD 66 times, and HELL 23 times. It all spirals downward from here.

Most Christians are shocked to learn anytime a word change is made away from the King James Bible, the NKJV new word matches identically the *New World Translation* - the Jehovah Witness Bible. If you were to try to lead a Jehovah Witness to Christ using the NKJV, you would not be able to show any difference in several key places. The word changes in the NKJV are so far removed from the originals God breathed that its own Introductory Preface concedes:

> A large percentage of the material has never been fully collated... We were forced to rely on von Soden's work.[2]

Many point to the subtle "666 logo" openly displayed on the NKJV cover. Thomas Nelson, the publisher, insists it is an ancient graphic device that represents the Godhead. Huh? How does that square with Acts 17:29?

> Acts 17:29
> ...we ought not to think that the Godhead is... graven by art and man's device.

For the record, the publishers of the NKJV were charged with fraud in 1997 by the Securities and Exchange Commission. They were ordered to pay approximately $400,000 in fines.[3]

In line with fraudulent practices, the Thomas Nelson edition of KJV/NKJV Parallel Bible falsified the *Translator To The Reader* preface by replacing the word "perfected" with "completed". This further removes the 1611 KJB from its rightful throne of Divine Perfection.

The NKJV is not a simple 1980's revision of the King James Bible. This futuristic "Sci-Fi" scripture replaces the KJB word *strangers* with *aliens* in Hosea 8:7. Its text is sullied with other adulterations that rouse suspicion. It is seemingly a sly attempt to credit the *New World Translation* Jehovah Witness bible. The *New* King James bible **should not be considered** to be a trustworthy update to the 1611 King James Bible.

Lead A Jehovah Witness (or Jew) To Christ With The 1611 King James Bible:

- Read Revelation 1:11, *"I am Alpha and Omega, the first and the last..."*
- Ask, Who is the **first** and the last? Who is speaking here?
- Every Jehovah Witness, or Jew, slightly versed in Scripture will respond, "Jehovah", based on Old Testament verses such as Isaiah 44:6, *"I am the first, and I am the last"*.
- Read Revelation 1:18, *"I am he that liveth, and was **dead**; and, behold, I am alive for evermore"*.
- Ask, "When was Jehovah dead?"
- They will then realize that Jesus Christ was "God manifest in the Flesh" (I Timothy 3:16). This technique is utilized to win many to Christ. It works, because the 1611 King James Bible is quick and powerful, always true to its original source.[4]

2.   Oldest scripture manuscripts are always the best manuscripts.

False. The age of manuscripts is not the measure of quality. NIV Concordance co-author Edward Goodrick realizes,

> Nor should the textual critic go by the *age of the manuscript alone* as if the older would always be better, for we don't know how old the parent manuscript was when its offspring was born. A 7th century manuscript might have been copied from a 6th century manuscript, but a 15th century manuscript might have been copied from a 3rd century manuscript.[5]

Even James White, author of *The King James Only Controversy,* reluctantly concedes,

> While it is not true in every instance that the older a manuscript is the better it is, it is generally true.[6]

In any event, scholars agree that the L A R G E R a family is, the older the original sources must be, relating to growth over time. Zane Hodges explains,

> ...an ancient book will...multiply in a reasonably regular fashion with the results that the **copies nearest the autograph [original] will normally have the largest number of descendants**. The further removed in history a text becomes from its source the less time it has to leave behind a large family of offspring. Hence, in a large tradition where a pronounced unity is observed...a very strong presumption is raised that this numeral preponderance is due to direct derivation from the very oldest sources.
> In the absence of any convincing contrary explanation, this presumption is raised to a very high level of probability indeed.
> Even the leading 19th century *Textus Receptus* critic, Fenton Hort conceded, A theoretical presumption indeed remains that a majority of the extant documents is more likely to represent a majority of ancestral documents at each stage of transmission than vise versa.[7]

According to even liberal experts, the oldest documents are not always indicative of the most reliable documents. The largest "family" of like documents, however, are a more valued signature of historical acceptance and authenticity. The Majority Text represents 95-99% of **all** ancient Scripture documents. The Critical text squeaks out less than 5% of all ancient scripture documents. By sheer numbers, it is obvious to conclude why the Majority Text enjoys its place as the inspired "Received Text" from the first century days of Christ and the early church.

P64 (Magdalen Papyrus) is considered to be the oldest Greek New Testament document dating 60 A.D. Its Matthew 26:22 reads different by a few words than the Critical text. While the difference is minor, **if** the *oldest* manuscript is to be considered *more original*, a change must occur beginning with the 1885 English Revised version and all subsequent bible versions. P64 has the same reading as the 1611 King James Bible. Thus, the perfect Majority Text New Testament is represented by both the **oldest and largest** family of inspired Holy Scripture documents.

3.   The 1611 King James Bible has obvious word errors.

False. When a supposed "error" in Scripture is found, to the critic it is always the Holy Bible that has a problem. It is the Bible that needs changing in the mind of a critic.

God has not called readers to check his Holy Bible for errors. He has called his Holy Bible to check us for errors.[8]

Gail Riplinger
Best Selling Author, *New Age Bible Versions*

Examples of declared "errors":

a) Acts 12:4 *" And when he had apprehended him, he put him in prison, and delivered him to four quaternions of soldiers to keep him; intending after **Easter** to bring him forth to the people."*

Although the Greek word *"to pascha"* is translated "Passover" in 28 out of 29 appearances in the King James Bible, critics claim it is incorrectly translated "Easter" in Acts 12:4. Why is "Easter" the **correct** word for Acts 12:4?

The Passover was celebrated <u>at the same time</u> of a pagan **Easter** festival called *Ishtar*. (Dating back to a pagan Phoenician festival in the Old Testament in honor of Ashteroth - a feminine Baal - the original term for Easter). This is the festival most likely being celebrated in Acts 12 by the Roman Governor of Judea, Herod, since he was unarguably a pagan official with little regard for Jewish tradition. "Easter" and "Passover" are possibly interchangeable in this passage, but the King James Bible committee CORRECTLY followed Tyndale's inspired New Testament and many other vernacular **Majority Text Bibles** to reflect the pagan mood during Herod's arrest of Peter.

Furthermore, Verse 3 of Acts 12 says that the Apostle Peter's arrest by Herod was during *"...the days of unleavened bread."* Hence, critics lump the Passover and the Feast of Unleavened Bread together incorrectly to be one in the same.

According to Leviticus 23:6, the precise date of the Feast of Unleavened Bread is the **15th** day of the first month. The exact celebration date of the LORD's Passover is the **14th** day of the first month. If the word in question were mistranslated "Passover", and Herod was waiting until AFTER the Passover (14th) to try Peter in court, how could the *"days of unleavened bread"* (15th) come before the 14th? This would be the case if the normal usage of the word *"to pascha"* were mistranslated "Passover". However, thankfully the King James Bible follows the inspired Majority Text of Scripture and avoids this confusion by correctly keeping the word "Easter" in its proper place.

Besides, isn't "Easter" (14th) during the "days of unleavened bread" on the 15th? It would be like saying Hanukkah (week of December 25) is during "the days of Christmas" (December 25th).

The Holy King James Bible is **never** in error when factual data is thoroughly reviewed. Spastic accusations assail from the textual criticism community when good faith in God's established Words, or the facts, are slighted, because it does not fit the modern bible version template.

Sometimes "errors" to us are limitations we put on God. The reader is encouraged to apply *faith* when it seems that God's Words do not make human sense. Truth is what sets us free from any confusion. If you want to know the truth behind a difficult passage or word of Holy Scripture, ask God for understanding in *faith* trusting that God *and His Words* are perfect. GOD LOVES YOU. He fulfills desires from your heart that give credit to His perfection.

b) Matthew 12:40 says, *"For as Jonas was three days and three nights in the **whale's** belly"*. Jonah 1:17 says, *"Now the LORD had prepared a **great fish** to swallow up Jonah"*. A great fish is a **fish**. A "whale" is a **mammal.** A mammal and a fish are two different classes of animals. Critics claim this to be an "error".

If I said, "The antelope was eaten by the *"king of the jungle"* in the open plain. The "king of the jungle" means who?......a human being, or a lion? A king is a (human) man. Yet, when we say "king of the jungle", everybody knows we are referring to a lion (animal) - not a man with a golden crown on his head bent over an antelope carcass eating raw meat in the middle of a field.

Likewise, a "great fish" is a common synonym for whale. This could loosely be called an "idiom", a descriptive narrative phrase. Other idioms in the Bible are Isaiah 27:1, *"leviathan that **crooked serpent**; and he shall slay the dragon that is in the sea"*, Mark 1:10, *"the Spirit **like a dove** descending upon him."*, and Mark 7:35, *"the **string of his tongue** was loosed."* Idioms are not errors. "Errors" mostly originate with critics who read their own thoughts into what the Scripture correctly says.

c) Hebrews 10:23, *" Let us hold fast the profession of our **faith** without wavering;"*

According to kingpin critic of the King James Bible, James White, author of *The King James Bible Only Controversy*, 13 times the Greek word for "hope" appears in the *Textus Receptus*. However only in Hebrews 10:23, it is once translated "faith". Gasp. It must be a "faulty error".

First of all, White bases his Greek word studies on a Von Sodon's halfway-house Greek text, which represents less than 10% of all 5,000+ Greek documents. Since White's book never cites the interchangeable Greek word for *"faith"* and *"hope"* on pages 131, 132, and 226 of his book, the claim of error distorts the truth of the actual word.

The actual Majority Text Greek word in Hebrews 10:23 is *elpidos* (a form of *elpis*) translated as faith, hope, or trust, many more times in the **entire** *Textus Receptus* readings, than White's 12.

The King James committee correctly stated in their governing rules that sometimes one Greek word can be **formally** translated by more than one English word *in context* of the Majority Text Scripture passage. The Golden Rule of Scripture Interpretation says, *First answer Scripture with Scripture.* The CONTEXT of Hebrews chapter 10 give us an *"...assurance of faith"* in verse 22, and a *faithful* God in the latter part of verse 23. In context, the type of trust here is correctly translated *faith*, rather than hope. Even Critical text pacesetter, Dr. Kittel, spotlights the "interrelating" of the Greek words for faith and hope.

d) Acts 5:30, *" The God of our fathers raised up Jesus, whom ye slew and hanged on a tree."*

Critical text bloodhounds bark like mad up this tree-verse thinking they have caught the King James Bible translators out on a limb of error. Attack dog scholars object to the word *"and"* in verse 30, because it is too "ruff" an interpretation. To them, it implies the Jews first killed Christ **and then** hung his body on the cross. Therefore, the New King James version, as well as the New American Standard version, replace the word *"and"* with the word *"by"* (...*by* hanging him...).

However, the basic premise of this suggestion misprojects the text of the King James Bible reading to say *"...whom ye slew and THEN hanged on a tree"*, which it does not say.

Basic English rules tell us the word *"and"* is a conjunction, linking two words or thoughts together **to become one.**

The King James Bible word *"and"* is used correctly as meaning the word *"further"*. Allow Dr. Thomas Holland to calm the yapping critics,

> We understand the text to mean that the Jews were responsible for killing their Messiah.

Further, they were responsible for having him placed on the cross ...When one assumes that the text is stating that the Jews murdered the Lord *and then* crucified him, they are reading their own thoughts into the text.[9]

This "error dog" won't hunt.

e) Genesis 36:24, *"...this was that Anah that found the **mules** in the wilderness..."*

New versions mistranslate the Hebrew word *yemin* as "hot springs" or "water", rather than "mules". This is based squarely upon Jerome's Catholic Latin Vulgate bible *interpretation* of this word (see Gesenius, "Hebrew and Chladee Lexicon", p.351). Again, this displays the telling difference between the Critical text, and the Majority Text Scriptures of Luther, Calvin, and Clarke, which side with the King James Bible reading of "mules"[10]

Because Hebrew words have as many as three meanings with the same letters, and as many as ten meanings when traced back to the roots, which word is God's Word? The inspired, Word-equals-Word Hebrew Scripture lost nothing in its formal translation from its original Divine source. The Majority Text did not lose or gain any extra parts. "Mules" mirrors the original inspired Scripture, because we know *how* it was copied.

Be assured, that any *new* bible version translated by the carefreeness of dynamic equivalency from the Critical Greek text gains extra parts and loses parts. This is more than likely why the usage of "hot springs" or "water" differ from the

Majority Text "mules". At least 5,604 word changes were made in the Critical Greek text which is the root of the first English bible version in 1885, representing an average of 15 changes per page.[11] This places it as being *further removed from the original God-inspired books*, thus devaluing all subsequent versions after it (RSV, ASV, NIV, NASV, etc.) of Divine authority.

f) I Samuel 2:25, *"If one man sin against another, the **judge** shall judge him…"*

Have you ever heard that a bully intimidates to mask his own fear and insecurities? Critics are their own double standard a lot of times. A shortsighted critic is quick to point out, even exploit, perceived weaknesses in others that they never see in themselves. Contrary opinions sound intelligent to the critic, until the same standard is applied to them. The rules of change apply to everyone, but the critic.

New King James bible version Old Testament editor, James Price, assaults the 1611 King James Bible committee for translating the Hebrew word *elohim* as "judges", instead of "God". Yet, his beloved NKJV does the very same thing in Exodus 21:6, 22:8, 22:9. To imply that *elohim* is **always** translated "God" cancels his own work's credibility. Even worse, the Critical text NIV uses **40** different words, such as, *idols, angels, goddesses,* and *heavenly beings*, to translate the Hebrew *elohim* (This demonstrates the ludicrousy of the carefree word choice translations of **dynamic equivalency**).

James Strong, L.L.D., author of *Strong's Exhaustive Concordance*, notes that *elohim* is "occasionally applied by way of deference to magistrates…judges."[12] The King James Bible's "judges" is correct after all the badgering by critics.

Doesn't the Holy Bible say a thing or two about *"For with what judgment ye judge, ye shall be judged"* (Matthew 7:2), and *"...judge not that ye be not judged"* (Matthew 7:1, Luke 6:37)? Critics of Holy Writ continue to shoot holes through their own criticism with harsh judgment toward a perfect, God-breathed, Holy Bible. It must frustrate the critic who swoons over finding "errors" in the 1611 King James Bible, only having them later splinter into pieces, by the **errors of their own misjudgment** and misrepresentation of truth. Against the anvil of God's Scripture, the critical hammer reigns down blow upon blow on the solid King James Bible. The hammer may break, but the anvil always remains the same.

g) Acts 19:2, *" He said unto them, Have ye received the Holy Ghost since ye believed?"*

Naysayers tout a false claim of false theology in the King James Bible's Acts 19:2. The word *"since"* is mistakenly pointed out to imply a "second reception" of the Holy Spirit for believers. All modern bible versions re-translate the word in question, *"since"*, to be *"when"*. The anxious claim of critics is that this verse is responsible for founding entire charismatic theologies of a second "Baptism of the Holy Spirit". To the critic, it is the Holy King James Bible who has the problem.

The Greek phrase *Ei pneuma agion elabete pisteusantes,* in the same word order in English says, "The Ghost Holy did ye receive having believed?" This phrase is settled in the Greek aorist tense, meaning it refers to **PAST** time. The aorist past tense is checked in the verse by the words "received" and "believed".

The word "since" holds similar value to the word "because". We understand the meaning of the verse to read, *Have ye received the Holy Ghost, **because** ye* *believed.* The word "since" clearly affirms a past action, one that was attained through a past decision (aorist tense). The word "when" does not hold such strong, past tense value. "When" could imply today, yesterday, even tomorrow, thus annulling the aorist past tense.

Noted Greek linguists H.E. Dana and Julius R. Mantey explain,

> The aorist is employed in this meaning when...verbs signify effort or progress, the aorist denoting the attainment of **the end** of such effort or process.[13]

Dr. George Ladd vouches,

> The Greek participle is *having believed*, and it is capable of being translated...**since** ye believed.[14]

The English word *since* is correct in the King James Bible as it relates to the Majority Text Greek reading in the aorist past tense. It is a stronger past tense word than the drifty word *"when"*.

The reader should recognize by now that it is never worth it to align oneself in a contrary, fault-finding approach to written perfection, the 1611 King James Bible. It ultimately ends in having to eat the terrible combination of "crow" for dinner and "humble pie" for desert. To assert "errors" against Holy Scripture is a blatant limitation on God. Take caution. God is smarter than us all. He wrote it. There is a reason why it says what is says. Our Bible cravings should be aligned to a diet of God's perfection.

Job 23:12

I have esteemed the **words of his** mouth more than my necessary *food.*

4.   The   Lucian   Recension   suppressed   true Scripture readings.

False. Lucian was an early church father who built his testimony upon Majority Text Scripture in 312 A.D. Critical text advocates Brooke Westcott and Fenton Hort (1870) chaired the translation committee that spawned the first non-Majority Text bible version in 1885 (the failed English Revised version). They believed that the Majority Text did not exist until the middle of the 4th century. To prop up their erroneous theory they spawned a "Lucian Recension".

Supposedly, an empire-wide Church Council met twice in Antioch 250-350 A.D. to suppress and condemn "true scripture readings" (Critical Alexandrian texts), while yet endorsing the "false" readings (Antiochian, or Majority Text). Hort tops off his debunked theory by insisting the inspired Majority Text was "conflated" (mixed together with other Greek texts, Alexandrian and Western) by Lucian of Antioch at that time.

Hort in his own words,

> The Syrian text must be in fact the result of a 'recension' in the proper sense of the word, a work of attempted criticism, performed deliberately by editors and not merely by scribes. An authoritative Revision at Antioch…was itself subjected to a second authoritative Revision carrying out more completely the purpose of the first. At what date between AD 250 and 350 the first process took place, it is impossible to say with confidence.

The final process was apparently completed by
AD 350 or thereabouts.[15]

There's a slight problem. Where is the historical
documentation for this? There is none. This allegedly
imposed, ecclesiastical boom left no crater or footprint in
the sands of time in any church records. Zero. Zippo.
Nada. Church history is silent, and Hort offered no proof.
The Lucian Recension Theory has been subsequently
abandoned by all serious textual scholarship.

> Even Kenyon, who supported the Critical Text,
> noted that we know the names of several
> revisers of the Septuagint...It seemed
> unbelievable to him that such a council could
> have taken place without any historical record
> whatsoever.[16]

Scrivener (leading conservative Anglican scholar
who contested with Hort for the Textus Receptus readings
throughout the decade of translation by the 1st revision
committee of 1871-1881) cuts to the chase,

> Such recensions never occurred. There is not a
> trace of them in history. It is a mere dream of
> Dr. Hort. They must be 'phantom
> recensions'...But Dr. Hort, as soon as he found
> that he could not maintain his ground with
> history as it was, instead of taking back his
> theory and altering it to square with facts,
> tampered with historical facts in order to make
> them agree with his theory.[17]

Today scholars like Colwell and Greelings agree
that such a recension did not occur. However, it is fanciful
theories like this that have misled believers and church

leaders alike, who are not engaged enough to check out the evidence for themselves. The Lucian Recension not only tainted the good name of an early church father and Majority Text advocate, it is a foundational cornerstone that props up all modern bible versions today. **And, the entire church, in this author's humble opinion, has been suffering for it, ever since the textual debate arose a sore issue by the likes of Hort and Wescott.**

Any reader of this information, who vouches for the Greek Critical text of all new bible versions, must strain over lack of historical basis to believe this misleading story which boldly emanates from the leading *Textus Receptus* critic of modern time, Dr. Fenton Hort. The only obvious fact about this conspiracy theory is that it gave new meaning to the word "conflated", as it mixed together fiction with gullibility to project with popularity misleading King James Bible criticism.

An honest believer seeking refuge in honest Scriptures may rest in the documental Majority Text that *flourished* through believers at Antioch (Syriac Peshitta Bible), where the first Bible teachers were (Acts 13:1), where the first missionary trip was commissioned (Acts 16:1-6), and where the word "Christian" originated (Acts 11:26).

5. The 1611 King James Bible translators gave "alternate renderings" in the margins of the King James Bible, because they believed they were not infallible. Neither should we.

False. Rule # 6 of *"The Rules Framed By The King James Bible Translators"* says,

> No marginal notes at all to be affixed, but **only for the explanation** of the Hebrew or Greek words which cannot, without some circumlocution [words to express a thought or idea], so briefly and fitly be expressed in the text.

This particular rule guiding the King James Bible translators means that "archaic" or "difficult" words and phrases were <u>left in the text</u> to ensure it remain a **pure text** with an *explanation* allowed in the margin. This rule guaranteed Word-equals-Word Scripture transcription from the original, inspired Hebrew (Old Testament) and Greek (New Testament) into English, untainted by human intellectual error.

Circumlocution in Rule 6 means "words to express an idea". Difficult, yet INSPIRED words would <u>correctly remain</u> in Majority Text English Scripture with a helpful, marginal reference explaining them. An explanation is not an "alternate reading or rendering". The King James Bible committee were not confusing the Scripture, but making "difficult" readings more crystal clear with an insightful explanation *in the margins*. This follows the Word-equals-Word, **perfect** translation integrity that the Majority Text is known for.

The opposite side of this would be the 1967 *New Scofield bible*, which inserts C.I. Scofield's marginal notes from the 1917 *Old Scofield Bible* into the text of Scripture. Sadly, this has become a translation standard for new bible publishers. Likewise, the NIV inserts the footnotes of anti-Semitic, Rudolf Kittel and his Old Testament *Biblical Hebraica* **as the text of scripture itself**, without being italicized. New bible version editors are guilty of the very same translation faux-pas today in closed-door committees.

By default, this egotistically elevates the translator himself to a falsely perceived scholarship superiority over God's Holy Words. Isn't it interesting the year 1870 was marked by the Papal declaration of *infallibility*? This is the same year that the Revised version committee first came together to make over 36,000 arbitrary word changes in their new English bible contrary to the Majority Text King James Holy Bible.

Of course, the King James Bible committee members were not infallible. *They did not need to be*. The Majority Text Scripture was **already infallible**, mirroring and equaling the inspired, original Words of God. Their exact job was to *copy* it perfectly so. They did, thanks to Rule #6.

6.   1611 King James Bible has been copyrighted.
False. The royal printer of the 1611 King James Bible was Robert Baker, who printed with *Cum Privilegio* (with privilege) under authority of the Crown. Some critics consider this a "copyright" that barred anyone else from printing copies the first 100 years before 1711.

Royal historian, John Dore, has dated a 1642 folio edition of the King James Bible printed in Amsterdam, a Geneva printing, a 1628 Scotland edition, various editions published outside of England in 1642, 1672, 1683, 1708, and in England itself in 1649. A special dispensation was granted to the University of Oxford edition of 1628, and the University of Cambridge edition of 1675; all of these without the *Cum Privilegio.*

Thus, this assault is unwarranted. Of course, the King James Bible is the only Bible in existence for all time that has *never been copyrighted* by any incorporation. Why? Because, it is not a vested part of the derivative copyright law's $400-million-dollar-a-year market of today's new bible versions. If you see a copyright on the front flap of a King James Bible, it is a copyright **only** on the marginal reference notes, indexes, additional materials, maps, etc. (all the other "extras" included), but there never has been a copyright on the Scripture text itself.

7. The Greek actually corrects the King James Bible reading in several places.

False. If you hear someone say, "the Greek corrects or improves the King James Bible", ask this person, "Which Greek text are you referring to? Majority Text or Critical text?" Things that have different labels are not the same thing. These two original sources are separated one from the other. That's why they have different names.

Example: We correctly compare Shakespeare to Shakespeare, Milton to Milton, apples to apples, oranges to oranges.

What would be the reaction in the literary world if we decided to change the wording of Shakespeare's plays to make them sound more like Milton? The great playwright's influence would die in one generation if these things were done. Cries of protest would be heard from every hall of learning. Shakespeare should never be revised against an unoriginal source. Neither should the Holy Bible.

Statements such as, "the Greek improves the King James Bible readings", confuses the facts by comparing the King James Bible incorrectly to the Critical text, instead of correctly to the Majority Text. The Critical text is *not the parent* of the King James Bible. It would be like comparing apples to oranges. It would be the comparison of a Chinese baby to Ethiopian parents. It would be the comparison of a pony to a snail. It would be the comparison of a rose to field grass. It would be the comparison of a pure breed Samoyed to an alley cat. Different parents do not make siblings.

To say the King James Bible must be "held to the same standard" as all other new versions is to plant a subliminal suggestion that the King James Bible is kin in its origin to all modern day bible versions. Majority Text and Critical text parents are two separate and different Greek and Hebrew texts! Which Scriptural parent are you adhering to - the Majority Text or the Critical text? The King James Bible can only be correctly compared to its **Majority Text** Hebrew and Greek parents.

8.   King James himself insisted the committee include certain words in the text of Scripture.

False. King James I was not a translator. The "ecclesiastical language" of the King James Bible was congruent with words familiar to the church. That is, equal words translated were checked and tuned into harmony with Tyndale's English New Testament and other fine English Majority Text Scripture. The King James Bible committee did not create a *new* Bible, but rather fine tuned the Bishop's Bible. Equal words such as "church" instead of "assembly", "bishop" instead of "elder" brought it back to Majority Text purity. The only word that was *rumored* to be a preference of King James is the word "baptize" rather than immerse. He never did insist on it. Any particular word that critics want to challenge in this regard, check it against the Tyndale New Testament.

9.   We need a bible that is easier to read, because the King James Bible is too hard for children and most adults to understand.
      False. The purpose of advertising is to make you dissatisfied with what you have. The unspoken purpose for advertising new bibles is to separate you from a perfect Bible.

II Peter 2:3
And through covetousness shall they **with feigned words** make merchandise of you...

      THE TRUTH IS, **everyone**, both adults and children, find portions of the King James Bible difficult to understand or read. Educated ministers, theologs, and Bible teachers of the highest degree ALWAYS use dictionaries, concordances, lexicons, and reference materials. No one has a total handle on this Book of books. Why? If we understood *everything* there is to understand about God or His Words, then He wouldn't be much of a God.
      In Awe of thy Word, authored by linguistic expert Gail Riplinger, grammatically lays out the know-how to read King James Bible words with contextual understanding. **The King James Bible contains its own *built-in dictionary*, defining each word, in its context. When difficult words are first used, there is a definition in the same passage or verse! The "Golden Rule of Scripture Interpretation" says, *First answer Scripture **with** Scripture.*

Robert Loweth (1710-1787) was just one among many who have observed and written about the **Bible's own built-in dictionary.** As Bishop of London and Professor of poetry at Oxford, Loweth observed that the Bible had parallelisms which reiterate God's thoughts.[18]

The KJV contains both the 'elevated' word, as Stanford Professor Lerer calls them, *and* the simpler word. They are placed in parallelism near each other so that the definition of the harder word is clearly understood. The **easy word** usually comes from an **Anglo-Saxon** root, while the more **difficult word** is sometimes of **Latin** origin.[19]

This speaks volumes for the **ANGLO SAXON-**derived Majority Text King James Bible compared to the **LATIN** Vulgate-derived Critical text bible versions ESV, RSV, NASV, NIV, et al.

Since the King James Bible contains **both** root word languages, it becomes a global text of the Gospel of Christ. "Those who read Spanish, Portuguese, French, Romanian, and Italian will recognize the Latin words. Those who read German, Dutch, Norwegian, Finnish, and Swedish will recognize the Anglo Saxon words. New versions omit one or the other or both!"[20]

The King James Bible is 80% one syllable and 95% one or two syllable words (Anglo-Saxon English). New versions ("Latinized" English), by factual data, have **more** dysfunctional reading challenges than the Holy King James Bible.

Manual computations by the *Flesch-Kincaid Grade Level Formula* reveals which Bible is easier to read overall:

The King James Bible is at the **fifth** grade level. The *New* King James version and the New American Standard version are **sixth** grade level. Good News For Modern Man version is **seventh** grade level. The New International version is **eighth** grade level.[21]

"*All About Bibles,* by Dr. John Kohlenberg III, lists additional reading analyzations, via study by two Texas A&M University professors. The NIV rated at **7.80** grade reading level, and the NASV at a **11.5** grade reading level."[22] The bottom line is any fifth grader can read the King James Bible with comprehension.

A Christian prisoner was advised that he was reading at a **fifth grade level** when he put his name on a long waiting list to enroll in the prison's high school equivalency program. He then began reading the King James Bible daily. Re-examination the next year showed that he was now reading at the **17th grade level** - post graduate! How did reading *one* book, which some falsely claim is difficult, manage to help him, rather than frustrate him?[23]

The Adventures of Tom Sawyer contain words that may be difficult for the average child to follow, such as: *cruelly, reckon, procured, fetched.* Anyone for having Mark Twain's timeless masterpiece revised? No one would dare revise such a classic book. Oh, by the way, the words - *cruelly, reckon, procured, fetched* - are also found in the 1611 King James Bible. Care to retake the same vote for revising God's Holy Word?

Approximately 1,000 difficult words exist within the 1611 King James Bible. In this age of advanced technology, there is **absolutely no excuse** for not being able to understand every one of them. Consider adjusting knee-jerk reactions such as "the difficult words need to be changed" to enhancing your reading and study habits. Instead of answering the challenge with a "dumbed-down" bible, let's rather "smarten-up" the next generation. Young people, as well as adults, are capable of looking up the meaning of difficult portions of Holy Scripture, just like the experts have to do.

The following 7 resources make difficult Bible words easy to understand. They may be obtained from A.V. Publications, Bible for Today, and Chick Publications:

1. *By Definition*, authored by Pastor James W. Know (KJB difficult words study and definitions).
2. *Archaic Words and the Authorized Version*, by Lawrence Vance, Th.D. (examines every "archaic" KJB word).
3. *The King James Bible's Built-in Dictionary*, by Barry Goddard (KJB's own definition of over 800 Bible words).
4. *1828 American Dictionary of the English Language*, edited by Daniel Webster * Defines (KJB) words of the English language used in 1611 A.D.
5. *B.F.T. # 1060* (Bible for Today) by Dr. D.A. Waite (618 difficult Bible words defined).
6. *The Defined King James Bible* by Bible For Today [B.F.T. #3000L] (a leather-bound 1611 King James Bible with definitions of each difficult word in the margins!).
7. *The King James Bible Companion*, by David Daniels (over 500 uncommon KJB words defined).

Part of our growth as Christians is to seek to understand what we do not fully comprehend about God. To "contemporize" the Holy Bible with new versions is not growth. By default, this detracts from the opportunity for growth in our spiritual walk. God's grace furthers His truth about *His preserved Word.* Human understanding can deepen only in search of HIS **truth**. Seek God's purposeful truth <u>behind</u> the difficult Bible word or passage. When you totally eliminate a difficult Scripture Word, you also cancel an opportunity to increase spiritual knowledge and understanding.

John 5:39
Search the scriptures; for in them ye think ye have eternal life: and they are they which testify of me.

Acts 17:11
...they received the word with all readiness of mind, and **searched the scriptures** daily...

Jesus' exhortation to the temple Pharisees at Jerusalem in John 5, and Luke's assessment of the Church of Berea in Acts 17 were likewise the same. Search the Scriptures, not correct them. These verses refer to copies of inspired Majority Text Holy Scripture, not the originals, just like we have today in the King James Bible. Teach the next generation to follow the call of Christ to *"search the Holy Scripture"*.

II Timothy 3:15
And that **from a child** thou hast known the holy scriptures, which are able to make thee wise...

Chapter Six

imperfect bibles

Most modern English translations go to the **opposite extreme**, *constantly translating the same word with different English equivalents...all these examples can be seen to have* **doctrinal or theological implications**... *The loss is immeasurable, not only in terms of aesthetics [constructive taste] but also in terms of meaning.*

The Literary Guide to the Bible
Harvard University

One of the serious **problems** *with almost all modern English translations is that they rely heavily on Hebrew and Greek manuscripts of the Bible developed by liberals, rationalists, and evolutionists,* **none of whom believed in the inspiration of the Bible**.

Henry Morris
(1918 -2006)
Creation Research Society, Founder
Institute for Creation Research, Founder

The latest "storefront versions" come with a lot of chest-pounding nonsense about how advanced they are. The purpose of modern bible marketing is to make you dissatisfied with what you own. Having Bible options seem to be a progressive step in improvement. However, scripture gyrations are a step *away* from real Biblical conservatism, hoodwinking religious consumers with narratives of "easier reading" or "better accuracy" platitudes.

The most important thing to know is that any bible that has a man-made Scripture origin, makes it IMPOSSIBLE to be the Words of God.

Modern bibles today are self-accredited by gumming onto catchy labels such as "most trustworthy", "most reliable", originating from the "most ancient manuscripts", ad nauseam. Nothing could be further from the truth. Isn't it a shame that publishers have turned modern bible versions into little more than a game of religious "one-ups-manship"? As a result, most Christians are so focused on the "better" word changes in new bible versions that <u>theological</u> errors go virtually undetected. The greatest *myth* of all is that new English bible versions are doctrinally sound.

> The impurity of the texts exhibited by Codices B [Vaticanus] and Aleph [Sinaiticus] is not a matter of opinion, but a matter of fact. These are two of the **least trustworthy documents in existence**... Codices B and Aleph are, demonstrably, nothing else but specimens of the depraved class thus characterized.[3]
>
> **Dean JOHN WILLIAM BURGON**
> (1813-1888)
> Venerated Conservative Anglican Church Scholar

By a narrow line of Critical text manuscripts (*Vaticanus* and *Sinaiticus*), new bible editors shortchange themselves in translation. It is next to impossible to stay on track theologically, when the documental course leading them is as spiritually unresourceful as a trickling stream. "Cotton candy bibles" are new versions fluffed with "new-and-improved" word flavors devoid of doctrinal substance. This unspiritual, marketing decision has resulted in entropic (chaotic) consequences. God's original Words become falsified in Critical text, new English bibles.

In spite of a life-threatening, 6-year illness, author Gail Riplinger mastered the definitive exposé on new version word changes, additions, and omissions. When the Majority Text is rejected by new version editors, bible manuscript pickins' become very slim. She records for us the small basis for new bible diversions into doctrinal error.

> Today we have over 5200 manuscripts of the Greek New Testament. KJV critics ignore the fact that over 99% agree with the KJV [King James Bible]. Only .008, much less than one percent, agree with the NIV, NASV, NKJV notes, NRSV, CEV, NCV, NAB, NJB, and NLB.[4]

The liberal sway of new versions today have everything to do with the editor's viewpoint of Scripture. There are three distinct views about the Divine Inspiration of Holy Scripture today:

1. Conservatives believe we hold the very Words of God in our hands when clutching the Holy Bible.
2. Moderates (neo-liberals) believe the Holy Bible *was* the very words of God only in the originally

inspired written books. It is not purely in any Bible today.

3. Liberals believe bibles today contain the message of God mixed with human error.

"Those who hold to the first, high view of Holy Scripture find it appalling to learn that virtually all new bible version editors adhere to the 2nd or 3rd views of Scripture."[5]   This is most obviously seen in Kenneth Taylor's Living Bible II Timothy 3:16, *All scripture* **was** *given by inspiration of God...*

The friend of Critical text editors is **dynamic equivalency** translation style. Dynamic implies *change* or movement. Webster's dynamic is defined, "pertaining to *change* or process."[6]   New bible version committees believe dynamic equivalency grants authority needed to make endless word changes to Holy Scripture. Here, Scripture text evolution opens up "the better rendering" latitude for the copyright law, man-altered versions. Modern versions, therefore, become *further removed from the original* Scripture books. Consequently, sound Bible doctrine is adversely affected. Modern English bible versions are more like over-stressed, problematic drafts of scripture.

Let's be clear, so as to not miss the obvious. Dynamic equivalency reduces textual criticism to a series of unnecessary man-made options, that merits "this reading" over "that reading", "this manuscript" over "that manuscript", "this word" over "that word". It brings the critic to an area where personal opinion, even personal bias, can easily determine translation decisions. It leaves the scholar free to choose words in or out of Scripture in terms of his own prejudice.

We've already seen Marcion (110 A.D.) to Clement (150 A.D.) to Origen (185 A.D.) to Eusebius (265 A.D.) to Jerome (420 A.D.) to the Roman Catholic

Inquisition (5th - 16th centuries) to Tischendorf (1844) to Wescott and Hort (1881) - **all** of these were driven by wacky theologies and dissent from the God-breathed Majority Text Scripture. The facts supporting their adverse prejudgment toward Scriptures received by Christ, His disciples, and the New Testament early church, are indisputable.

The English offspring of man-made scriptures from the Critical text have been enrolled into the textual halfway-house of modern bible publishers. These are exonerated by secularized churches and higher theological academia, which birth armchair theologs of every religious brand and stripe.

Removing scripture further away from the God-breathed original books today is the *Derivative Copyright Law*. Any new translation of the bible in America today must adhere to a "Derivative Copyright Law" in order to be published by all major press companies who market new versions. This law is placed upon the text of all "new and improved" scripture.

Translation committees follow this publishing law, "To be copyrighted, the work must be different enough *from the original* to be a new work. It must contain substantial amount of new material. Making minor changes will not qualify a copyright."[7] The incomparable King James Bible has never been assaulted by any copyright injuring its pure text.

The first challenge to the King James Bible's perfection began with Henry Hammond's *A Paraphrase and Annotations Upon All the Books of the New Testament* in 1644. By 1881, there were 90 different translations and paraphrases in view. Over 311 bible versions, new testaments, and paraphrases since 1611 have ransacked the Scriptures up to a 1991 count. And critics accuse King James Bible advocates of "dividing the body of Christ".

Creationist Dr. Henry Morris points to 45 bibles and 100 new testaments in his own lifetime (1918-2006). He mentions trying to use at least 20 of them, and concludes, *"So what if it* [KJB] *does not sound like a modern newspaper or novel? The fact is, it should not, for* **God is speaking!** *I believe, therefore after studying, teaching, and loving the Bible for over 55 years, that Christians--especially creationists!--need to hang on to their old King James Bibles as long as they live."*[8]

Consider this compelling comparison of modern bible kinships,

> Visit a Christian bookstore and compare the texts of their Catholic *New American Bible* with the often matching texts of a TNIV, NIV, HCSB, ESV, or NASV. The TNIV, NIV, NASV, ESV, and HCSB, Jehovah Witness Version and most new versions are the corrupt Roman Catholic Latin Vulgate, under a different cover. Examine the **identical wording**. [9]

American History interpreter Bill Grady interestingly points out 3 United States Presidents met death by gunfire immediately after 3 major bible versions were shot-gunned onto the American public. Abraham Lincoln occupied the White House during the release of the American Bible Union version. President James Garfield was shot in July 1881, a 46-day snap-of-the-finger after the infamous Revised Version was marketed to the public. Only a blink of 11 days after the September 6, 1901 release of the American Standard version was President McKinley shot by a polish gunman in New York.

In earlier days of America's founding, children were actually taught in school to read by means of the King James Bible. At the founding of Harvard University (1636), every student underwent Bible courses and ministerial training for 3 years before focusing on their vocational preference. Which Bible brought life and vitality to the United States of America?

A hallway of Critical text imperfect bibles and their doctrinal misgivings are listed below:

BEN ASHER HEBREW OLD TESTAMENT CRITICAL TEXT

Jacob ben Asher (1270-1340 A.D.) was an anti-Semitic, German-born rabbi. He moved to Spain with his father, also a Rabbi, who was his principal teacher. His commentaries on the Pentateuch (Genesis-Deuteronomy) are printed in virtually all modern Jewish editions of the Pentateuch. His commentaries consist of symbolic references within the Torah (Jewish Law, same as Pentateuch), because of his leanings toward Hellenistic mystery religions.

The *New* King James version Old Testament is directly translated via the ben Asher Hebrew text. Modern English Old Testament versions, since 1901, have paternal lineage kinship to the Ben Asher Hebrew Critical text.

SEPUAGINT (Chapter 4, #5)

APOCRYPHA (Chapter 4, #7)

ROMAN CATHOLIC VULGATE BIBLE (Chapter 4, #9)

CODEX VATICANUS (Chapter 4, #11)

TAVERNER'S BIBLE

Richard Taverner was a layman protégé of Thomas Cromwell, a vicegerent in ecclesiastical affairs for King Henry VIII. This opportunist became a lawyer and clerk of the king's signet. Taverner was a former student of Cardinal College.

Because of the success of the Matthew's Bible, Taverner revised this Bible to form his own. It was published by "John Byddell for Thomas Barthlet" in 1539 and dedicated to King Henry VIII.

The unauthorized use of another production, especially infringement of a copyright, was as illegal then as it is now. This was, in fact, what would now be called **"piracy"**, being Grafton's Matthew Bible revised by Taverner, a learned member of the Inner Temple and famous Greek scholar. He made **several alterations** in the Matthew Bible.[10]

The Taverner's bible takes a step backwards highlighting textual alterations taken from Catholic Latin Vulgate idioms (native language expressions). Whenever possible, he substituted Bible words of original repute for foreign expressions. Taverner's bible never attained prominence due to Critical text translation and lack of Divine authority.

Taverner's illegal revision of the Matthew's Bible had little influence on subsequent Majority Text Scripture preservation. It did, not surprisingly, influence heavily the English translation of the Catholic New Testament in 1582. This would later become the mainline Douay-Rheims bible version of today's Catholic Church.

DOUAY-RHEIMS VERSION

Catholic scholar Gregory Martin, while exiled in France, translated the Catholic Latin Vulgate into English in 1582 and 1609. This is the bible in use today within mainline Roman Catholic Churches.

The New Testament was issued in 1582 by the English College in Rheims, France. The Old Testament publication was released by the same English College in 1609 after its move to Douay, Flanders. It was translated strictly from the Critical text Latin Vulgate bible of Rome.

The Catholics have always been put on the defensive by Majority Text Bibles. Why? Protestant Bibles rub Catholic tradition crossways, historically freeing the Holy Scriptures to the hand of common men. Centuried Catholic tradition dictates scriptural directives to her children exclusively through the Roman Catholic Church. For this reason the Catholic Church felt they must protect themselves by providing an English translation of their own.

The Douay-Rheims bible version underwent a revision by Bishop Challoner in 1750. This has been the best known English bible version for Catholics into our present century. It officially became the approved English version for Catholics in America in 1810.

CODEX SINIATICUS (Chapter 4, #11)

WESCOTT AND HORT GREEK NEW TESTAMENT (Chapter 4, #12)

NESTLE/ALAND GREEK NEW TESTAMENT

This Critical text Greek New Testament was published first in 1898 by German textual critic and evolutionist, Eberhard Nestle (1851-1913). He published several handbooks of scholarly criticism. He is primarily remembered for his critical revisions of the Greek New Testament. He somehow convinced the *British and*

Foreign Bible Society to adopt his Nestle Greek New Testament in place of the time-honored *Textus Receptus.* The Nestle Greek New Testament is a textual splicing of Tischendorf's *Codex Sinaiticus*, Wescott and Hort's Greek text, and Weymouth's *Resultant Greek Text*, all grafted from the Critical text tree. In 1901, Weymouth's readings were purged out for Bernhard Weiss's textual work, another Critical text bud. In 1927, Nestle's son, Erwin, issued the 13th edition after his father's death. It was at this point that the inspired Greek Majority Text was systematically abandoned by the editor in translation.

In 1952, Kurt Aland, also a German textual critic and evolutionist, became the associate editor of the 21st edition. As more Critical text manuscripts were subsequently discovered they were instantly inserted up to the 25th edition in 1963. Since Aland was a member of the United Bible Society, he submitted this Nestle/Aland Greek text to their editorial Greek committee. It became the basis of the United Bible Society's 3rd edition Greek New Testament (UBS[3]) in 1975.[11]

The 1979 26th edition of the Nestle/Aland Greek text became the basis for the UBS4 (4th edition of United Bible Society Greek New Testament). Expected to be published in the fall of 2009, the 28th edition of Nestle/Aland Greek text will incorporate more textual changes. It is now completely devoid of any inspired Majority Text readings.

Since its inception in 1898, the Nestle/Aland text have produced an updated edition every 3.1 years. This lets us know with common sense certainty that these editors have absolutely no assurances whatsoever of what are and what are not the exact Words of God in the Greek New Testament.

Numerical words changes applied to the 26th edition of Nestle/Aland Greek text were counted by Rev. Jack Moorman in 1988. His *"Missing in Modern Bibles-- Is the Full Story Being Told?"* reveals the Nestle/Aland text to be **2,886** words shorter than the inspired *Textus Receptus*. This would be the equivalent to deleting the entire books of I and II Peter. Five scholars actually make up the 26th edition committee. Four are deceased. Conservative Bible scholar, Dr. D.A. Waite, exposes their brief, yet telling biographic sketch of dubious distinction.

> It was made up of a committee consisting of Kurt Aland (who is an unbeliever), Matthew Black (an unbeliever), Carlo M. Martini [still living] (a Cardinal of the Roman Catholic Church), Bruce Metzger (who is from Princeton, a man who demonstrated his apostasy as editor of the *Reader's Digest Bible*), and Alan Wigren (from Chicago, an apostate also).[12]

The Nestle/Aland Greek New Testament is the translation basis for the 1885 *English Revised version,* the 1901 *American Standard version,* the 1970 *New English version,* the 1971 *New American Standard version*, the 1978 *New International version,* and scores of others lesser known versions.

RUDOLF KITTEL'S HEBREW BIBLE (Chapter 5, #1)

NEW KING JAMES VERSION (Chapter 5 #1)

NEW SCOFIELD REFERENCE VERSION

The original 1907 & 1917 *Old Scofield Reference Bible* were the King James Bible with C.I. Scofield's marginal notes added as a reference guide. Some of Scofield's notations were wacky, rather not doctrinally sound. Some notes suggest a "better rendering" for certain words. Other notes suggest omissions of fundamental, doctrine-based verses altogether, such as I John 5:8. Scofield also bought into the intelligent-sounding "the older manuscripts say..." to stake his claim of word changes or verse omissions.

The 1967 *New* Scofield Reference bible **inserts** the marginal word change suggestions and verse deletions of Scofield's notes into the scripture text. While C.I. Scofield is a trusted name, because it is attached to the word "Bible", let us not fail to remember that the text of Holy Scripture is inspired, the marginal references are not.

NEW AMERICAN STANDARD VERSION

"I under God **renounce every attachment to the New American Standard Version** ...I'm afraid I'm in trouble with the Lord...We laid the groundwork; I wrote the format; I helped interview some of the translators; I sat with the translators; I wrote the preface...I'm in trouble; I can't refute these arguments; it's wrong; it's terribly wrong; it's frighteningly wrong; and what am I going to do about it?...You can say **the Authorized Version [KJB] is absolutely correct.**[13]

Dr. Frank Logsdon
NASV Preface Author

The 1901 American Standard version was originally the melding of the failed 1885 English Revised version and the 1611 King James Holy Bible. From its inception, the ASV is fraught with doctrinal defects. "In the book, *The Life of Schaff*, arch liberal ASV chairman Phillip Schaff, an evolutionist, is quoted as stating that he only selected translators to be a on the ASV translation committee who **denied the inspiration** of the Scriptures."[14]   Schaff was tried by his denomination not once, but twice, for heresy. He taught at very liberal Union Seminary.

James Strong, author of the recognizable *Strong's Exhaustive Concordance*, was one of the members on the ASV translation committee. As a side note, few realize his main objective for the *Strong's Concordance* was to lead the reader to his lexicon in the back that indexed changes for "correcting" the King James Bible's "wrong translations". Strong's Hebrew and Greek word definitions are made up of his own collection of the beleaguered ASV readings.

Erasmus was a scholar ahead of his time. He forewarned over 500 years ago of lexicons (Dictionary of Bible words) that would feign accurate word descriptions of the Majority Text Bible. Erasmus cited "heresy would be faction" in future lexicons.[15]   Consider this <u>exact word change</u> in modern versions I Corinthians 11:19,

> **KJB** - "heresy"   to   **NASV** - "faction"
> **KJB** - "heresy"   to   **NKJV** - "faction"

A *faction* is "a party or group marked by dissension." A *heresy* is "a denial of revealed, religious truth" (Merriam-Webster's Dictionary 11th Collegiate Version 3.0, 2003). The softer, more noble-sounding word choice "faction" is the very denial of Scriptural truth and the heresy I Corinthians 11:19 warns us of.

There were over 4,000 word changes in the 1901 NASV apart from the Holy King James Bible.

> Only about 400 affect the sense; and of these 400 only about 50 are of real significance for one reason or another, and **not one of these affect an article of faith**.[16]
> **Dr. Phillip Schaff**
> 1901 American Standard version Chairman

Oh, contraire. Dr. Phillip Schaff was an eclectic leader who felt comfortable in religious circles of Baptists to Buddhism to Catholicism. He tried to be a pleaser of all brands of conservatives and liberals to sell the idea of an ASV for all. Who respects a religious opportunist? Is it any wonder that the ASV went *bankrupt* only 15 years after being on the market?

The 1995 NASV has mutated itself by **24,338** word changes since its 1901 publication. This 1995 5th edition of the NASV is a revision of the ASV, which was a revision of the failed 1885 English Revised version. The readings only get worse.

Mark 10:24 reads, *"Children, how hard is it for them that trust in riches to enter into the kingdom of God!"* By omitting 6 words and reverting the words "is it" to "it is", listen to the NASV and NIV retort, *"Children, how hard **it is** to enter the kingdom of God!"* Imagine the ludicrousy of making it **hard** for children to enter into Heaven.

Jesus and Lucifer (the devil) are akin by Critical text word choices within the NASV <u>and</u> in the NIV Isaiah 14:12 and I Peter 1:19:

Isaiah 14:12		II Peter 1:19
KJB	Lucifer	Jesus
NASV	star of the morning	morning star
NIV	morning star	morning star

The Hebrew word for "star" is not found in the Majority Text (Masoretic) Hebrew Old Testament Isaiah 14:12. The actual meaning of Lucifer is "light bearer". Therefore, the King James Bible remains accurate and doctrinally pure in its formal translation into English. However, because the NASV and NIV were dynamically translated into English from the revenant Ben Asher and Catholic Vulgate Old Testament, a breakdown occurs in sensible, sound doctrine.

> In pagan **Roman** mythology, Lucifer was vaunted as 'the day star', Christ himself.
> The **Roman** Catholic church continued this myth in their Latin Vulgate bible…New versions' use of the word 'star' is *not* a translation, but an *interpretation*, from lexicons that **follow Roman mythology.**[17]

Paul the Apostle combats Gnostic heresy to truth in the King James Bible, Philippians 2. The Gnostics of Paul's day believe as the Jehovah Witness do today that Jesus (physical man) and Christ (spiritual God) are not the same person.

The NASV robs Jesus of His deity in Philippians 2:5-6,
…who, although He existed in the **form** of God, did **not regard equality with God** a thing to be grasped.

The correct reading of the King James Bible,

Philippians 2:5-6

Let this mind be in you, which was also in **Christ Jesus**: Who, being in the form of God, thought it not robbery to be **equal with God**:

The correct reading of the King James Bible lets us know that God the Son (Jesus) did not rob God the Father of His deity, because Jesus <u>is</u> God Incarnate. In fact, the angel of the Lord foretold Jesus' birth to Mary and Joseph in Matthew 1:23, calling Him Emmanuel, "God with us".

THE LIVING BIBLE

Kenneth Taylor, who published the Living bible **paraphrase** in 1971, told his psychotherapist years later that the reason why his life had been so plagued, was because he had perverted the Word of God. He died believing the 1611 King James Bible was the true Holy Bible.

Forty million people own a Living bible in the United States. The *New Living Translation* is an update to the Living bible. Touted as the easiest bible on Earth to read, the Preface itself disclaims its readings begin at <u>High School</u> levels and above. Doesn't seem as "reader friendly" to the national 6th grade reading score average. However, the King James Bible is at 5th grade reading level, according to the Flesch-Kincaid Grade Level Formula.

The oxymoronic claim of the Living bible in name only to contain the Words of God is found in its own preface. Pick up any Living bible, open the front flap, read the Preface, which states, *"To paraphrase is to say something in <u>different words than the author</u> used....This **book** is a paraphrase of the Old and New Testaments."* If the Living bible categorizes itself as a paraphrased book, not a bible, why should we?

NEW INTERNATIONAL VERSION

> And the New International Version...Here we can see the diminishments consequent upon tinkering with the **original** syntax.[18]
>
> **The Literary Guide to the Bible**
> Harvard University

There is valid reason why the NIV is a more "gay friendly" bible than other modern versions. Who can forget the 70's decade of dance, liberation love, and open moral reversals that pushed liberty to new excess? Child abortion on demand was legalized in 1973. The year 1975 launched the *International Women's Year*. The 1978 New International version seeped into religious circles on this cultural momentum.

The author possesses a taped radio interview of Dr. Virginia Mollenkott, NIV stylist and consultant, who openly discloses her own homosexuality. She is quoted in 1993 as saying, "Jesus remained chromosomally female throughout life".[19]

According to Ms. Mollenkott, she worked for several years in the 1960's & 70's as a stylistic consultant throughout the final years when the initial NIV translation was fine tuned.

In her own words,

> Edwin   Palmer   {NIV   Executive Secretary}...knew me, had heard me speak, and sent me sheaf after sheaf of translations to review over a period of three or more years including several gift editions for the committee members when the work was first completed.[20]

The Reverend Wally Bee Bee knew Mollenkott in college to be "an avowed homosexual". She was dismissed from the faculty of Bob Jones University in the late 1950's for attempting to seduce female students into lesbian affairs. As a linguistic stylist, Mollenkott placed her discretionary taste upon the text of scripture. The words "sodomy" and "sodomite" have been summarily **removed** from the NIV bible.

Forensic Stylonomy is a method used to reflect an author's character. By employing this method, it can be determined who wrote a letter, or if a certain person did, based on sentence structure, style, and the number of certain words and letters used, etc. The NIV has an **effeminate** "forensic stylonomy".

"Mr. Martin Woodstra, Chairman of the Old Testament NIV committee, is a known homosexual."[21]

An example of the sweeping theological shift in the NIV, contrary to inspired Majority Text Scripture, would be I Corinthians 7:1.

King James Bible I Corinthians 7:1
It is good for a man not to touch a woman.

NIV I Corinthians 7:1
It is good for a man not to marry.

A reoccurring problem in the NIV is its propensity to change proper nouns to mere pronouns. A murky example is Genesis 35:9 *"And God appeared unto Jacob again, when he came out of Padanaram, and blessed him."* The NIV changes "Jacob" to "him", and the KJB word "he" to "Jacob", even though the Majority Hebrew Text says otherwise. How does this make it any clearer to read? Just leave it the way the Holy Spirit breathed it, eh?

In Acts 8, God led Philip into the desert to cross paths with a eunuch serving Ethiopian Queen Candace. The Ethiopian eunuch was reading an allegoric passage of Scripture from Isaiah portraying Christ as Saviour. Philip navigated the eunuch's understanding into the prophetic fulfillment that Jesus is the risen Messiah. Seeing an oasis pool of water, the eunuch inquired about baptism, and asked Philip a common question regarding when is the proper time to be baptized?

Philip answers the Ethiopian Eunuch in Acts 8:37, And Philip said, If thou believest with all thine heart, thou mayest. And he answered and said, I believe that Jesus Christ is the Son of God.

The NIV completely erases this all-important verse 37. This crucial verse is breached out of the NIV. The rift in the NIV passage goes from the eunuch's question to Philip about baptism in verse 36, directly to the eunuch's baptism by Philip in verse 38. What a tragedy, since verse 37 is the _**only verse in the entire Bible**_ that answers this doctrinally significant question about WHEN to be baptized. This key doctrinal verse about baptism is omitted as well in the NLT (New Living Translation), the RSV, and the NRSV. Other modern versions bracket verse 37, or deduce it to *italics*, to further obscure it as authentic in Critical text scripture.

There is no longer a sacred "veil" in the Gospels and Hebrews. It was replaced by a domestic "curtain". There are at least three Hebrew words for "curtain", and a specific Hebrew word for "veil". The inspired Majority Text specifically reads the exact Hebrew word for "veil". Also, the "mercy seat" has been removed from Hebrews 9:5. What has it been replaced with? Nothing. A cobwebbed empty space is where the mercy seat used to be in the NIV scripture. Intentional or not, these changes uproot and plunder anchor words of the Christian faith.

II Corinthians 2:17 **KJB**
For we are not as many, which **corrupt** the word of God...

II Corinthians 2:17 **NIV**
Unlike so many, we do not **peddle** the word of God for profit...

Random omissions of crucial words, as well as erasing whole verses in the NIV New Testament, account for severe doctrinal quakes in its structure. JESUS is completely left out of 45 passages. CHRIST is completely left out of 42 passages. LORD is completely left out of 26 passages. GOD is completely left out of 3 passages. "The NIV omits 64,000 *doctrinally* important words and 17 whole verses!"[22]   The excess of theological abuses within this spiritually impoverished "scripture" is disturbing at minimum, and sinister at worst.

The King James Bible has 64,098 more words than the NIV. The NIV omissions account for 10% less of the bible, reducing it by 170 pages. It has not only declined in content, but also in sound biblical authority.

This is irrefutably pointed out by author and linguistic expert, Gail Riplinger,

John 3:7

KJB	NIV
Marvel not that I say unto **thee**, **Ye** must be born again.	**You** should not be surprised at my saying, **You** must be born again.

In the NIV the word 'you' is used for both the singular (thee) and the plural (Ye).

The KJV is the **only** current version that *clearly teaches* that Jesus was not merely addressing Nicodemus alone. **All men must be born again.**[23]

King James Bible John 6:47 reads, *He that believeth on me hath everlasting life.* The NIV and NASV omit "on me" to read, *He who believes_(?)_ has everlasting life.* Seem harmless? Hardly. According to the NIV or NASV, in what or whom are we to believe for eternal life in Heaven? Is this making the true Gospel more easily understood, or more vague? More succinct, or more sloppy? More holy, or more holey? More trustworthy, or more truncated?

It has been duly noted by author Gail Riplinger that the owner of the NIV is Zondervan Publishers, which is owned by Harper Collins, which is owned by the not-so-Christian-friendly Rupert Murdoch. "Murdoch also owns several newspapers in England that feature topless photos of women."[24] His HarperSanFransisco Publishing House is home base to John Spong's inflammatory *Why Christians Must Change or Die.* Sound like a sterile maternity outlet to birth new bible versions?

NEW REVISED STANDARD VERSION

I Peter 2:2 instructs new born babies in Christ to *"...desire the sincere milk of the word that ye may grow thereby."* The Majority Greek reading is *ina en auto auxethete.* The Critical text Greek reading in the NRSV adds *eis soterian* (to salvation). This phrase tacked onto the end of the verse implies salvation is something that is grown into, and not instantaneous..."that by it you may grow into salvation."

The King James Bible correctly prevents this collapse of truth by its formal translation from God-breathed Majority Text Scriptures. The Critical text's NRSV annuls the divine doctrine of immediate redemption for a passively earned salvation fallacy.

21st CENTURY KING JAMES VERSION (KJ21)

Like the New King James Version, the KJ21 asserts itself as a mere update of the 1611 King James Bible. Sigh. Here we go again. "The writers - Barbara Graff, Florence Ronning, Mary Burkham, and William Prindle claim to enhance the Scripture text with 'modern synonyms'. In several places, even more difficult words replace the 'archaic' Words of the 1611 King James Bible."[25]

Jesus Christ is demoted in John 12:34,

KJB 1611	KJ21
Who is this *Son* of man?	Who is this *son* of man?

Glaring doctrinal variance from Colossians 1:3, and I Thessalonians 1:3, both muddy the waters of the pristine doctrine of the Trinity. Judas is also incorrectly made to be the son of none other than James the Apostle. The spirit of man is confused with the Spirit of God. And, Jesus, the Word in flesh, is confused with the Scripture, the written Word.[26]   Other hidden theological errors are as painful to point to as a hairy wart poking out of a sequined dress. The seduction of the KJ21 goes only as far as its JKV veneer. Its marketing ploy "Today's King James version" is a decorous mirage of truth, a mimicking wanna-be.

2012 THE VOICE

The latest "novel" approach to misconstruing Divine Scripture is a Hollywood screen play version of God's Word "The Voice". Simply put, it is the newest scripture sell that minimizes sound, Bible doctrine – intentional or not. Entirely omitting the words Christ, angel, apostle, and Lord (Yahweh), this contemporary church bible version has reached a new low to heighten confusion that already exists over God's true name. Claiming "new Christians" must have an easier read to understand "archaic language" of traditional Bibles, scraggly-bearded Pastor and author Chris Seay of Houston's Ecclesia Church is known for his "coffee-house, peer-driven" techniques of ministry.

CRITICAL TEXT

I John 1:7 reads, *"But if we walk in the light, as he is in the light, we have fellowship one with another, and the blood of **Jesus Christ** his Son cleanseth us from all sin."*

Holy Majority Text Scripture equally reflects John the Apostle's divinely inspired words "Jesus Christ". Holey Critical text modern versions shorten it to "Jesus". So, what's the big deal?

In the first century A.D., a massive front of heresy called "Gnosticism" threatened sound doctrine of early New Testament churches and teachings of Christ. The

Gnostics taught that Jesus and Christ were two separate beings who "got together". Accordingly, the Jesus born to Joseph and Mary was physical. At His baptism, the spiritual Christ entered into Jesus' body. At the crucifixion, Christ left the body of Jesus to die. At the resurrection, only the spiritual Christ was seen by the disciples. Gnostics taught the mortal (physical) Jesus remains in the tomb.

Once we understand the heresy that John was dealing with, the correct Scripture reading in the King James Bible makes perfect sense. By inspiration of the Holy Spirit and Divine preservation, both words together "Jesus Christ" confronts the heresy of Gnosticism. Both the physical (mortal) and spiritual (immortal) God-man, Jesus Christ, triumphed in both death and resurrection to ultimately pay the sin debt of the entire human race. If John would have written just "the blood of Jesus", he would have been in agreement with the theological apostasy of Gnosticism.

How does your bible version read I John 1:7?

The King James Bible Luke 2:11 reads, *"For unto you is born this day in the city of David a Saviour, which is Christ the Lord."* Notice the old British-English spelling of the word Saviour with the letter "u". Critical text bibles scrub this key letter out to read "Savior". Webster's 1959 Dictionary gives two, separate definitions for the words Saviour and savior.

> **Saviour:** Jesus Christ, the Redeemer, who is called Saviour *by way of distinction.* The Saviour of men, who has opened the way of everlasting salvation by his obedience and death, the Saviour of the world.
> **Savior:** one who saves or preserves, or delivers from danger.

A savior can be anybody. For example: A grateful, yet potential victim of a robbery, whose perpetrator was overcome by a good Samaritan could exclaim, "This person stopped my mugger from attacking me. He is my savior." Or, a person who was rescued from drowning could report, "If it weren't for the skilled efforts of the paramedic, I would not be alive today. My savior rescued me."

In the Bible, there is only one Saviour of mankind from the fires of hell for Heaven, Jesus Christ, by "way of distinction". The King James Bible correctly retains this clarity of meaning. The omission of one, single letter "u" seems trite, but it also takes away the exclusivity of Jesus Christ within our English language. Would you rest your faith and eternal destination in a savior, or the Saviour? How does your bible version read Luke 2:11?

Alarming as it may sound, Applied Digital Solutions was given the green light in April 2002 by the FDA to manufacture and begin selling a "Verichip" that goes directly beneath the skin on the hand. The rice-sized chip may be utilized for a variety of security, emergency, or healthcare applications. The wearer's data on the chip is received by radio frequency to an external scanner.

The Associated Press in Washington reported in 2002 that a spokesman for Applied Digital Solutions appeared on Pat Roberson's *700 Club* to assure Christian viewers that the chip does not fit the Biblical description of the "mark of the beast". Why? Because, the chip is embedded *under* the skin from plain view, and not stamped <u>on top</u> of the skin, as the Bible warns against, said Applied Digital. Just a second. Hold the phone. Which new bible version was the spokesman referring to?

King James Bible Revelation 13:16 reads, *"And he causeth all, both small and great, rich and poor, free* *and bond, to receive a mark **in** their right hand, or **in** their foreheads."* The readings of the NASV, NIV, NKJV, ESV, and TNIV modern versions all say, *"...**on** the right hand."* By incorrectly changing the letter "i" to "o", millions of believers vested false assurance in contemporary scripture. The spokesman for Applied Digital quoted from a new bible version.

How does your bible version read Revelation 13:16?

Can you begin to see how end-time believers, as well as Israel herself, will be duped into believing, then follow, the end-time antichrist? Apparently, it won't take much with new bible versions **in advocacy** of believers receiving a digital mark in the body. Does this one-word change, yea, one-letter change, devalue new bible versions as not quite trustworthy? You decide. *New Age Bible Versions* made this observation and warned of textual changes that soil pure Bible doctrine years ago. The Majority Text 1611 King James Bible was built letter by letter, word by word, with sound doctrinal consistency that perfectly fulfills the **trustworthy** label this and other books give it.

Hall of imperfect bibles

132 B.C. Septuagint (Hebrew to Greek)
1st - 3rd Centuries A.D. Apocrypha (Greek)
405 A.D. Jerome'sRomanCatholicVulgatebible (Latin)
1270 A.D. ben Asher Critical Hebrew text (Hebrew)
1475 Codex Vaticanus (Greek)
1539 Taverner's bible
1609 Douay-Rheims version
1844 Codex Sinaiticus (Greek)
1870 Wescott and Hort Greek text
1885 English Revised version

1898 Nestle/Aland Greek New Testament (Greek)
1901 American Standard version
1909 Rudolf Kittel's *Biblical Hebraica* (Hebrew bible)
1926 Moffat bible
1931 Goodspeed version
1950 Watchtower bible (Jehovah Witness) New World Translation
1952 Revised Standard version
1958 Phillips New Testament version
1965 Amplified bible
1967 New Scofield Reference bible
1966 Jerusalem bible
1970 New English version
1970 New American version
1971 Living bible
1971 New American Standard version
1971 Revised Standard version
1976 Good News Translation(Today's English version)
1978 New International version
1982 New King James version
1985 New Jerusalem bible (Catholic)
1986 International Children's bible
1997 NewCenturyversion (InternationalChildrenbible)
1989 Jewish New Testament
1989 New Revised Standard version
1991 Contemporary English version
1993 The Message bible
1994 21st Century King James version (KV21)
1995 Contemporary English version
1996 New Living bible (New Living Translation)
2001 English Standard version
2002 The Message updated
2004 Holman Christian Standard bible
2007 KJVer [easy read]
2009 bible Across America (Handwritten NIV)

2011 New American bible (Catholic)
2012 The Voice

The Holy Bible doesn't need to be re-written.

It needs to be re-read.

Chapter Seven

Conclusion

*We have as a rule used the King James Version...our reasons for doing so must be obvious...it is still arguably the version that best preserves the **literary effects of the original languages.***

*The Authorized Version has the kind of transparency which makes it possible for the reader to see the **original clearly.***

*Through its transparency the reader not only **sees the original** but learns how to read it.*

*The Authorized Version [KJB] emerges from comparison with twentieth century versions as more attractive and **more accurate.***

The Literary Guide to the Bible
Harvard University

The undivided, thus, preserved Words of God span a time frame beginning with the first books being written by Holy Inspiration in 1400 B.C. *The exact, equal words* waft all the way into united completion at 1611. Onwards to 1769, today's King James Bible embodies par excellence in perfection.

The Majority Text *English* Bible is evidenced from first century part and parcel inspired Scripture, until its unification in the printed 1525 Tyndale English Holy Bible. Majority Text historian Gail Riplinger sums up nicely the paternity of Majority Text *English* Bibles as "Acts 2-to-You".

Gothic Bibles (apostles-500 A.D.)
Anglo Saxon Bibles (500-1000)
Pre Wycliffe Bibles (1000-1400)
Wycliffe and Tyndale Bibles (1384-1525)
Coverdale/Matthews/Great/Geneva   Bibles
(1536-1560)
Bishop's Bible (1568-1610)
King James Bible (1611) [2]

Pure Bible translation occurs as the picking up of words from the originally inspired Hebrew (Old Testament) and originally inspired Greek (New Testament), carrying those words over into English, or any language being translated into, and setting them down very gently *without losing any parts, gaining any parts, or changing any parts*. It means to simply copy from language to language. This solidifies Word-equals-Word purity. To mirror or equal its provenance (original source), copies must remain error free from word changes. Marvel this miracle in the King James Bible.

The 1611 King James Bible represents equally copied words in English as the God-breathed original Scripture books. Why? Because, we know **exactly how** the Majority Text Scripture has been historically copied (formal equivalent translation). The King James Bible DOES NOT represent changed words. Changed words cease to be Majority Text Scripture. Non-Majority Text scripture cease to be inspired Words of God.

Over 3,000 years of Divine unchanged Scripture places itself within your hands while handling a copy of the blessed 1611 King James Holy Bible. Compatriots of Holy Scripture have literally shielded this Divine Book with their own lives, honor, and bodies, amid centuries of assaults, for you to receive the Gospel of Jesus Christ in original purity.

Dr. D.A. Waite has studied this subject intimately for over 37 years. He draws his conclusion,

> It is my own personal conviction and belief,...that the WORDS of the Received Greek and Masoretic Hebrew texts that underline the King James Bible are the very WORDS which God has preserved down through the centuries, being the exact WORDS of the **ORIGINALS** themselves. [3]

This pinnacle of written love beacons God's revelation of Himself to mankind. The English language has become an end day, universal language. When the King James Bible was completed in 1611, there lived only 5 million English speaking people on the planet. Today, there are over 2 billion English speaking people, one third of the world population, scattered across planet Earth. Learning English as a second language is now required in most schools of the world. Most of these would not easily recognize the written "Americanized" English dialect. Instead ye ole' British spelling of 1611 (ex: musick, Saviour) is used outside of the United States. 33% of the entire population of the world could understand the

Gospel of Christ in the internationally recognized English language of the King James Bible.

On purpose, modernized new bible versions are not written in ye ole' British English dialect. So, only 1/6 of the world's English speaking people would be able to easily comprehend the Gospel of Christ from "Americanized" new bible versions. For these reasons, in Chapter 4, I specifically lay out why "thee" "thou" "ye" words are necessary to remain part of Scripture text. The King James Bible is the perfect missionary book to communicate to the rest of the world the love of God in words they will understand.

Because we understand the King James Bible's derivation (source), advocates get concerned when there is any hint of any attack upon it. We get upset when there is a misrepresentation of facts undermining its accuracy. This Book has to do with man's eternal destiny. To belittle the Holy Bible is like tampering with medicine for a sick man, like poisoning the bread of a hungry man.

Ponder an era of insight from the late pastor of America's largest church:

> When I was a young preacher, the battle was over how to interpret the Bible. Now, almost half a century later, **the battle is over the Bible itself.** Then, the battle was over what the Bible TAUGHT.
> Today the battle is over **what the Bible IS.** Then, it was a battle over interpretation. Now, it is a battle over inspiration and preservation. Then, it was a battle over difference of doctrine. Now, it is battle over where we get our doctrine. Then, it was a battle over the flow. Now, it is battle over the source. Then, it was a battle over what Truth says. Now the battle is over **what**

the truth is. I have given the few years that I
have left to...the King James Bible.[4]

Dr. Jack Hyles
(1926 - 2001)
23,000 member First Baptist Church, Hammond, IN, Pastor
Author, 26 books
Hyles-Anderson College, Founder

President Ronald Reagan alluded to the subject of
modern bible versions in a September 6, 1977 radio
broadcast series, *Reagan in His Own Words*. Hear the
greatest President of modern times criticize the attempt to
improve the King James Bible:

> ...boast that their bible is as readable as the daily
> paper...But do readers of the daily news find
> themselves moved to wonder, at the gracious
> words which proceeded out of his mouth?
> ...**horsing around with the sacred text**...to
> make   the   Bible   more   readable   and
> understandable...I can't help feeling we should
> instead be taking the people to religion and
> lifting them with the beauty of the language that
> has outlived centuries... [KJB] **it has already
> been gotten right**.[5]

Critical text advocate, James White, smugs in his
book, *The King James Only Controversy* (p. 248),
"antintellectualism is traditional to fundamentalism."
This mala fide claim White makes with bare words.
Notice at the same time, this KJB contrarian fiercely
flaunts <u>uncritical</u> loyalties toward a manuscript line that
was rummaged out of a trash can (Codex Sinaiticus).
Which seems more intellectual to you - believing God
preserved His Word in a Critical text manuscript that lay
dormant for 1500 years in a wastepaper basket, or
believing God preserved His Word in Majority Text

Scripture that enjoyed world-wide circulation beginning with the first century New Testament church at Antioch to present day?

To settle a precise, fact-based conviction in favor of Divine Word-equals-Word Scripture preservation, based upon historical data, is not "antintellectualism". On the other hand, a wastebasket manuscript speaks for itself.

New English bibles today are self-credentialed based on their own short lived merit, not on any historical track record of authenticity. Modern age versions of the Critical text reek of rancid doctrinal errors that have putrefied in layers over centuries beneath cosmetically sutured bible covers. Advocates of "better bible versions" unaware of this fact are familiarized first to an anti-King James Bible aroma within secularized Christianity, intoxicating the spiritual air breathed in contemporary churches, religious classrooms, even in the pulpit. It began long ago.

In the Middle Ages, European governments were nothing more than an appendage of the Roman Catholic Church. We have seen from its beginning, the Critical text was made prominent out of the bile of religious genocide. The Critical text has always elevated itself by stepping on the inspired Majority Text Scripture. Onwards to today, most modern versions (paraphrases) merit their existence on getting rid of the *"archaic language"* of the King James Bible. Never mind these lofty words equally mirror the original God-breathed books. Critical text bibles (NIV, NASV, ERV, RSV, NWT, NKJV, KJ21, et al) never claim to be <u>inspired,</u> only "better" scripture than the King James Bible.

This author has experienced personally the ultimate, ridiculous endgame of anti King James Bible sentiment in our current religious climate. Enrolled as a 19 yr. old Bible college student at a leading CHRISTIAN

University, I was shocked by its Vice President in the privacy of his own office, when I asked him a simple question, *"Do you mean to tell me that the King James Bible I hold in my hands is not really the Bible?"* His emphatic answer, *"Yes"*.

Eh? It seems to me that if there is any place in the world where you ought to have your faith in the Bible stabilized, it would be in a Christian college, a Christian church, or a Christian institution. However, in this author's own **personal** experience, that is all too often where traditional, conservative faith is shaken up these days. Elevated positions and higher degrees have unfortunately educated contemporary religious leaders beyond common sense more than you'd like to think.

Thankfully, Auburn University Professor, Allen Ward characterizes his Biblical studies of *"[T]he miraculous **perfection** of the Authorized Version <KJB>"* (Translating For King James, p.ix). So adds British Professor, David Daniell, *"The Authorized Version <KJB> became the acme of achievable literary perfection.."*(Daniell, pp. vii, ix, x, et al)

So, do the heretical leanings of Critical text fathers Origen, Marcion, Clement, Eusebius, Jerome, Tischendorf, Wescott, and Hort not matter? What part of their pedantic translations are sacred? These "halfway house manuscripts" yearly mill out new English bible versions that satisfy America's bible menu today. The newest scripture version item to pop up on the menu is simply the publisher's savvy for making another buck off the Holy Bible. How is this obvious pattern a non issue? How is it ignored by true Christians? Furthermore, exactly how many bibles did God write anyway? When is enough bibles, enough? Evolution of scripture becomes a way of life for Critical text, man-made bible versions.

What good is what you believe, if it is based upon misrepresented truth? What good is what you believe if it began in spiritual error? What good is what you believe if it comes from wrong? What good are modern day versions if they are offspring of Critical text parents which fog up the original Words of God?

Glance for a moment at a bible we all are opposed to. Why are we all opposed to the satanic bible? Is it because we hate the people who edited it? Of course not. God loves every human soul. We place the same value upon every soul, regardless, to love like Christ. We simply are against the doctrinal heresy of the editor's belief system. Likewise, fathers of the Critical text *embraced* theological error. Yet, "after criticizing Madalyn Murray O'Hair for expelling the Bible from America's *schoolrooms*, we are exposed to ministers who cannot even profess to have Bibles in their *studies*!"[6]

Well-intended believers are in line today to purchase, inadvertently support, and fund superfluous versions of scripture from out-of-touch committees, and off-track religious "intelligentsia". This means a Christian can directly support a Critical text bible, which originated diametrically juxtaposed to inspired Holy Writ. In *other words*, God's Words have been systematically omitted in Critical text, new English bibles. Mustn't serious Christians be wary of this madness?

Dual manuscript lineage separating Majority Text Scripture from the Critical text forge a necessary crossroad that complicates the issue for common believers. Unfortunately, these different Scriptures compete against one another for supremacy in the minds and hearts of the American Christian culture today. We have all seen the splintering effects.

We must know God's Word in truth. II Timothy 2:15 reads, *"Study to shew thyself...rightly dividing the* *word of **truth**."* Precise truth requires precise words. Could we study the Word of truth if we did not have it? Could we rightly divide the Words of God if it exists only in the "lost original books"? The Critical text arose based on these unsettling assumptions as fact. However, Majority Text Scripture is home to perfectly *preserved Words of **original inspiration.***

The reader, therefore, must wade into whose textual stream he or she will sail – that of the Divine Majority Text, as nestled within the King James Bible of 1611, or the Critical text, being the evolving reversions of ancient dissent, as represented inside all "new-and-improved" bible versions of modern times.

If we select the latter bias, we must remember that marginal notes become <u>textual</u> words, and the dubious Apocryphal (Roman Catholic) books become <u>books of scripture</u>. Furthermore, if critics do not know what *books* should be in the Bible, how can they know what ***words*** should be in the Bible? This explains the dual, polar-opposite, streams of Scripture in history.

TWO STREAMS OF SCRIPTURE

Majority Text	Critical text
Moses Pentateuch 1400 B.C. (Old Testament Original)	Ben Asher text 1270 A.D. (old testament original)
Masoretic Old Testament 200 B.C. (Hebrew)	Septuagint 132 B.C. (Hebrew to Greek)
Mishnah 200 A.D. (Sopherim & Masoretes 500 B.C.-500 A.D.)	Apocrypha (Latin Catholic books, 1st-3rd centuries A.D.)
Rabbinic Bible (Hebrew Bible, 1524 B.C.)	Rudolf Kittel *Biblical Hebraica* (Hebrew bible, 1909 A.D.)
Apostles (New Testament Original) 30-100 A.D.	Apostates (new testament original) 100-200 A.D.
Vernacular Scripture from Antioch (Italian, French, Syrian, Dutch, Latin, 60-1300)	Greek neo-scripture from Alexandria (Marcion, Clement, Origen, Eusebius, Jerome, 100-420)
Waldensian Bible (*Itala*, 120)	Roman Catholic Vulgate bible (Latin, 405)
Erasmus (early church Greek New Testament, 1466)	Codex Vaticanus 1475 / Codex Sinaiticus 1844 (Catholic Greek new testaments)
Tyndale Bible (English Received Text, 1525)	Douay-Rheims bible (English Catholic bible, 1582)
1611 King James Bible	Wescott & Hort 1885 English Revised version

To say that we do *not* have in existence today an every-Word-inspired Holy Bible is to side against logic, reason, and fact. We factually know the 1611 King James Bible can be traced upstream to the original roots of Holy Scripture.

The first stream which carried the Received Text in Hebrew and Greek **began with the apostolic churches,** and reappearing at intervals down the

Christian Era among enlightened believers, was protected by the wisdom and scholarship of the pure church in her different phases: precious manuscripts were preserved by such as the church at Pella in Palestine where Christians fled, when in 70 A.D. the Romans destroyed Jerusalem. [7]

This stream continued its path through the Syriac Church of Antioch sling-shotting missionaries armed with powerhouse Majority Text Bibles of vernacular languages sanitizing all major nations with the pure Gospel of Jesus Christ. Coursing through the Italic Church in northern Italy, and the Gallic Church in southern France, then upwards into the Celtic Church of Great Britain the mighty bellows rolled into a tide of Divine Revival. The Waldensian churches bridged the Word to the churches of the Reformation.

The Majority Text's unscathed Holy Writ, in spite of taking on entrenched authorities inflicting havoc upon its copyists, and the understanding of Word-equals-Word translation by these expert copyists, thus preserving every inspired Word of God, is unmatched by the Critical text.

By 1637, the King James Bible had replaced the Geneva Bible throughout the Massachusetts Bay Colony. The first King James Bible printed in the U.S.A. was the Aitken Bible in 1782. It has been the only Bible authorized by Congress. The Holy Bible is the basis of our U.S. Constitution. The history of the free Protestant world is inseparable from the Received Majority Text Holy Bible.

This day, I trust, the reign of political protestantism will commence. The rights of the colonists as Christians...are to be found clearly written and promulgated in the New Testament.[8]

Samuel Adams
(1722-1803)
Father of the American Revolution
Upon signing the Declaration of Independence

Freedom shines bright into the heavens as the greatest nation on Earth was established upon this rock. Time-honored Holy Writ surrounds its people with grace and moral majesty. Lawlessness could easily break loose and plunge our nation into anarchy without this solid, historic anchor. The adverse Critical text gave us versions which speaks in faltering tones, whose music is discordant, whose legacy runs crosswise to peace. The King James Bible is harmonious. It agrees with itself. It is self-proving, and it creeps into the affections of the heart.

"It is popular nowadays to compile lists of difficult words found in the KJB as reason for more simplicity. The following examples are words that may be difficult for the average reader: *onslought, ferule, cruelly, gesticulation, filial, geniality, garrett, forlorn, fetched, well-nigh, reckon, palpable, auspicious, oaken, labyrinth, tallow, and stalmart.* The above list did not come from the Elizabethan English of the Authorized Version, but from four chapters of the narrative of Mark Twain's children's classic, *The Adventures of Tom Sawyer.*"[9]

What would be the reaction if the scholarly world decided to change the wording of Shakespeare's plays to make them more understandable to the modern mind? Instead of *"To be, or not to be,"* it became, *"I reckon I don't know if want to live or die."* Or yet, what if the publishing companies began producing many different "versions" of Shakespeare for profit? The great playwright's influence would die in one generation if these things were done. Cries of protest would be heard from every hall of learning. Shakespeare should never be revised. Neither should the Bible.

We resist the howling ninnies swept up in cultural withdrawals from the King James Bible demanding "easier versions". Christians aren't built today like they were in times of persecution. Our forefather-brethren of the Protestant Reformation resisted ease, and stood for a higher standard. So should we.

To amend a single word in the United States Constitution would require the approval of two-thirds of Congress and three-fourths of the states. To change every chapter in the Book that has been the foundation of our culture, our morals, our ideals, and our society as a nation requires nothing but the approval of a single publisher. Many Christians are ok with this today, sadly.

The problematic bible versions milled out by Nelson, Zondervan, Lockman, and American Bible Society over the past 50 years, all have serious weaknesses. Unfledged bible versions are in severe doctrinal disarray. Up to this point, none of them compare even remotely to the quality and authority of the Holy English Bible our forefathers liberated America with and used in our homes, our courtrooms, our schools, and our churches for almost 400 years (Mayflower, 1620).

The Ben Asher text Old Testament and the Alexandrian (Critical) text New Testament make up an Inquisition-enforced Latin Vulgate bible, puting an impossible strain on divine authorship. This juggernaut sub-scripture parents the *English Revised version, Revised Standard version, American Standard version, New Revised Standard version, New International version, New American Standard version, Living bible,*

International Children's bible, New King James version, 21ˢᵗ Century King James version, New World Translation, and the English Standard version, et al.

The next popular bible edition of Zondervan Publishers will be handwritten by 31,000 Americans in 2008. A 90-city, 15,000 mile cross-country tour kicks off to attend special events, churches, and national landmarks, to give the public a chance to write out Bible verses. The "Bible Across America Scriptorium" grants anyone seeking to contribute, the opportunity to translate a scripture verse of your own. Won't it be amusing to see what America's armchair theologists come up with? Is Zondervan going to administer any screening process to ensure verses are being translated by people who are sober, not high, and sane, I wonder? Are any world religions excluded from participation? Can atheists participate?

By contrast, ever noticed how the hottest, new versions nowadays are also going back to re-marketing the 1611 King James Bible? (ie: New King James version, 21ˢᵗ Century King James, KJ21, KJVer [easy read] All of which do not liken to one another) Religious or not, big business keys on cultural wants and needs. Re-tapping, re-packaging, and re-commercializing the King James Bible clearly demonstrates a grassroots pivot back to the trusted KJB. Capitalizing on widespread loyalties to the 1611 King James Bible, manufacturers of the latest versions for too long have played a constant game of "one-ups-manship" with one another to their own profit and the doom of Scriptural church unity.

I will say what we all feel is the heart and soul of the issue. Everybody knows the 1611 King James Bible represents the Words of God more authentically than any other. Always has. Always will. Why? This Book of God embodies preserved Words of original inspiration. The

King James Bible are God's Holy Words copied equally and perfectly into English. Clearly, history validates this fact.

Although we all tend to stray from the truth we know, life unfailingly cycles us back around to what is right. The real question is, can the American church survive its lusty consumerism?

How many bible versions will be enough, until we get it --- our pro choice view of Holy Scripture is doing us more harm than good? When the gaming of scriptures for profit is over, God will checkmate us back to HIS original Word in English, the 1611 King James Bible.

Although the *New International version* has surpassed the King James Bible as the best selling among Christian book dealers today, Majority Text advocates need not feel in the minority.

> A 1995 poll concerning Bible translations showed that nearly all Americans own at least one version of the Bible, and that approximately two-thirds of those   surveyed   claim   the Authorized [King James] Version as their main translation.
> Additionally, in 1997 the Barna Research Group established that the **King James Version is more likely to be read** than the New International Version   by a ratio of five to one. Other   polling   through   the   Internet   has established the King James as the most likely favored English translation.[10]

A professional cleaning crew entered a museum to clean a priceless painting. Somehow the cleaning solution was mixed incorrectly. The wrong solvent was used. A few hours later, the priceless picture being cleaned was destroyed. It is the author's humble opinion that the

Words of God are being inadvertently destroyed by perhaps well-intended, professional Christians, who are using a disfiguring solvent (Critical text) to clean up the issue of which Bible is God's Word.

Appropriately administered solvent should be used. Historical fact, faith, and the Word-equals-Word divinely preserved Majority Text are the perfect solution. When truth is applied *correctly* to the issue of which Bible is the Word of God, the 1611 King James Bible is beautified.

Preserved copies of ancient Majority Text Scripture are nestled in museums around the world.

- Corpus Christi College, Cambridge.
- Cambridge University Library.
- British Museum, Cotton Library.
- Bodleian Library, Oxford.
- Beron Institute, Rome.

Antiquarian booksellers today offer early, genuine King James Bibles and its leaves. Visit on the Internet *HistoricBibles.com, greatsite.com, davidclachman.com, historicprints.com,* and *rarebiblesandmore.com* to purchase your own portion of English Scripture from its original era.

The Holy King James Bible is one that floats down to us perfectly upon the blood of Christian martyrs, our religious forefathers. Through millennia of time, God has incubated His saving Gospel Plan in written purity for 3,400 years beginning at 1400 B.C.

From its foretelling in the day of Moses, through the day of Christ, up to this very moment, God's recorded holiness abounds. Evil never has and never will annul the written witness of God's perfection. In fact, God chose the most *unlikely* writers just to demonstrate the power of His eternal Words. Almost one-third of the entire Holy Bible is penned by converted felons, ex-murderers: King David, Moses, and the Apostle Paul. The inspired Word is supernatural property, able to cleanse, heal, restore to health. God can save, then use anybody. Human reason is often confounded by the foolish things of this world in God's Plan. It points the glory to God alone.

The inspired Majority Text from the New Testament church is the true and perfect Scripture used in <u>unbroken succession</u> for centuries into the Protestant Reformation's zenith of 1611. This perpetual revelation of our Creator is an untainted piece of Heaven on Earth. It is a perfect witness for mankind to receive and believe in the Lord Jesus Christ as a personal Saviour.

Only one continent, of all the great nations, both ancient and modern, can lay claim to the Holy Bible as the basis for its Constitution - North America. The English Majority Text Scripture came to rest in 1611, a few years before the Puritans fled religious intolerance in England. They carried with them the King James Bible across stormy seas (1620) to lay a firm foundation of the greatest nation this world has ever known. God's Holy Word has as much to do with the laying of the foundation of our great country as the Declaration of Independence did. The first building erected on American soil by decree of its first Governor Bradford, was a church assembly house. Observance to the inspired Holy Scriptures took place 5-6 hours every Sunday in the cradle of our country's infancy.

American independence thrives on this foundation. It has foretold the fall of nations who forget or refuse to honor the Almighty God of this perfect Book. When empires disappeared, the Bible survived. It has warned succeeding kingdoms. It has honored generations who honor the Bible. Inventions, entire branches of science, human hospitory care, archeological discoveries, have lifted society in lieu of the Bible's hidden treasures of knowledge. No living being can stabilize a life, a home, a heart, until following its moral precepts within our God-given structure of reality.

Today's religious leaders more and more are wanting to fit in with the rest of the world. Even the Christian community has shifted its mission of spreading Gospel truth to a quest for gaining relevance in American society by peace-offering its own Scripture into "modernesque lingo". We're trying to fit in. God wants us to stand out. That's what America does. That is what America is all about.

God's truth is what liberated our nation's fathers from the inside out. Nestled in individual soul liberty, America flourished apart from earthy governments. And, God's truth not only became our foundation, but loyalty to its guiding principles have kept us free. With eternal light of its radiance, the King James Bible beacons Heavenly hope this United States of America shines into a dark and hungry world.

It has been justly said, *"Our Holy Bible is the only eternal thing human hands will ever touch."* True that. We have God's unending Words on Earth that directly descended from Heaven long ago. Trustworthy. Precise. Alive. Perfect. Teeming with eternal value.

However the reader chooses to handle Heaven's perfection on Earth today - good, bad, or indifferent - there may be only one thing admittedly lacking in the 1611 King James Bible. Our faith. Is your faith at rest in the perfect Words of God?

The mighty God, even the LORD, hath spoken,
and called the earth from the rising of the sun
unto the going down thereof.
*Out of Zion, the **perfection** of beauty,*
God hath shined.

Psalm 50:1,2

Holy Bible and
United States Presidents

*The Bible is the best gift God has ever given to man. All
the good from the Savior to the world
is communicated to us through this book.*
President Abraham Lincoln 1865

...the Bible is the best book in the world.
President John Adams 1826

*The first and almost the only Book deserving of universal
attention is the Bible.*
President John Quincy Adams 1848

*The foundations of our society and our government rest
so much on the teachings of the Bible that it would be
difficult to support them in faith if these teachings would
cease to be practically universal in our country.*
President Calvin Coolidge 1933

*The purpose of a devout and united people was set forth
in the pages of the Bible.*
President Dwight D. Eisenhower 1969

*...it is a habit of mine to read a chapter in the Bible every
evening.* **President James A. Garfield** 1881

*Hold fast to the Bible as the sheet anchor of your
liberties. To the influence of this Book are we indebted
for all the progress made in true civilization.*
President Ulysses S. Grant 1885

*...we must seek revival of our strength in the spiritual
foundations which are the bedrock of our republic...
its highest embodiment is the Bible.*
President Herbert Hoover 1964

That Book, sir, is the rock upon which our republic rests.
President Andrew Jackson,
in reference to the Bible 1845

*I do believe in Almighty God! And I believe also in the
Bible.* **President Andrew Johnson** 1875

*The more profoundly we study this wonderful Book, the
better citizens we will become
and the higher will be our destiny as a nation.*
President William McKinley 1901

*Therefore, be it Resolved by the Senate and House of
Representatives...Now, therefore, I, Ronald Reagan,
President of the United States of America, in recognition
of the contributions and influence of the Bible on our
Republic and our people, and our national need to study
and apply the teachings of the Holy Scriptures, do hereby
proclaim 1983 the Year of the Bible in the United States.*
President Ronald Reagan October 4, 1982
Authorized by a joint resolution of the 97th Congress

*We cannot read the history of our rise and development
as a nation, without reckoning with the place the Bible
has occupied in shaping the advances of the Republic. As
Commander-in-Chief, I take pleasure in commending the
reading of the Bible to all who serve in the armed forces
of the United States.*
President Franklin Delano Roosevelt 1941,45

*...the teachings of the Bible are so interwoven and
entwined with our civic and social life.*
President Theodore Roosevelt 1919

It was for the love of the truths of this great Book that our fathers abandoned their native shores for the wilderness.
President Zachary Taylor 1850

It is impossible to rightly govern the world without God and the Bible.
President George Washington 1799

I am sorry for the men who do not read the Bible every day...The Bible is the one supreme source of revelation of the meaning of life.
President Woodrow Wilson 1924

In all my perplexities and distresses, the Bible has never failed to give me light and strength...I fully accept it as the infallible Word of God, and receive its teachings as inspired by the Holy Spirit.
General Robert E. Lee 1870

When we all...draw our guidance and inspiration...and moral direction from the same general area, the Bible,...we have every reason to believe...[we] should live together in the closest of harmony.
President John F. Kennedy 1961[11]

ENDNOTES

CHAPTER ONE

1   Lee Roberson,
     http://amazinggracebaptistchurchkjv.com/gpage4.
     html, Amazing Grace Baptist Church Website,
     April 13, 2008.
2   Bill Grady, *Final Authority*, Schererville, Ind.,
     Grady Publications, 1993, p. 17.
3   G.A. Riplinger, *King James Version Ditches Blind
     Guides*, Ararat, Va., A.V. Publications Corp.,
     2000, p. 49.
4   G.A. Riplinger, *The Language of the King James
     Bible*, Ararat, Va, A.V. Publications Corp., 1998,
     p. xv.
5   Josh Mc Dowell, *A Ready Defense*, San
     Bernardino, Ca., Here's Life Publishers, Inc.,
     1990, p.35.
6   Daniel Webster, *Webster's New Collegiate
     Dictionary*, 1949, p.257.
7   G.A. Riplinger, *Which Bible Is God's Word?*,
     Oklahoma City, Oklahoma, Hearthstone
     Publishing, Ltd., 1994, p.69.
8   D.A. Carson, *The King James Version Debate*,
     Grand Rapids, Mich., Baker Book House Co.,
     1979, p.74.
9   Josh McDowell, *A Ready Defense*, San
     Bernardino, Ca., Here's Life Publishers, Inc.,
     1990, p.51.
10   G.A. Riplinger, *The History Of The Bible*, Ararat,
     Va., A.V. Publications Corp., 2000, p.14.
11   T.C. Smith, *How We Got Our Bible*, Macon, Ga.,
     Smyth and Helwys Publishing,, Inc., 1994, p.5
12   Ibid, p.5.

13   Ibid, p.7.
14   Josh Mc Dowell, *A Ready Defense*, San Bernardino, Ca., Here's Life Publishers, Inc., 1990, p.49.
15   Rene Pache', *The Inspiration And Authority Of Scripture*, Chicago, Ill., Moody Press, 1969-1978, p.166.
16   G.A. Riplinger, *In Awe of thy Word*, Ararat, Va., A.V. Publications Corp., 2003, p.109.
17   Henry W. Coray, *Valiant for the Truth*, New York, New York, McGraw-Hill Book Co. Inc., 1961.
18   Rene Pache', *The Inspiration And Authority Of Scripture*, Chicago, Ill., Moody Press, 1969-1978, p.128.
19   D.A. Waite, *Defending The King James Bible*, Collingswood, NJ, The Bible For Today Press, 2002, p.35.

CHAPTER TWO

1.   William Bell Riley, http://en.wikipedia.org/wiki/William_Bell_Riley, May 2008, p.1.
2.   D.A. Carson, *The King James Version Debate*, Grand Rapids, Mich., Baker Book House Co., 1979, p.18.
3.   G.A. Riplinger, *The Language of the King James Bible*, Ararat, Va, A.V. Publications Corp., 1998, p. xv.
4.   G.A. Riplinger, *Riplinger Lectures*, tape 2 – side A.
5.   Jeffrey, Sheler, *Is The Bible True?*, New York, NY, Harper Collins Publishers, Inc. 1999, p.19.

6.   Hershel Hobbs, *Getting Acquainted With The Bible*, Nashville, Tenn., Thomas Nelson, Inc., 1982, p.140.

7.   G.A. Riplinger, *In Awe of thy Word*, Ararat, Va., A.V. Publications Corp., 2003, p.850.

8.   Jeffrey, Sheler, *Is The Bible True?*, New York, NY, Harper Collins Publishers, Inc. 1999, p.32.

9.   Ibid, p.32.

10. Josh McDowell, *The Bible*, p. 65.

11. Thomas Holland, *Crowned With Glory*, Lincoln, Nebraska, Writers Club Press, 2002, p.43.

12. Bill Grady, *Final Authority*, Schererville, Ind., Grady Publications, 1993, p.31.

13. Herbert Gordon May, *Our English Bible In The Making*, Philadelphia, Penn., The Westminster Press, 1952, p.11.

14. Bill Grady, *Final Authority*, Schererville, Ind., Grady Publications, 1993, p.35.

15. Rene Pache', *The Inspiration And Authority Of Scripture*, Chicago, Ill., Moody Press, 1969-1978, p.175.

16. http://www.newble.co.uk/hall/kjv/whichbible.html , The Scottish Ministers' Hall of Fame, June 2008, p.1.

17. *Ante-Nicene Fathers*, Volume 1, Grand Rapids, 1953, pp.434-435.

18. T.C. Smith, *How We Got Our Bible*, Macon, Ga., Smyth and Helwys Publishing,, Inc., 1994, p.24.

19. Bill Grady, *Final Authority*, Schererville, Ind., Grady Publications, 1993, p.86.

20. G.A. Riplinger, *New Age Versions,* 1993, & Bill Grady, *Final Authority,* pp. 84-95.

21. Bill Grady, *Final Authority*, Schererville, Ind., Grady Publications, 1993, pp.91-95.

22. McClintock and Strong Cyclopedia, *Origen*, 1895.

23. J.J. Ray, *God Wrote Only One Bible*, 1955.
24. G.A. Riplinger, *In Awe of thy Word*, Ararat, Va., A.V. Publications Corp., 2003, p.963.
25. G.A. Riplinger, *In Awe of thy Word*, Ararat, Va., A.V. Publications Corp., 2003, p.983.
26. http://en.wikipedia.org/wiki/Church_of_England, May 2008, p.1.
27. G.A. Riplinger, *In Awe of thy Word*, Ararat, Va., A.V. Publications Corp., 2003, p.962.
28. http://www.battleoflife.org/history.html, June 2008, p.1.
29. http://www.newadvent.org/cathen/08026a.htm, Catholic Encyclopedia: Inquisition, April 2008, p.15.
30. http://mr_sedivytripodcom/med_hist3.html, Medieval History, April 2008, p.4.
31. http://www.newadvent.org/cathen/08026a.htm, Catholic Encyclopedia: Inquisition, April 2008, p.16.
32. William J. Federer, *America's God and Country*, Coppell, Texas, FAME Publishing, 1994.
33. Bill Grady, *Final Authority*, Schererville, Ind., Grady Publications, 1993, p.193.
34. G.A. Riplinger, *In Awe of thy Word*, Ararat, Va., A.V. Publications Corp., 2003, p.835.
35. Bill Grady, *Final Authority*, Schererville, Ind., Grady Publications, 1993, p.193.
36. John Foxe, *Acts and Monuments (Foxe's Book of Martyrs),*vol.8, p.408.
37. Herbert Gordon May, *Our English Bible In The Making*, Philadelphia, Penn., The Westminster Press, 1952, p.16.
38. G.A. Riplinger, *In Awe of thy Word*, Ararat, Va., A.V. Publications Corp., 2003, p.789.
39. Ibid, p.788.

40. Bill Grady, *Final Authority*, Schererville, Ind., Grady Publications, 1993, p.123.
41. G.A. Riplinger, *In Awe of thy Word*, Ararat, Va., A.V. Publications Corp., 2003, p.760.
42. Bill Grady, *Final Authority*, Schererville, Ind., Grady Publications, 1993, p.126.
43. Ibid, pp.127-141.
44. D.A. Carson, *The King James Version Debate*, Grand Rapids, Mich., Baker Book House Co., 1979, pp.49,50.
45. Ibid, pp.49,50.
46. G.A. Riplinger, *The History Of The Bible*, Ararat, Va., A.V. Publications Corp., 2000, p.2a.
47. G.A. Riplinger, *In Awe of thy Word*, Ararat, Va., A.V. Publications Corp., 2003, p.109.
48. G.A. Riplinger, *The History Of The Bible*, Ararat, Va., A.V. Publications Corp., 2000, p.9.
49. Ibid, p.50.
50. Ibid, p.51.
51. Ibid, p.51
52. Herbert Gordon May, *Our English Bible In The Making*, Philadelphia, Penn., The Westminster Press, 1952, p.41.
53. G.A. Riplinger, *In Awe of thy Word*, Ararat, Va., A.V. Publications Corp., 2003, pp.819,835.

CHAPTER THREE

1. Robert Alter, *The Literary Guide To The Bible*, Cambridge, Mass., Harvard University Press, 1987, p.656.
2. Ronald Reagan, G.A. Riplinger, *In Awe of thy Word*, Ararat, Va., A.V. Publications Corp., 2003, p.28.

3.   Sam Jones,
      htpp://en.wikipedia.org/wiki/Sam_Jones_%28evan
      gelist%29, May 2008, p.2.
4.   G.A. Riplinger, *In Awe of thy Word*, Ararat, Va.,
      A.V. Publications Corp., 2003, p.830.
5.   Ibid, p.834.
6.   Ibid, p.848.
7.   Herbert Gordon May, *Our English Bible In The
      Making*, Philadelphia, Penn., The Westminster
      Press, 1952, p.36.
8.   G.A. Riplinger, *In Awe of thy Word*, Ararat, Va.,
      A.V. Publications Corp., 2003, p.834.
9.   Ibid, p.833.
10.   Herbert Gordon May, *Our English Bible In The
      Making*, Philadelphia, Penn., The Westminster
      Press, 1952, p.46.
11.   Bill Grady, *Final Authority*, Schererville, Ind.,
      Grady Publications, 1993, p.160.
12.   http://www.reformedreader.org/gbn/igb.htm, The
      Reformed Reader, May 2008, p.5
13.   G.A. Riplinger, *The History Of The Bible*, Ararat,
      Va., A.V. Publications Corp., 2000, p.9.
14.   Bill Grady, *Final Authority*, Schererville, Ind.,
      Grady Publications, 1993, p.332
15.   G.A. Riplinger, *In Awe of thy Word*, Ararat, Va.,
      A.V. Publications Corp., 2003, p.891.
16.   Herbert Gordon May, *Our English Bible In The
      Making*, Philadelphia, Penn., The Westminster
      Press, 1952, p.49.
17.   Bill Grady, *Final Authority*, Schererville, Ind.,
      Grady Publications, 1993, p.147.
18.   Ibid, p.28.
19.   Ibid, p.153
20.   Ibid, p.157.

21. Hershel Hobbs, *Getting Acquainted With The Bible*, Nashville, Tenn., Thomas Nelson, Inc., 1982, p.150.

22. Thomas Holland, *Crowned With Glory*, Lincoln, Nebraska, Writers Club Press, 2002, p.67.

23. Josh McDowell, *A Ready Defense*, San Bernardino, Ca., Here's Life Publishers, Inc., 1990, p.51.

24. G.A. Riplinger, *The Language of the King James Bible*, Ararat, Va, A.V. Publications Corp., 1998, Intro, p. xvii.

25. Thomas Holland, *Crowned With Glory*, Lincoln, Nebraska, Writers Club Press, 2002, p.91.

26. Bill Grady, *Final Authority*, Schererville, Ind., Grady Publications, 1993, pp.166,67.

27. Waite, D.A., *Defending The King James Bible*, Collingswood, NJ, The Bible For   Today Press, 2002, p.75.

28. G.A. Riplinger, *In Awe of thy Word*, Ararat, Va., A.V. Publications Corp., 2003, p.608.

29. Thomas Holland, *Crowned With Glory*, Lincoln, Nebraska, Writers Club Press, 2002, pp.212-14.

30. G.A. Riplinger, *In Awe of thy Word*, Ararat, Va., A.V. Publications Corp., 2003, p.28.

CHAPTER FOUR

1. Oliver B. Greene, *Bible Prophecy*, p.4, *The Landmark Anchor Newsletter*, February 2004, p.4.

2. Josh Mc Dowell, *A Ready Defense*, San Bernardino, Ca., Here's Life Publishers, Inc., 1990, p.49.

3. Josh McDowell, *The Bible,* p.52.

4. G.A. Riplinger, *In Awe of thy Word*, Ararat, Va., A.V. Publications Corp., 2003, p.865.

5. Thomas Holland, *Crowned With Glory*, Lincoln, Nebraska, Writers Club Press, 2002, p.7.
6. Don Stewart, <u>The</u> *Bible*, p. 66.
7. Ibid. p.66.
8. Josh McDowell, *A Ready Defense*, San Bernardino, Ca., Here's Life Publishers, Inc., 1990, p.49.
9. Linsell, Harold, *The Battle For The Bible*, Grand Rapids, Mich., Zondervan Publishing House, 1978, p.36.
10. G.A. Riplinger, *In Awe of thy Word*, Ararat, Va., A.V. Publications Corp., 2003, p.550.
11. Bill Grady, *Final Authority*, Schererville, Ind., Grady Publications, 1993, p.156.
12. Thomas Holland, *Crowned With Glory*, Lincoln, Nebraska, Writers Club Press, 2002, p.89.
13. Ibid, p.90.
14. Josh McDowell, *A Ready Defense*, San Bernardino, Ca., Here's Life Publishers, Inc., 1990, p.49.
15. I. Mac Perry, *The Bible: Why Trust It?*, Plainfield, NJ, Logos International, 1980, pp.103,104.
16. Josh McDowell, *A Ready Defense*, San Bernardino, Ca., Here's Life Publishers, Inc., 1990, p.51.
17. Josh McDowell, <u>The</u> *Bible*, p. 52.
18. Edward W. Goodrick, *Is My Bible The Inspired Word Of God?*, Portland, Oregon, Multnomah Press, 1988, p.60.
19. Herbert Gordon May, *Our English Bible In The Making*, Philadelphia, Penn., The Westminster Press, 1952, p.10.
20. Jeffrey, Sheler, *Is The Bible True?*, New York, NY, Harper Collins Publishers, Inc. 1999, p.18.

21.   Hershel Hobbs, *Getting Acquainted With The Bible*, Nashville, Tenn., Thomas Nelson, Inc., 1982, p.137.

22.   Thomas Holland, *Crowned With Glory*, Lincoln, Nebraska, Writers Club Press, 2002, p.120.

23.   Ibid, pp.121,22.

24.   Bill Grady, *Final Authority*, Schererville, Ind., Grady Publications, 1993, pp.166,67.

25.   Hershel Hobbs, *Getting Acquainted With The Bible*, Nashville, Tenn., Thomas Nelson, Inc., 1982, p.137.

26.   Ibid, p.140.

27.   G.A. Riplinger, *In Awe of thy Word*, Ararat, Va., A.V. Publications Corp., 2003, p.963.

28.   G.A. Riplinger, *The History Of The Bible*, Ararat, Va., A.V. Publications Corp., 2000, p.7.

29.   G.A. Riplinger, *The Language of the King James Bible*, Ararat, Va, A.V. Publications Corp., 1998, Intro, p.133.

30.   Thomas Holland, *Crowned With Glory*, Lincoln, Nebraska, Writers Club Press, 2002, pp.103,104.

31.   John William Burgon, http://amazinggracebaptistchurchkjv.com/gpage4.html, Amazing Grace Baptist Church Website, April 13, 2008.

32.   Thomas Holland, *Crowned With Glory*, Lincoln, Nebraska, Writers Club Press, 2002, p.117.

33.   Bill Grady, *Final Authority*, Schererville, Ind., Grady Publications, 1993, p.31.

34.   Thomas Holland, *Crowned With Glory*, Lincoln, Nebraska, Writers Club Press, 2002, p.43.

35.   Hershel Hobbs, *Getting Acquainted With The Bible*, Nashville, Tenn., Thomas Nelson, Inc., 1982, p.137.

36.   G.A. Riplinger, *Riplinger Lectures,* tape 1, side B.

37. John Charles Ellicott, *Submission of the Revised Version to Convocation,* 1881, p.27.
38. Bill Grady, *Final Authority*, Schererville, Ind., Grady Publications, 1993, p.249.
39. F.C. Cook, *Revised Version of the First Three Gospels,* p.226
40. Bill Grady, *Final Authority,* Schererville, Ind., Grady Publications, 1993, p.252.
41. Edwin Cone Bissell, *Origin of the Bible,* New York, Anson D.F. Randolph & Co., 1889. p.357
42. Thomas Holland, *Crowned With Glory*, Lincoln, Nebraska, Writers Club Press, 2002, pp.38,39.
43. Bill Grady, *Final Authority*, Schererville, Ind., Grady Publications, 1993, pp.243,44.
44. http://www.seekgod.ca/ghostsociety.htm., The Chapham Sect, Wescott and Hort, June 2008, p.1.
45. Bill Grady, *Final Authority*, Schererville, Ind., Grady Publications, 1993, p.259.
46. John Charles Ellicott, *Addresses*, p.118.
47. Samuel Hemphill, *History of the Revised Version*, London, England, E. Stock Publishers, 1906. pp.54-55.
48. Bill Grady, *Final Authority*, Schererville, Ind., Grady Publications, 1993, p.259.
49. Ibid, p.262.
50. D.A. Waite, *Defending The King James Bible*, Collingswood, NJ, The Bible For Today Press, 2002, p.41.
51. G.A. Riplinger, *Riplinger lectures,* Tape 1 – Side B.
52. Bill Grady, *Final Authority*, Schererville, Ind., Grady Publications, 1993, p.269.

CHAPTER FIVE

1. Bob Jones, Sr., *The Sword Scrapbook*, Murfreesboro, Tennessee, Sword of the Lord Publishers, 1969, *The Landmark Anchor newsletter,* February 2004, p.4.

2. G.A. Riplinger, *Which Bible Is God's Word?*, Oklahoma City, Ok., Hearthstone Publishing, Ltd., 1994, p.72.

3. G.A. Riplinger, *The Language of the King James Bible*, Ararat, Va, A.V. Publications Corp., 1998, p.125.

4. G.A. Riplinger, *King James Version Ditches Blind Guides*, Ararat, Va., A.V. Publications Corp., 2000, p. 42.

5. Edward W. Goodrick, *Is My Bible The Inspired Word Of God?*, Portland, Oregon, Multnomah Press, 1988, p.55.

6. White, James, *The King James Only Controversy*, Minneapolis, Minn., Bethany House Publishers, 1995, p.153.

7. Bill Grady, *Final Authority*, Schererville, Ind., Grady Publications, 1993, p.29.

8. G.A. Riplinger, *In Awe of thy Word*, Ararat, Va., A.V. Publications Corp., 2003, p.956.

9. Thomas Holland, *Crowned With Glory*, Lincoln, Nebraska, Writers Club Press, 2002, p.189.

10. G.A. Riplinger, *King James Version Ditches Blind Guides*, Ararat, Va., A.V. Publications Corp., 2000, p.53.

11. Bill Grady, *Final Authority*, Schererville, Ind., Grady Publications, 1993, pp.261,62.

12. G.A. Riplinger, *King James Version Ditches Blind Guides*, Ararat, Va., A.V. Publications Corp., 2000, p.53.

13. Thomas Holland, *Crowned With Glory*, Lincoln,
    Nebraska, Writers Club Press, 2002, pp.186,87.
14. Ibid, p.187.
15. Bill Grady, *Final Authority*, Schererville, Ind.,
    Grady Publications, 1993, pp.32,33.
16. Thomas Holland, *Crowned With Glory*, Lincoln,
    Nebraska, Writers Club Press, 2002, p.38, footnote
    75.
17. John William Burgon, *Causes of Corruption in the
    Traditional Text,* Cambridge, England, 1896, p.93.
18. Robert Loweth,
    http://shop.avpublications.com/product_info.php?c
    Path=23&products_id=231&osCsid=0, May 2008,
    p.1.
19. G.A. Riplinger, *In Awe of thy Word*, Ararat, Va.,
    A.V. Publications Corp., 2003, p.286.
20. Ibid, p.286.
21. G.A. Riplinger, *Which Bible Is God's Word?*,
    Oklahoma City, Ok., Hearthstone Publishing, Ltd.,
    1994, p.8.
22. Thomas Holland, *Crowned With Glory*, Lincoln,
    Nebraska, Writers Club Press, 2002, p.206.
23. G.A. Riplinger, *The Language of the King James
    Bible*, Ararat, Va, A.V. Publications Corp., 1998,
    back cover.

CHAPTER SIX

1. *The Literary Guide to the Bible*, Cambridge,
   Mass., Harvard University Press, 1987, pp. 652,
   663.
2. Henry Morris, "A Creationist's Defense of the
   King James Bible", Institute for Creation Research
   Website,

http://www.icr.org/home/resources/resources_tract s_kjv/, August 6, 2008.

3. John William Burgon, *The Revision Revised*, pp. 315-16.

4. G.A. Riplinger, *The History Of The Bible*, Ararat, Va., A.V. Publications Corp., 2000, p.4.

5. G.A. Riplinger, *King James Version Ditches Blind Guides*, Ararat, Va., A.V. Publications Corp., 2000, p.60.

6. Daniel Webster, *Webster's New Collegiate Dictionary,*1949, p.257.

7. http://www.copyright.gov/circs/circ14.pdf, 1-28-09.

8. Henry Morris, http://www.icr.org/home/resources/resources/_trac ts_jkv_, August 3, 2008.

9. G.A. Riplinger, *In Awe of thy Word*, Ararat, Va., A.V. Publications Corp., 2003, p.7.

10. http://en.wikipedia.org/wiki/Taverner's_Bible, June 2008, p.1.

11. http://en.wikipedia.org/wiki/Novum_Testamentum _Graece, May 2008, p.1

12. D.A. Waite, *Defending The King James Bible*, Collingswood, NJ, The Bible For Today Press, 2002.

13. Frank Logsdon, *New Age Bible Versions* brochure, Ararat, Va, A.V. Publications, p.1.

14. G.A. Riplinger, *In Awe of thy Word*, Ararat, Va., A.V. Publications Corp., 2003, p.877.

15. G.A. Riplinger, *The History Of The Bible*, Ararat, Va., A.V. Publications Corp., 2000, p.14.

16. G.A. Riplinger, *In Awe of thy Word*, Ararat, Va., A.V. Publications Corp., 2003.

17. Ibid, p.966.

18. *The Literary Guide To The Bible*, Cambridge, Mass., Harvard University Press, 1987, p.660.
19. G.A. Riplinger, *Riplinger Lectures*, tape 1, side B.
20. G.A. Riplinger, *King James Version Ditches Blind Guides*, Ararat, Va., A.V. Publications Corp., 2000, p.56.
21. G.A. Riplinger, *Riplinger Lectures*, Tape 2, Side A.
22. G.A. Riplinger, *In Awe of thy Word*, Ararat, Va., A.V. Publications Corp., 2003, p.269.
23. G.A. Riplinger, *The Language of the King James Bible*, Ararat, Va, A.V. Publications Corp, 1998, p.117.
24. G.A. Riplinger, *In Awe of thy Word*, Ararat, Va., A.V. Publications Corp., 2003, p.12.
25. G.A. Riplinger, *The Language of the King James Bible*, Ararat, Va, A.V. Publications Corp, 1998, pp.164,65.
26. Ibid, p.165.

CHAPTER SEVEN

1. *Literary Guide to the Bible*, Cambridge, Mass., Harvard University Press, 1987, pp. 7,663,664.
2. G.A. Riplinger, *In Awe of thy Word*, Ararat, Va., A.V. Publications Corp., 2003.
3. D.A. Waite, *Defending The King James Bible*, Collingswood, NJ, The Bible For Today Press, 2002, p.48.
4. Bill Grady, *Final Authority*, Schererville, Ind., Grady Publications, 1993, Introduction - iii.
5. Ronald Reagan, G.A. Riplinger, *In Awe of thy Word*, Ararat, Va., A.V. Publications Corp., 2003, p.28.

6. Bill Grady, *Final Authority*, Schererville, Ind.,
    Grady Publications, 1993, p.20.
7. G.T. Stokes, *Acts of the Apostles Volume 2*, p.439.
8. William J. Federer, *America's God and Country*,
    Coppell, Texas, FAME Publishing, 1994, p.22 /
    "American Minute", Oct. 31,2008,
    mail@AmericanMinute.com.
9. Thomas Holland, *Crowned With Glory*, Lincoln,
    Nebraska, Writers Club Press, 2002, p.205.
10. Ibid, p.105.
11. William J. Federer, *America's God and Country*,
    Coppell, Texas, FAME Publishing, 1994.

BIBLIOGRAPHY

Carson, D.A., *The King James Version Debate*, Grand Rapids, Mich., Baker Book, House Co., 1979.

Comfort, Philip, *How We Got The Bible* (pamphlet), Torrance, Ca., Rose, Publishing Co., 1998.

Dolan, John P., *The Essential Erasmus*, New York, New York, Mentor-Omega Books, 1964.

Federer, William J., *America's God And Country*, Coppell, Tx., AME Publishing, Co., 1994.

Fuller, David Otis, *Valiant for the Truth,* New York, McGraw Hill Book Co. Inc., 1961.

Fuller, David Otis, *Which Bible?*, Grand Rapids, Michigan, Institute for Biblical Textual, Studies, 1990.

Goodrick, Edward W., *Is My Bible The Inspired Word Of God?*, Portland, Oregon, Multnomah Press, 1988.

Grady, William P., *Final Authority*, Schererville, Ind., Grady Publications, 1993.

Grady, William P., *What Hath God Wrought!*, Schererville, Ind., Grady Publications, 1996.

Hobbs, Hershel, *Getting Acquainted With The Bible*, Nashville, Tenn., Thomas, Nelson, Inc., 1982.

Holland, Dr. Thomas, *Crowned With Glory*, Lincoln, Neb., Writers Club Press, 2002.

Lackey, Bruce, *Why I Believe The Old King James Bible*, Chattanooga, Tennessee, 1987.

Linsell, Harold, *The Battle For The Bible*, Grand Rapids, Mich., Zondervan Publishing House, 1978.

May, Herbert Gordon, *Our English Bible In The Making*, Philadelphia, Penn., The Westminster Press, 1952.

McDowell, Josh, *A Ready Defense*, San Bernardino, Ca., Here's Life Publishers, Inc., 1990, *www.josh.org*.

Miller, Gary, *Why The King James Bible Is The Perfect Word Of God*, Ontario, California, Chick Publications, 2006.

Pache', Rene, *The Inspiration And Authority Of Scripture*, Chicago, Ill., Moody Press, 1969-1978.

Perry, I. Mac, *The Bible: Why Trust It?*, Plainfield, NJ, Logos International, 1980.

Riplinger, G.A., *In Awe of thy Word*, Ararat, Va., A.V. Publications Corp., 2003.

Riplinger, G.A., *Lecture Series*, Ararat, Va., A.V. Publications Corp., 1998.

Riplinger, G.A., *King James Version Ditches Blind Guides*, Ararat, Va., A.V. Publications Corp., 2000.

Riplinger, G.A., *The Language of the King James Bible*, Ararat, Va., A.V. Publications Corp., 1998.

Riplinger, G.A., *The History Of The Bible*, Ararat, Va.,
A.V. Publications Corp., 2000.

Riplinger, G.A., *Which Bible Is God's Word?*, Oklahoma
City, Oklahoma, Hearthstone Publishing, Ltd.,
1994.

Sheler, Jeffrey, *Is The Bible True?*, New York, NY,
Harper Collins Publishers, Inc. 1999.

Smith, T.C., *How We Got Our Bible*, Macon Ga., Smyth
and Helwys Publishing, Inc., 1994.

Steward, Don, & McDowell, Josh, *The Bible*, San
Bernardino, Ca., Here's Life Publishers, Inc.,
1983.

Vines, Jerry, *A Baptist And His Bible*, Nashville, Tenn.,
Southern Baptist Press, 1987.

Waite, D.A., *Defending The King James Bible*,
Collingswood, NJ, The Bible For Today Press,
2002.

Waite, D.A., *The Authorized Version 1611 Compared To
Today's King James Version,* Collingswood, NJ,
The Bible For Today Press, 1985.

Webster, Daniel, *Webster's New Collegiate Dictionary*,
1949.

White, James, *The King James Only Controversy*,
Minneapolis, Minn., Bethany House Publishers,
1995.

Contact, More Publications

INVITE DR. TROY CLARK
to speak for your event or organization
Hotline@TroyClark.net

Dr. Troy G. Clark
P.O. Box 805
Southmont, NC 27351

General Inquiries
Info@TroyClark.net

See All Publications by Dr. Troy Clark
www.amazon.com/author/troyclark
www.TroyClark.net

Paperback, Ebook, Audiobook:
Amazon.com, Kindle, Smashwords, Barnes-n-Nobles,
Apple iBooks, Sony Reader, Kobo, Palm Doc, Audible.com,
iTunes

Video: **http://www.youtube.com/user/DrTroyClark**

www.FinalExpenseSuccess.com
Leads Resource
Coaching Session
Master Sales Training
Executive Consultation
Sales Script MANUAL
Master Sellinar Event

Made in the USA
Coppell, TX
10 April 2025

48136022R00184